DISCARDED

VIEWS IN TEXAS, 1895-96

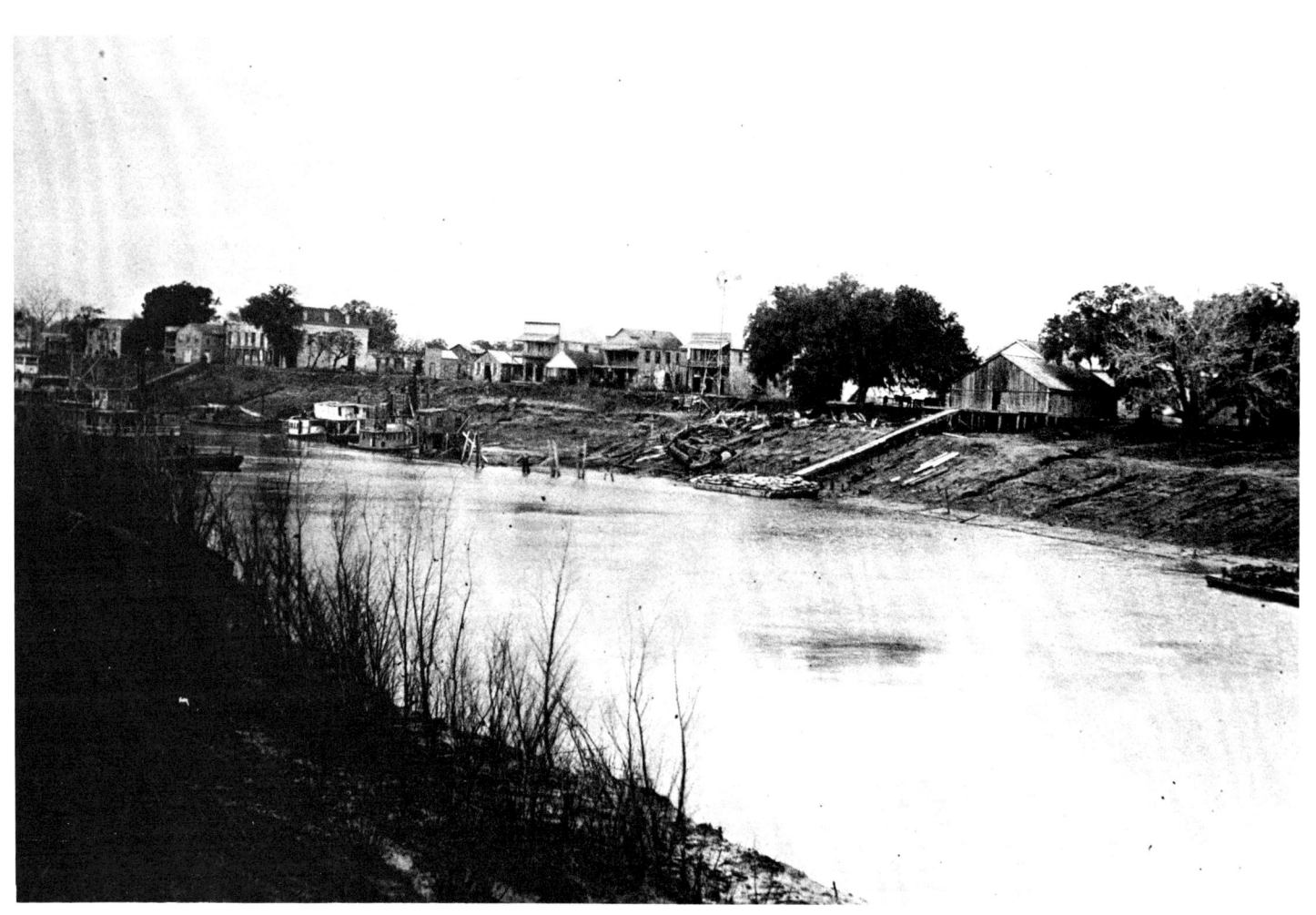

VIEWS IN TEXAS

A Photographic Tour of Texas made in the Winter of 1895-96 by HENRY STARK ★ To which has been added A Historical Commentary by A. C. GREENE ★ The Encino Press, Austin ★

1895-96

First Edition
© 1974 : THE ENCINO PRESS
510 Baylor Street : Austin

THE ENCINO PRESS wishes to acknowledge with sincere appreciation the help of the following people in producing this book:

ELIOT GREENE, who assisted in copying Henry Stark's original prints, which were too fragile to survive the handling necessary to the book production process.

JOHN CHRISTIAN, himself a photographer of sensitivity and determination, who laboriously made a set of reproduction prints faithful to Stark's originals.

SARA CLARK and PHYLLIS GREEN, whose frank and cheerful ways made the final selection of photographs published in this book a joyful task.

JOHN JENKINS, who first brought Stark's book of photographs to the attention of the Encino Press.

Typesetting : SARA CLARK / Printing : CAPITOL PRINTING COMPANY / Paper : LONE STAR PAPER COMPANY

Binding : CUSTOM BOOKBINDERS / Design : WILLIAM D. WITTLIFF

FOR ELIOT
My personal cameraman

VIEWS IN TEXAS, 1895-96

VIEWS IN TEXAS

THESE PHOTOGRAPHS
WERE MADE IN THE
WINTER OF 1895-96
BY
HENRY STARK
ST. LOUIS, MO.

VIEWS IN TEXAS, 1895-96

IN THE WINTER OF 1895-96 a Saint Louis resident named Henry Stark visited Texas, taking photographs as he traveled over the state. Fortunately for us, he made good pictures, and he visited every major city except Beaumont and Brownsville, and every section of Texas save the Panhandle. Beaumont was a lumbering center (population 4,000) but Spindletop and world fame were six years away. Perhaps because it was located off the route of the rail lines he used, Mr. Stark felt it was not worth a special trip to visit. Brownsville's omission is simpler: it had no rail connection with the rest of the state: the steam cars stopped at Corpus Christi, going south. And surely our visitor can be excused for skipping the Panhandle. Amarillo, while on a railroad, had only 800 inhabitants, and Lubbock, trackless, had fewer than 155.

Henry Stark's visit was, we believe, unique in one sense. He was the first person known to have done a straight photographic record of Texas. There had been any number of *writings* about travels through Texas, beginning with Cabeza de Vaca, proliferating into the hundreds by 1895, and some of the works, especially in the second half of the nineteenth century, were illustrated by woodcuts, drawings, lithographs, or engravings of the Texas scene, but no earlier such complete photographic document survives. Mr. Stark went back to Missouri and put together a book containing 250 of his original photographic prints, which he titled *Views in Texas*. While he may have produced more than one copy, only a single example is known. The book is entirely hand-done (the charming title page is reproduced at left), and was expertly sewn and bound into a leather cover. The captions, hand inscribed on the photographic paper pages, are exceedingly brief: "Res. in Bonham" or "Farm in Denton Co." No accompanying notes or further descriptions are included—and a few captions are inaccurate, although none is misleading. The photographs were taken with a camera using glass plate negatives. Film speeds were only about one-tenth to one-twentieth of a second, so all exposures had to be made from a tripod and movement is often blurred. It was not the casual kind of photography we practice on our travels today.

We know very little about Mr. Stark or the party that accompanied him (he seems not to have been alone). We think the man lying on the winter grass, looking back at the camera in "A scene near Abilene" may be Stark, or that he is one of the group pictured before the large Spanish dagger plant at Rockport. It is undoubtedly over-romantic to hope that Henry Stark is the young man in this picture, that the pretty girl is perhaps his bride, and that the Texas expedition was in the nature of a honeymoon trip—although lugging around the amount of clumsy equipment required for this type of photography would indicate a rare dedication to the craft or a rare attitude on the part of a bride, one.

Facts (or fancies) aside, Henry Stark performed a historic service which, in several instances, verges on the artistic.

1895 WAS A CURIOUS TIME in Texas history, stranded between the frontier and the future. The frontier was gone, ended suddenly and irrevocably by the railroads; the future was coming faster than any future had before . . . but it would have taken unbelievable prescience to have grasped even part of the next decade.

Behind 1895, but close enough in time to be the vital part of Texas social dogma, were Indian raids, the wars with Mexico, the Confederacy, and the long cattle drives. Still powerful in public life and decision-making was the influence of pioneering that old *terra incognita* which had edged the Texas map since the province was named—till now. Now, it was all dead... but with ghosts more powerful than its reality. The reality made Texas history, the ghosts made Texas myth.

Ahead—in only two, three, ten years—would be automobiles on the streets, airplanes, the petroleum revolution, picture shows, the wireless. But the most important changes were already taking place—changes in Texas attitudes toward status in society, morals, living habits: changes in something for which the word would not be invented for another sixty years—lifestyle. It is the kind of thing photographs convey better than words: electrical wires along the streets, streetcar tracks, sidewalks, advertising signs—even the dress and faces of the people who pass before the camera in an incidental way. Look at the school children, for example, the depot crowds, or the strollers on Avenue I in Galveston. Occasionally, as with the bearded horseman of Greenville, there will stalk across the scene a face which, at a distance (ours and the camera's), seems to show a dead-set defiance to the changing ways—but with few exceptions the subtle evidence is there in every picture: this could not be ten years before 1895 anymore than it could be ten years after.

THE PLATES

1. A FARM IN BOWIE COUNTY, NEAR TEXARKANA.

HENRY STARK entered the Lone Star State at Texarkana, straddling the Texas-Arkansas border, a gateway which the railroads had begun in 1873. From there he took the northern line of the Texas & Pacific which passed through the Red River valley by way of Bowie, Red River, Lamar, Fannin, and Grayson counties.

What we would call a small town now was a sizable city in 1895. There were no places which approached the size we call a big city today. Texas was many years away from being urban. Here are the twenty largest Texas towns with their population figures:

1. San Antonio	45,000	2. Dallas	40,000		
3. Houston	36,000		12. Paris	9,000	
4. Galveston	32,000		13. Marshall	7,500	
5. Fort Worth	24,000		14. Corsicana	7,400	
6. Austin	18,000		15. Tyler	7,400	
7. Waco	17,000		16. Gainesville	7,000	
8. El Paso	12,500		17. Palestine	6,500	
9. Laredo	12,000		18. Brownsville	6,000	
10. Denison	11,000		19. Greenville	5,300	
11. Sherman	9,100		20. Cleburne	5,000	

2. A SCENE AT NAPLES.

3. PUBLIC SQUARE, PARIS.

THE CENTER of Paris was around the square (and was destroyed by fire in 1916). The federal building is an imposing piece of architecture, both in size and style, befitting a place many times the size of Paris. But this building housed not just the federal court of the Texas district it served, but the courts for the Choctaw and the Chickasaw Nations, as well as a piece of vastness called Oklahoma Territory—all of which lay across the Red River. The building saw some of the nation's legal oddities in its years—in fact, Judge David Bryant, who sat for twenty years, sentenced three boys (aged 13 and 14) to life in federal prison for murder "because, on account of their age, they could not be hanged." This took place not long after Stark made the photograph.

4. FEDERAL BUILDING, PARIS.

5. A FARM IN FANNIN COUNTY, NEAR BONHAM.

THERE was some added excitement in Fannin County as Stark was passing through; coal had been discovered by a Negro sharecropper and 5,000 acres had been put under a mineral lease. It didn't lead to any large-scale mining. Fannin was one of those northeastern Texas counties Stark visited which had twice the population in 1895 it would have eighty years later.

6. A RESIDENCE AT DENISON.

DENISON, a strong young rival ten miles to the north of Sherman, had been built and named by the Katy Railroad in 1872. Fame was already guaranteed for Denison, although neither Stark nor the city knew it.... In 1890, David J. and Ida Eisenhower had become parents of a son, Dwight David, in a Denison cottage the photographer almost certainly passed by.

7. BUSINESS PART OF TRAVIS STREET, SHERMAN.

8. AUSTIN COLLEGE, SHERMAN.

SHERMAN had the biggest cottonseed oil mill in the world in 1895 (which would begin producing Mrs. Tucker's brand shortening in a few years). Austin College (Presbyterian) had moved to Sherman from Huntsville in 1876; then Mary Nash College and North Texas Female College (later Kidd-Key) opened, and finally (1894) Carr-Burdette College, to make Sherman the state's major academic center.

9. NORTH TEXAS STATE NORMAL, DENTON.

DENTON was a growing town of 3,200, where North Texas State Normal had been made a state school (there were only four) in 1891. The belfry of Old Normal was believed to be haunted because of the shrieks and cries of agony and the tolling of the bell which issued from the tower on certain nights. The bell was removed when it caused the brickwork to crack, and in the twentieth century it became the victory bell for North Texas State University. Old Normal was struck by lightning and burned to the ground in 1907.

10. PUBLIC SCHOOL, DENTON.

FREE PUBLIC SCHOOLS had really gotten started only after 1883 in Texas because that was when local taxation was authorized and state tax money given to independent school districts. But even in 1896 the boys and girls were kept separate in most schools, sometimes (as in Abilene) going to class in separate rooms—especially high school classes—and having to stay on the "girls' side" or the "boys' side" of the building at recess.

11. ALLIANCE MILLING CO., DENTON.

12. A GREENVILLE STREET SCENE.

POLITICS, as usual, was strong in Texas in 1895-96. Both William Jennings Bryan and Senator Joe Bailey were speaking over the state. "Sound money" and "Free Silver" were on every tongue, and the People's Party (a Populist group) came within 20 per cent of electing its candidate to the governor's chair later in '96. The Prohibition Party, after an unsuccessful attempt a few years earlier to dry up Texas, was coming back strong—

and even though women couldn't vote, their zeal added strength to the anti-liquor issue.

13. HOPKINS COUNTY COURTHOUSE, SULPHUR SPRINGS.

14. SCHOOL AT SULPHUR SPRINGS.

15. A RURAL ROAD AND WELL IN FRANKLIN COUNTY.

16. A FARM IN CAMP COUNTY, NEAR PITTSBURG.

IN A GOOD YEAR, cotton made everybody happy, despite the work ... but as a crop, it was notoriously fickle. Statistics on production in Texas swung widely from year to year and without any means of predicting the good years—until after the crop was over. Anything, right up to the last days when rains could ruin the picking, could play cain with your cotton. For example, as Stark passed through, several of the counties of northeast and north Texas reported the 1895 crop was "distressingly short," running only one-third of 1894's production in Camp, Cass, and surrounding counties. Cotton farmers didn't know it but they had something to be thankful for: the boll weevil wouldn't arrive for another five years!

17. A SCENE IN TERRELL.

18. COMPRESS AT TERRELL.

BESIDES COTTON FARMING there was cotton manufacturing, and every town of any size had one or more gins (there were 4,000 in Texas), and the larger towns had compresses and cotton oil mills. (Stark took several pictures of these which are not included because they tend to look very much alike.) In 1895 when you said "oil" you were much more likely to mean cottonseed oil than petroleum.

19. LOOKING TOWARD DALLAS FROM OAK CLIFF.

THE ONLY TIME Dallas was the largest city of Texas was in 1890 when the census gave her 38,000 population. Oak Cliff was still a separate city from Dallas, and looking at Stark's photograph of a streetcar—which has just crossed the Trinity River on the "causeway" (as the rail bridge was called)—we sense what a lovely place Hord's Ridge (its pioneer name) must have been—and why "oak" was in the name later.

Oak Cliff Park was the sports arena for Dallas, and just a couple of weeks before Stark visited, the University of Texas football team "wiped up some Oak Cliff real estate with Dallas," according to a report from the park. The score was 10-0. The annual game (Dallas had a town team) was a social event. "Lots of pretty girls out, accompanied by strong lunged young men decked in ribbons," the same writer noted. On Christmas Day the Dallas team whipped Fort Worth 14-0 on the same field to recover some prestige.

20. LOOKING EAST FROM THE ORIENTAL HOTEL, DALLAS.

THE BIGGEST news event in Texas during the last months of 1895 was a sporting event—or rather the fact that one wasn't taking place. The World's Heavyweight Boxing Championship match between Gentleman Jim Corbett, the titleholder, and England's Bob Fitzsimmons was supposed to take place in Dallas on October 31. Stands seating thousands were under construction. But bowing to pressure from a large group which felt boxing to be "barbaric and immoral," Governor Culberson (despite being from Dallas) called a special session of the legislature and a bill was passed to stop the fight. Both the fighters hung around Texas, and the heavyweight battle was announced for Hot Springs, Arkansas, then, Little Rock. . . . But the Arkansas governor almost called out the militia to stop it. In December an El Paso group swore (in the newspapers) they would hold the fight, possibly just over the line in New Mexico Territory, but despite it remaining front page news for three months, the match didn't take place in Texas; in fact, it didn't take place anywhere until 1897 when, in Nevada, Fitzsimmons took Gentleman Jim's crown.

21. TRINITY OIL COMPANY, DALLAS.

22. FORT WORTH DRESSED MEAT AND PACKING CO.

FORT WORTH wasn't a national meat packing center in 1895 (Armour and Swift & Co. came after 1901), but it was an important livestock market and shipping point. The Fort Worth Dressed Meat and Packing Co. had opened in 1890 with thirty local men pitching in $10,000 apiece to try and rescue some of the income which had ended with the final cattle drives through Fort Worth.

23. STOCKYARDS HOTEL & EXCHANGE, FORT WORTH.

24. HURLEY OFFICE BUILDING, SOUTH MAIN, FORT WORTH.

FORT WORTH Republicans were pushing the "Lily-White Movement," trying to get the Texas GOP out of the hands of the Negroes who had held party power since Reconstruction days. "Gooseneck" Bill McDonald, one of the shrewdest political figures in Texas history, with the support of white millionaire E. H. R. Green, kept the "reformation" from sweeping Texas, and in April 1896 when the "Lily-Whites" met in a separate session, they elected two Negro delegates to the Republican National Convention.

25. FORT WORTH HIGH SCHOOL, JENNINGS AND DAGGETT STREETS.

26. SATURDAY AFTERNOON ON THE NORTH SIDE OF THE SQUARE, WEATHERFORD.

WEATHERFORD'S FAME as a watermelon town came in the next decade, but it was already a truck producer. In January 1896 a strange affliction called "watermelon wilt" was being puzzled over in Texas agriculture circles. One G. L. Taber, a Floridian, toured Texas in November 1895 and warned would-be orange growers if they tried citrus culture—he privately thought Texas was too cold in winter—they'd best go to the Satsuma orange. The lower Rio Grande valley, one of the great citrus producing areas of America, was so cut off from commerce in 1895 that no one thought about growing oranges (or much of anything) there.

27. PARKER COUNTY COURTHOUSE, WEATHERFORD.

28. A LIVERY HACK AT THE LAMAR MINERAL WELL, PALO PINTO COUNTY, NEAR MINERAL WELLS.

MINERAL WATERS served two functions, medical and social. Palo Pinto County's mineral springs, after the famous "Crazy Water" well was bored in 1885, were said to cure "hysterical manias as well as other maladies." The town of Mineral Wells was already becoming a fashionable vacation spa: in 1897 the Hexagon House—first of its famed hotels—would be constructed, and by 1920 the town (once a robber's roost because of its secluded valley) would have 400 mineral wells for public use.

29. A STREET SCENE IN ABILENE.

LAPOWSKI BROS. (on left of street scene) had been an Abilene commercial leader since early in the '80s. The Abilene Light Infantry rented the upper floor of this building for weekly military drills and occasional social dancing. A Lapowski son went on to considerable financial fame as Clarence Dillon, a founder of Dillon, Read & Co., and a grandson, C. Douglas Dillon, was U. S. Secretary of the Treasury in the 1960s.

30. TAYLOR COUNTY COURTHOUSE, ABILENE.

31. A SCENE NEAR ABILENE.

32. ABILENE HIGH SCHOOL.

THE ABILENE PUBLIC SCHOOL, built in 1890, replaced another school building which had earlier been a warehouse and was called by the students the "Beer and Ice Seminary" because of what the owner, a Mr. Riney, had stored there. The new brick high school was so imposing it was called "The College." The T&P railroad tracks ran so close to it that classes often had to hold up until the train passed.

33. SCHOOL AT COLORADO CITY.

34. SALT WORKS NEAR COLORADO CITY.

35. EL PASO, NEAR THE DEPOT.

EL PASO, remote from the rest of Texas society, while an important health resort (for tuberculosis) and smelting and mining center, was still rather "wild" . . . the last spot toward which the old frontier of Texas had drifted to die. It was also a foreign sort of town, turning to Mexico more than to the home state. In August 1895 El Paso had seen the shooting death of John Wesley Hardin, the Methodist preacher's son who was probably the West's most dangerous gunman (he killed thirty men), by Constable John Selman in a saloon; shot from behind witnesses said. In April 1896 Selman himself was gunned down by U. S. Marshal George Scarborough, supposedly his friend. All three had come to El Paso after working their colorful way through the rest of West Texas.

36. SMELTER, EL PASO.

37. HILL COUNTY COURTHOUSE, HILLSBORO.

38. SCENE FROM THE COURTHOUSE AT HILLSBORO.

MANY SMALL THINGS had meshed by 1895 to produce larger changes. By 1890, for instance, the "safety" bike had begun to replace the high-wheeler, and the "bike craze" led to demands for better streets and roads. Bicycles were not just toys, either. In Texas in 1895 a good one cost $75 (two months wages), and its pneumatic tires could not take the punishment unpaved dirt roads gave buggy and wagon wheels. So bicycles, not autos, were leading the way to cheaper and quicker forms of paving. (Not too fast, however. You will notice that most Texas streets were dirt—and most were muddy.) The problem of paving was a major municipal headache. Less attention was given highways and inter-city roads because most passengers and freight rode the rails. Many things were tried as pavement, including bois d'arc blocks (which worked fairly well unless they swelled up and exploded from the roadbed) and macadam, which was a system of layered and packed crushed rock and gravel. Corsicana, going into an oil boom in 1895, was the first town to use heavy oil on its streets to prevent blowing dust . . . although Palestine and St. Jo (in Montague County) had used "native asphalt" on streets the year before.

39. BEATON STREET FROM EAST SIXTH, CORSICANA.

40. COTTON BELT AND HOUSTON & TEXAS CENTRAL CROSSING, CORSICANA.

CORSICANA, as noted, was getting started on an oil boom— Texas's first real one—when Stark arrived early in 1896— in fact, he may have gotten off the train about the time (January 15) a new well was being drilled on South 11th Street, one block north of the Cotton Belt station. Oil had been hit (an annoyance) in June of '94 when the city was trying to get artesian water, but commercial flow of oil didn't begin until the spring of '96. By spring of '97 wells were being drilled within a few feet of each other "on downtown street corners, in front or back yards . . . in gardens and horse lots." One result of the Corsicana oil boom was the Magnolia Petroleum Co., which became Mobil.

41. COTTON BELT STATION, WACO.

THE "CENTER OF GRAVITY" of population for Texas was out in the country between Waco and Marlin—about the village of Reisel—and the 1890 census had counted 2,235,527 souls (84 per cent of them rural), making Texas the seventh most populated state.

42. CAMERON MILLING CO., WACO, MCLENNAN COUNTY.

43. BAYLOR UNIVERSITY, WACO.

44. COTTON BELT STATION, GATESVILLE.

45. SCHOOL AT HEARNE.

THE HEARNE BROTHERS, for whom Hearne was named, established a 3,800 acre plantation in 1852 and after the Civil War hired many former slaves to continue operation of what was probably Texas' first big agribusiness endeavor. When Stark came through, Horatio ("Raish") Hearne was still alive and the plantation employed 700 to 800 hands. An 1896 account says, "Recently he has put in an apparatus to utilize the gas coming from the wells, and has so far succeeded that he now has gas to light his house and for cooking and heating purposes, and to run a four-horsepower engine in a blacksmithing and woodworking establishment . . . where he makes everything in the way of machinery needed on the plantation."

46. LOOKING NORTH ACROSS THE COLORADO RIVER FROM SOUTH AUSTIN.

47. AUSTIN, LOOKING SOUTHEAST FROM THE CAPITOL DOME.

48. LAKE MCDONALD, BEHIND THE AUSTIN DAM.

THE AUSTIN DAM on the Colorado River, built in 1893, was said to be the largest in the world. It was 1,150 feet long, 60 feet high, and developed an electric output of 16,500 horsepower. In April 1900 this dam broke (pieces may still be seen at the foot of the modern dam) and many lives were lost. Lake McDonald was drained and the little excursion steamer destroyed. The dam and lake were so popular that, at the time Stark visited, the Austin Dam & Suburban steam railroad was being built from downtown to the park.

49. VERANDA OF THE DRISKILL HOTEL, AUSTIN.

50. UNIVERSITY OF TEXAS, AUSTIN.

51. PUBLIC SQUARE, SAN MARCOS.

ICE MAKING and mechanical refrigeration advancements led to the ice cream parlor and the soda fountains which may be seen in some pictures—and which would not have been there five years before. The Westinghouse alternating current generator was what had spread electric lights across Texas so quickly, not Edison's electric bulb. Edison's direct current system was not suitable for sending current long distances. Each town had its own generator, however. The utilities grid systems were several years away.

52. CORONAL INSTITUTE, SAN MARCOS.

53. KATY STATION AT NEW BRAUNFELS.

IN 1895 TRAVELERS used trains to get places almost exclusively, and the Texas rail system was just becoming the longest in the nation, capable of delivering you to almost any hamlet in the state—with the exceptions noted. Notice the toy-like quality of the steam locomotives pulling the wooden, open-vestibule coaches. They are not just utilitarian; they are beautiful, with their dainty brass trimmings, their flashing siderods, their high wheels, tall stacks, and slender polished boilers. The depot was the social center of every town, particularly the small one, and some sort of crowd was always on hand when the train pulled in. In those days when newspapers carried no photographs, when neither radio nor television was around to bring you instant events, the railroad station was where your town met the outside world—even when it only paused to let off a few passengers and then fled.

54. STATION HOTEL, NEW BRAUNFELS.

55. ON THE MOUNTAIN ROAD, NEW BRAUNFELS.

56. A DAM ON THE COMAL RIVER, NEW BRAUNFELS.

57. LANDA ROLLER MILLS, NEW BRAUNFELS.

JOSEPH LANDA, a San Antonio merchant, was so attracted by the natural beauty of New Braunfels he moved there. In 1859 he bought Comal Springs and the surrounding land, eventually erecting a complex of waterpowered mills. When Stark visited the Comal Springs the Landa mills were among the largest in Texas. "The plants now being operated are a flour mill of 500 barrel capacity, a large electric light plant, and an 80-ton cottonseed oil mill," a January 1896 report states. "At the present time Mr. Landa is busy increasing the capacity of his oil mill to 100 tons per day and putting in a late improved water wheel of 260 horsepower to operate the oil mill. The company has also contracted for the erection of a new electric light station, and in addition to the new wheel, will put in another one to operate several new dynamos for light and the transmission of power. It handled last year (1895) 3,000 car loads of product."

Shortly after Stark's visit, Jay Gould's daughter Helen had the International & Great Northern Railroad (which her father controlled) buy the land along the river and make it into a park. Eventually it became the property of the city, but the mills remain in private hands. The Comal River is the shortest major waterway in the U. S. (four miles) to rise and empty wholly within the limits of one town. The springs have always been Texas' biggest, flowing, in 1896, 240,000,000 gallons per day and diminished only slightly by mid-twentieth century.

58. A FARM IN COMAL COUNTY.

59. A SCENE ON THE COMAL RIVER.

60. A FORD ON THE SAN ANTONIO RIVER.

SAN ANTONIO, in 1896, was not only the state's largest city and its cultural center, it was the military capital of the nation and the brewing center of the Southwest. It was, by far, the most cosmopolitan spot in the Southwest with its heavy mixture of Mexican and other Latin peoples, the largest concentration of Germans and Czechs and Irish Catholics . . . even a remnant of Indians . . . to go with the diverse Anglo community. Although the oldest large city and the most sacred shrine in Texas history, San Antonio was separate from the rest of the state, not just by statistics but (more importantly) by traditions and social codes.

61. ALAMO PLAZA, SAN ANTONIO.

62. SAN FERNANDO CATHEDRAL, SAN ANTONIO.

63. MILAM SQUARE, SAN ANTONIO.

64. "FIRST MONDAY" IN COTULLA.

COTULLA, now a fruit and vegetable center, was a typical South Texas brush country cattle town when Stark was there. The biggest roundup of wild mustangs in Texas had taken place nearby only a few years before. Despite its location in an area which had been visited and (in some cases) settled for more than a century and a half, it remained wild. Cotulla's last Indian raid (killing three) took place in 1878, years after the Comanches of the plains had been corraled in Oklahoma. Spanish and Mexican rancheros operated around Cotulla from the eighteenth century but Anglos only arrived in 1852.

65. A STREET SCENE IN LAREDO.

LAREDO, like El Paso, looked south of the Rio Grande for much more of its culture than it did Texasward. But in 1895 it was the most popular gateway to Mexico that the U. S. had. The Laredo Seminary was established in 1880 by the Methodist church on 26 acres along the river primarily to teach Mexican children. In 1895 it had expanded to seven buildings and Miss Nannie Emory Holding was its superintendent. She was such a powerful influence that when she retired in 1913, after thirty years, the name was changed to Holding Institute—and it still operates under that name today.

66. FORT MCINTOSH, LAREDO.

67. LAREDO SEMINARY, LATER THE HOLDING INSTITUTE.

68. MEXICAN CANDY VENDORS, LAREDO.

69. INTERNATIONAL BRIDGE, LAREDO TO NUEVO LAREDO.

70. CORPUS CHRISTI FROM THE BLUFF.

CORPUS CHRISTI was once called Kinney's Ranch and Trading Post, and during the Civil War it was twice shelled by Union gunboats—once with whiskey. Sailors, hiding their illicit grog, poured out the powder and filled the shells with liquor. When fired—through someone's oversight, so to speak—the shells failed to explode and the Corpus Christi defenders, puzzled, discovered that these "duds" packed their own kind of wallop.

In 1895, as the picture shows, Corpus Christi was still "below the bluff." The little port was a big wool market, in the forgotten days when sheep were a major item in the Rio Grande's lower reaches. The Laguna Madre Horticultural Co. was growing table grapes a few miles south of town and Sam M. Johnson said Corpus Christi would "export" fifteen tons of them in 1896.

71. A SPANISH DAGGER PLANT, ROCKPORT.

72. THE MOUTH OF THE BRAZOS RIVER.

73. BRAZOS LAND & IMPROVEMENT CO., VELASCO.

OLD VELASCO was where Stephen F. Austin's first settlers entered Texas in 1823 and where Texas and Mexico signed the peace treaty (shortly after San Jacinto) ending fighting in 1836. For decades it was a popular ocean resort, but after 1875, when hurricanes blew it away for the third time, Velasco removed itself four miles upriver, and in 1891 the site pictured opened for business.

74. COLUMBIA ON THE BRAZOS RIVER.

HISTORIC COLUMBIA was the first permanent capital of the Republic of Texas, and Santa Anna was held there after his capture at the battle of San Jacinto. Stephen F. Austin, the father of Texas, died in Columbia in a house on the street shown. (The village is now East Columbia.)

75. A SCENE ON AVENUE I IN GALVESTON.

76. ON THE BEACH, GALVESTON.

77. ON THE BEACH, GALVESTON.

78. GALVESTON WATER WORKS.

A NEW SOURCE of municipal pride in Texas was the waterworks—although in 1896 even in the larger cities they generally pumped raw water into the mains. It wasn't as bad as it sounds, perhaps: fire protection was the first job of the waterworks—note the prevalence of fireplugs. Fire was a constant risk. (Note also how many of the pictured buildings burned.) Water for drinking and cooking usually came from private wells, from water vendors, from cisterns which caught rain water from off the roof, or, in some lucky cities (Waco was one) from pure artesian wells.

79. BALL HIGH SCHOOL, GALVESTON.

GEORGE BALL, in 1883, gave $70,000 to build a high school "for the boys and girls of Galveston." He died before it was occupied, and his widow subsequently gave $40,000 more to add a mansard roof (she didn't like the flat style), and an additional $10,000 to furnish the building—making it far and away the most palatial school building, public or private, in the South. During the Galveston hurricane of 1900, the most destructive natural event in U. S. history, hundreds of persons were sheltered in the building (including the author's grandparents). The dome blew off but the families within were saved.

80. GRAIN ELEVATOR, GALVESTON.

81. MOODY COMPRESS, GALVESTON.

82. I&GN STATION, HOUSTON.

RAILROADING was the biggest industry and the most powerful business in the state, and only in 1891 had Governor Jim Hogg finally imposed some needed regulations on the corporations when he created his Texas Railroad Commission. His follower, Charles Culberson, inaugurated in January 1895, had already strengthened the commission with stronger controls over the railroads.

83. TRAVIS STREET AT TEXAS IN HOUSTON.

84. MARKET SQUARE, HOUSTON.

FURNITURE PRICES in most cities were about the same: a five-piece set of heavy rattan (very big this year) with settee was $42.75; high-backed, cane-seat, solid oak chairs were 85¢ each, or an oak rolltop desk was $17.95. A 74-piece dinner set of Queensware sold for $6.50 in Houston.

Men's suits ranged from $3.85 to $7.75, although cutaways and frocks went as high as $25. At that, most men had their suits tailored. Few readymade dresses were on sale, although some shirtwaists, skirts, and cloaks were in the stores. Even the non-wealthy women had their dresses made by a seamstress who often came to the house to work. Ladies' double-sole, high spliced-heel hose were 25¢ a pair, and silk crepe de chine (the finest cloth available for dresses) was 75¢ per yard.

85. THE AUDITORIUM, HOUSTON.

METHODIST Evangelist Sam Jones, the Billy Graham of his time, was holding a huge public meeting in Houston in November and he reminded his audience the rent on the auditorium was between $500 and $600 and, though he hated to keep bringing it up, "it must be paid." He added, "I notice there are fellows in almost every community whose mouths fly open and pocketbooks fly shut when you talk like that." One evening he sounded disgusted: "Houston is short on religion. It would take all of it in town pumped into one man to get up a good shout."

86. A WHARF AT HOUSTON.

87. BUFFALO BAYOU, HOUSTON.

88. INMAN COMPRESS, HOUSTON.

89. SAM HOUSTON STATE NORMAL, HUNTSVILLE.

SAM HOUSTON STATE NORMAL, which opened at Huntsville in 1879 in the old Austin College buildings, was the first "Normal" in Texas, and as late as 1892 was the largest school in the state system, with 313 students, compared to the University of Texas' 309. The Sam Houston students, in December 1895, had "an old fashioned candy pulling" to entertain the students.

90. A SCENE AT LUFKIN.

LUFKIN was a new town, begun with a townlot auction in 1885 by the Houston East and West Texas Railway—a narrow-gauge road more often called, from its initials, "Hell Either Way Taken." Lufkin had become the county seat of Angelina County in 1893.

91. A NEW SETTLER IN ANGELINA COUNTY.

92. A FARM IN CHEROKEE COUNTY, NEAR RUSK.

93. I&GN STATION AT PALESTINE.

94. POST OFFICE, TYLER.

ABOUT ONE MONTH before Stark visited Tyler, a Negro man named Robert Hilliard, accused of murdering and mutilating a young white woman, had been taken by a mob to the west side of the public square and roasted alive. He was chained to a rail and "many loads of boxing, oil barrels and such materials were piled up for the execution." Some 4,000 of

Tyler's 7,000 population watched. "His pleading for mercy fell in vain upon the ears of an angry populace, as the fumes of his burning flesh ascended," a Dallas *News* reporter told. "Pains were taken that the fire burned slow in order that the Negro's torture continue as long as possible. . . . After having been tortured in this manner for over an hour, the iron bar was pulled down and a large fire was built over him and the crowd dispersed."

95. HENDERSON MALE AND FEMALE COLLEGE.

96. A STREET SCENE IN MARSHALL.

MARSHALL was the original headquarters for the Texas & Pacific Railway. Before the Civil War it had one of the earliest railroads in Texas whose locomotive was called "Bull of the Woods" because of its habit, on curves, of leaving the tracks and plunging off into the forest.

97. HARRISON COUNTY COURTHOUSE, MARSHALL.

98. "WYALUCING" (BISHOP COLLEGE), MARSHALL.

SHOWPLACE of antebellum Marshall was "Wyalucing," built in 1850 by Beverly Lafayette Holcombe. His daughter Lucy, age 24, was married there in 1857 to Francis Wilkinson Pickens, a distinguished South Carolina politician, who was shortly afterwards appointed U. S. ambassador to Russia. Lucy became such a favorite at the St. Petersburg court that the Czarina Catherine became godmother to the Pickens' child, naming her Douschka. Pickens became governor of South Carolina in 1860 and, in that office, gave the order to fire the first guns of the Civil War. "Lady Lucy," as she was called, was such a beauty her face was used on Confederate currency. Lucy sold the jewelry Czar Alexander II had presented to her, and outfitted a Confederate Army unit which called itself the "Lucy Holcombe Legion." Meanwhile, "Wyalucing" was used as headquarters for the Confederate Trans-Mississippi post office. Pickens, who was thirty years older than Lucy (she was his third wife), died in 1869 and she moved back to Marshall. "Wyalucing" was bought, in 1880, by former Harrison County slaves and made part of the Bishop College campus. When Stark photographed the building it housed the music school. Bishop College moved to Dallas in 1961 and "Wyalucing" was torn down, to the dismay of all Texas.

99. CLARK & BOYCE LUMBER CO., JEFFERSON, MARION COUNTY.

LUMBERING had created a new class of Texas millionaire, over in the Piney Woods, and from 1895 to 1910 Texas ranked third or fourth among the states in lumber production. But in 1895 cotton was king. Not only was it the state's biggest crop, it was the *only* crop in county after county. It had to be worked by hand at almost every step of its yield: plowing, of course, to prepare the rows for spring planting; then it had to be kept clean of weeds by chopping with a hoe, and finally it was picked, or pulled, by hand. It never was a jolly kind of farming.

100. A FARM IN CASS COUNTY, NEAR ATLANTA.

MUCH of a family's food was grown and processed at home, especially in small towns and on farms. Bacon was 7½¢ per pound; whisky was as low as $1.22 per gallon, and could be sent through the mail.

In the market in the winter of 1895-96, cotton was bringing 6½ to 8½¢ per pound (which was rather low), top grade steers brought $3, while hogs ran $3-3.50. Milk cows cost $25, and even in big cities most families kept a cow. Horses were like automobiles, so far as prices went: you could pay almost any price for a fine one or get a "used" one dirt cheap, but with no guarantees. The horse trader corresponded closely to the modern used car dealer.

A NOTE about the railroad names: The *Cotton Belt* was (and is) the popular name given the Saint Louis-Southwestern, and the *Katy* railroad is the Missouri-Kansas-Texas. The International & Great Northern (I&GN) is still the corporate name for the road, but it is generally referred to now as the Missouri Pacific or *MoPac*. The Texas & Pacific is also part of the Missouri Pacific system, but only in the 1960s did it begin to carry that emblem or use that name. The Houston & Texas Central (H&TC) is now called the Southern Pacific in most places—although even in 1895 it was an SP property. The Cotton Belt today is SP controlled also.

BIBLIOGRAPHY

A History of Texas Revised, Anna J. H. Pennybacker
Texas Almanac (years 1911, 1926, 1936, 1941, 1968, 1972, 1974)
The Story of North Texas, James L. Rogers
The Red River Valley Then and Now, A. W. Neville
A Condensed History of Texas, Mary M. Brown
Texas the Lone Star State, 2nd ed., R. N. Richardson
A History of the Texas Railroads, S. G. Reed
How Fort Worth Became the Texasmost City, Leonard Sanders and Ronnie C. Tyler
Indian Wars and Pioneers of Texas, John Henry Brown
The Handbook of Texas, 2 vols., W. P. Webb and H. B. Carroll, eds.
Dallas Morning News (October-December 1895; January 1896)
Houston Daily Post (November 1895)
Chronology of the Modern World, Neville Williams
Concise Dictionary of American Biography, Jos. G. E. Hopkins, et al.
Who's Who in American History 1607-1896
United States History, R. N. Current, Alex. DeConde, Harris L. Dante
The History of Abilene, John Hutto, Hugh Cosby
John Selman, Texas Gunfighter, L. C. Metz
Oil! Titan of the Southwest, C. Coke Rister

ACKNOWLEDGMENTS

THE AUTHOR wishes to express his thanks to Mr. Lloyd Bockstruck and to Ms. Mary Kay Loomis of the Texas Collection of the Dallas Public Library; to Mr. Sidney Marks of Corsicana, and to Mr. George Johnston, Mr. Ben Garity, and Mr. Bill Porterfield, all of Dallas, for services and information. Thanks also to the Laredo Chamber of Commerce.

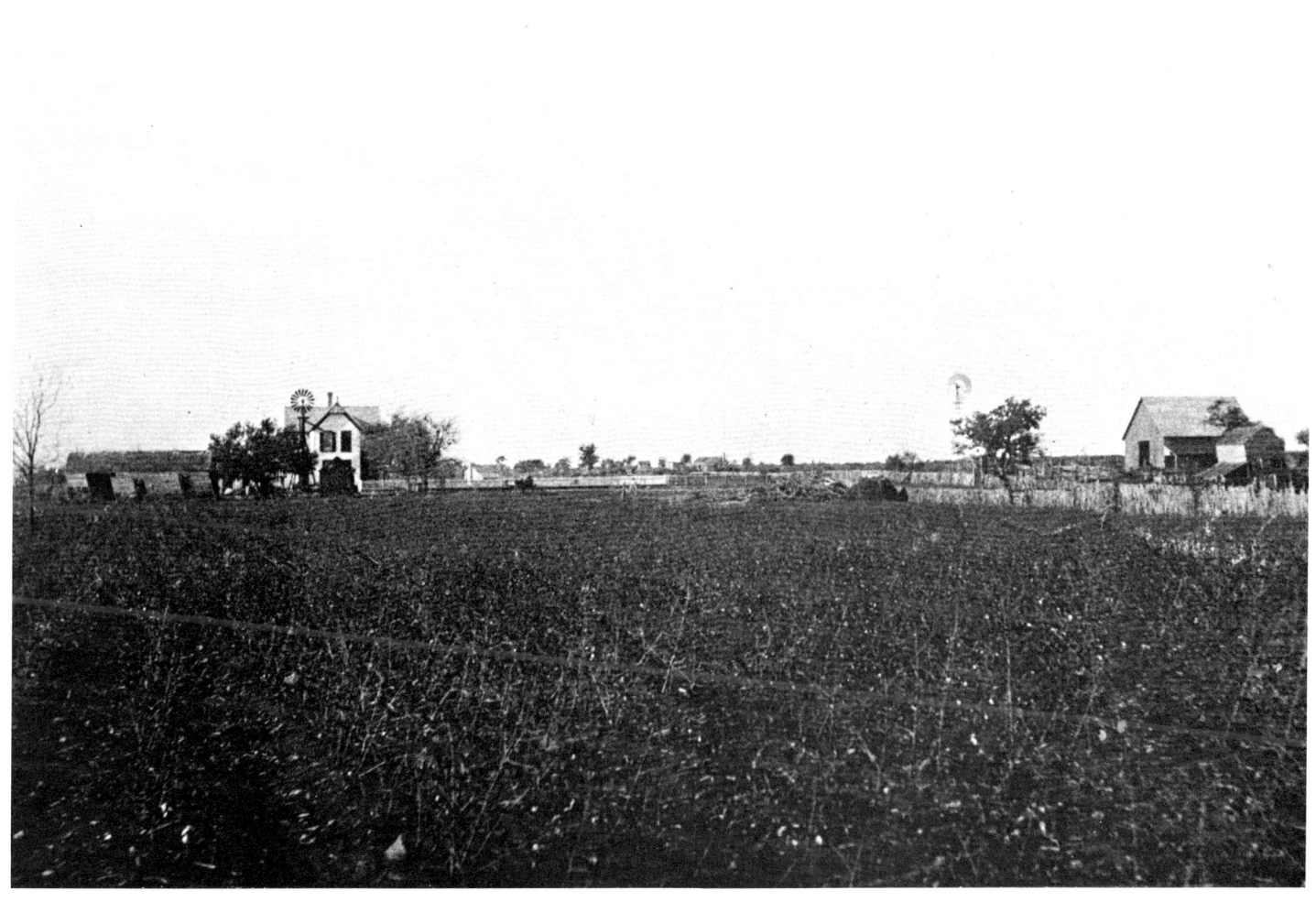

1. A farm in Bowie County, near Texarkana.

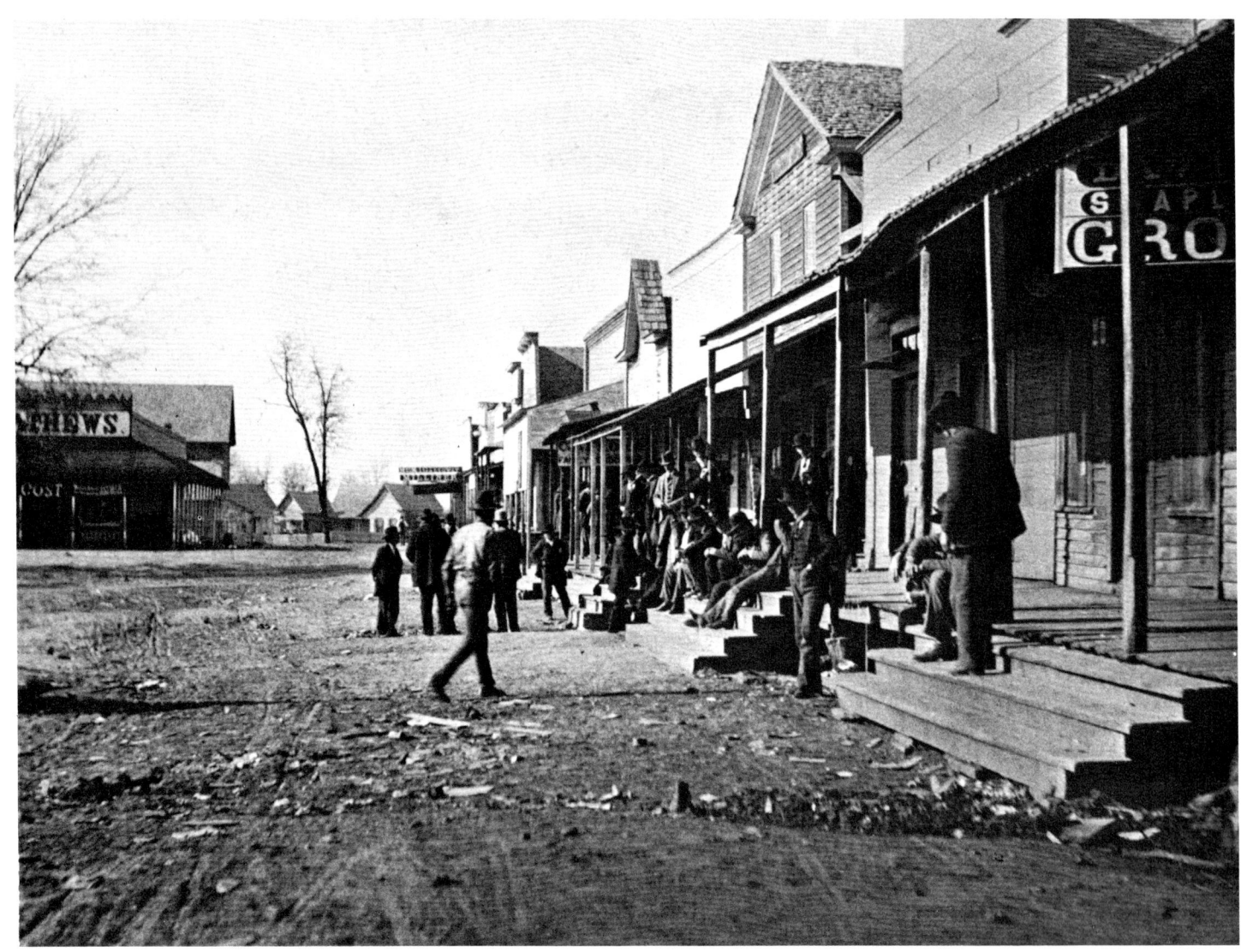

2. A scene at Naples. The name of the town had just been changed from "Belden."

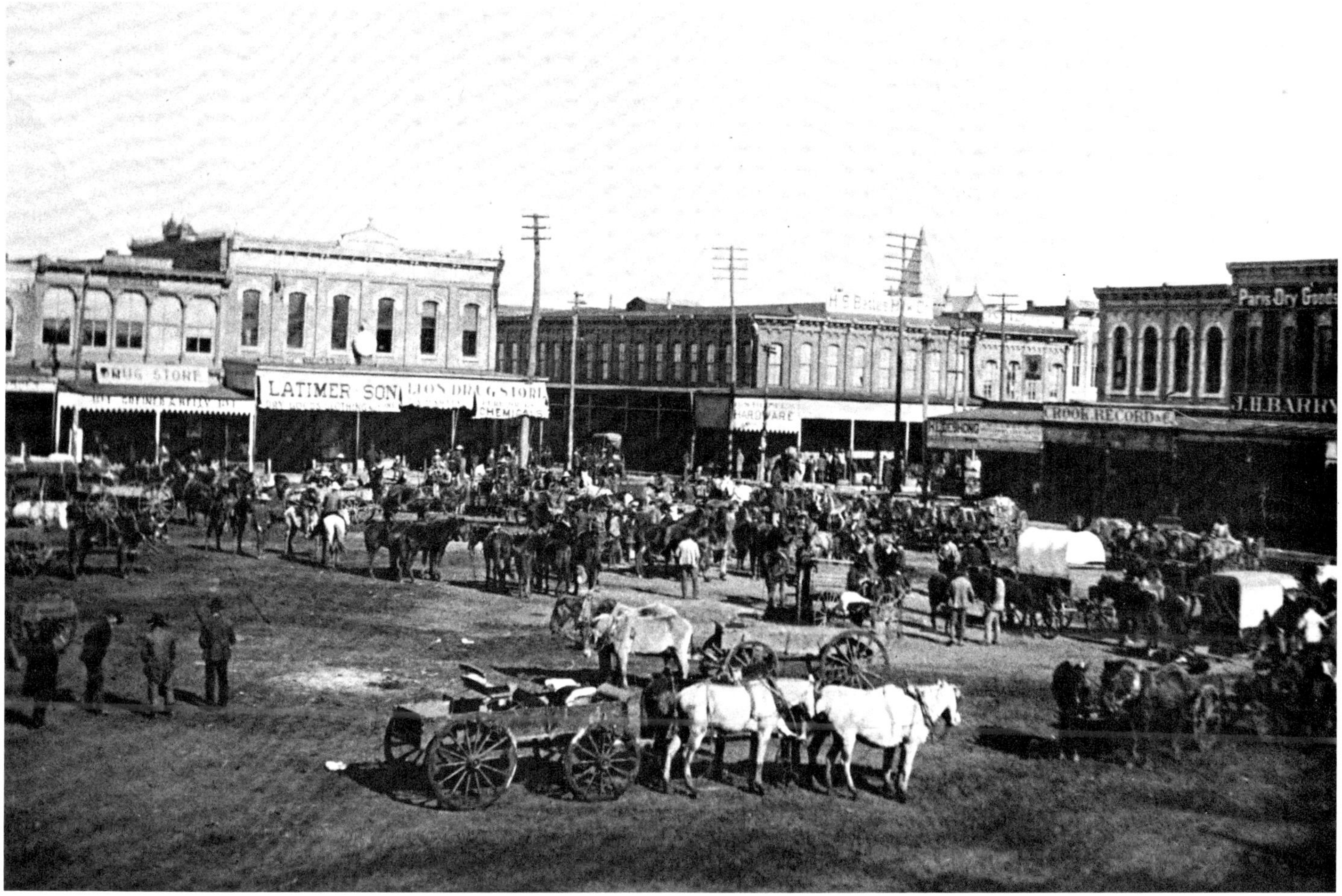

3. Public Square, Paris.

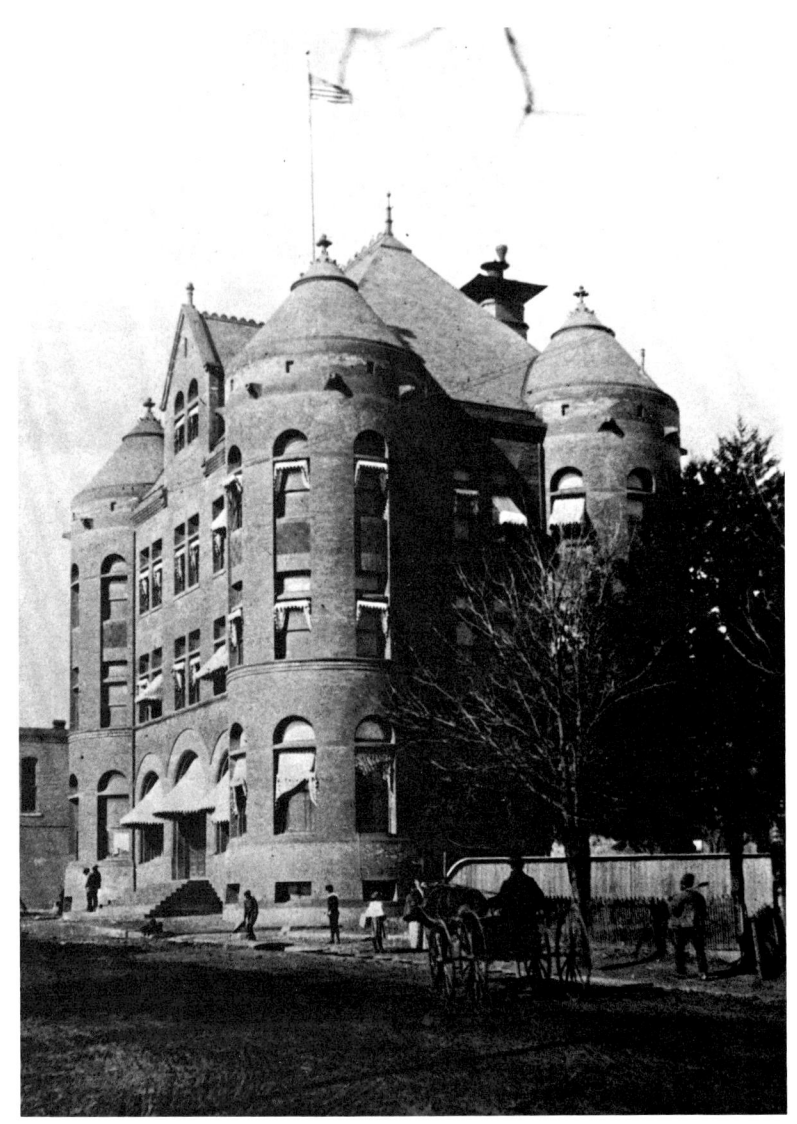

4. Federal Building, Paris.

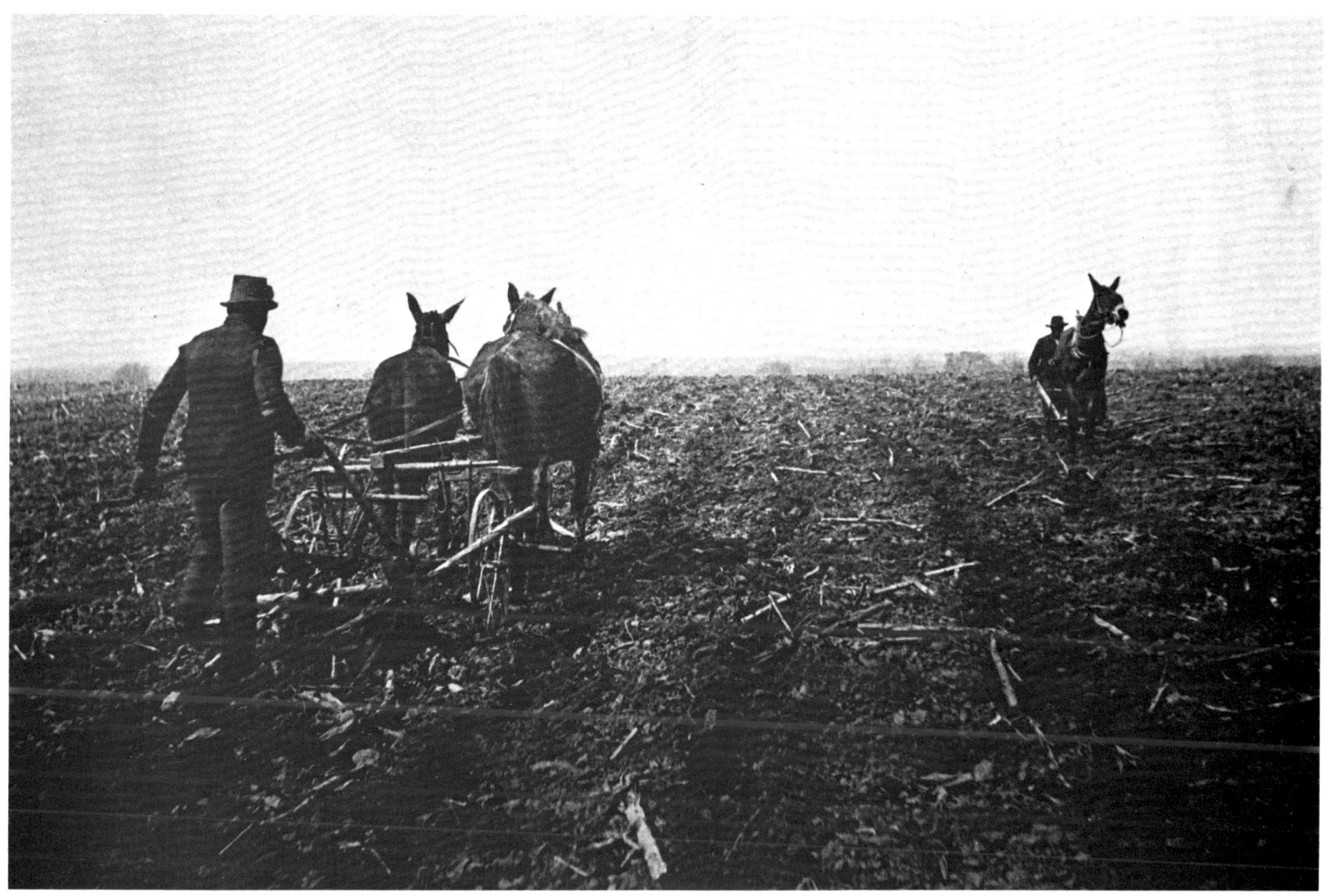

5. A farm in Fannin County, near Bonham.

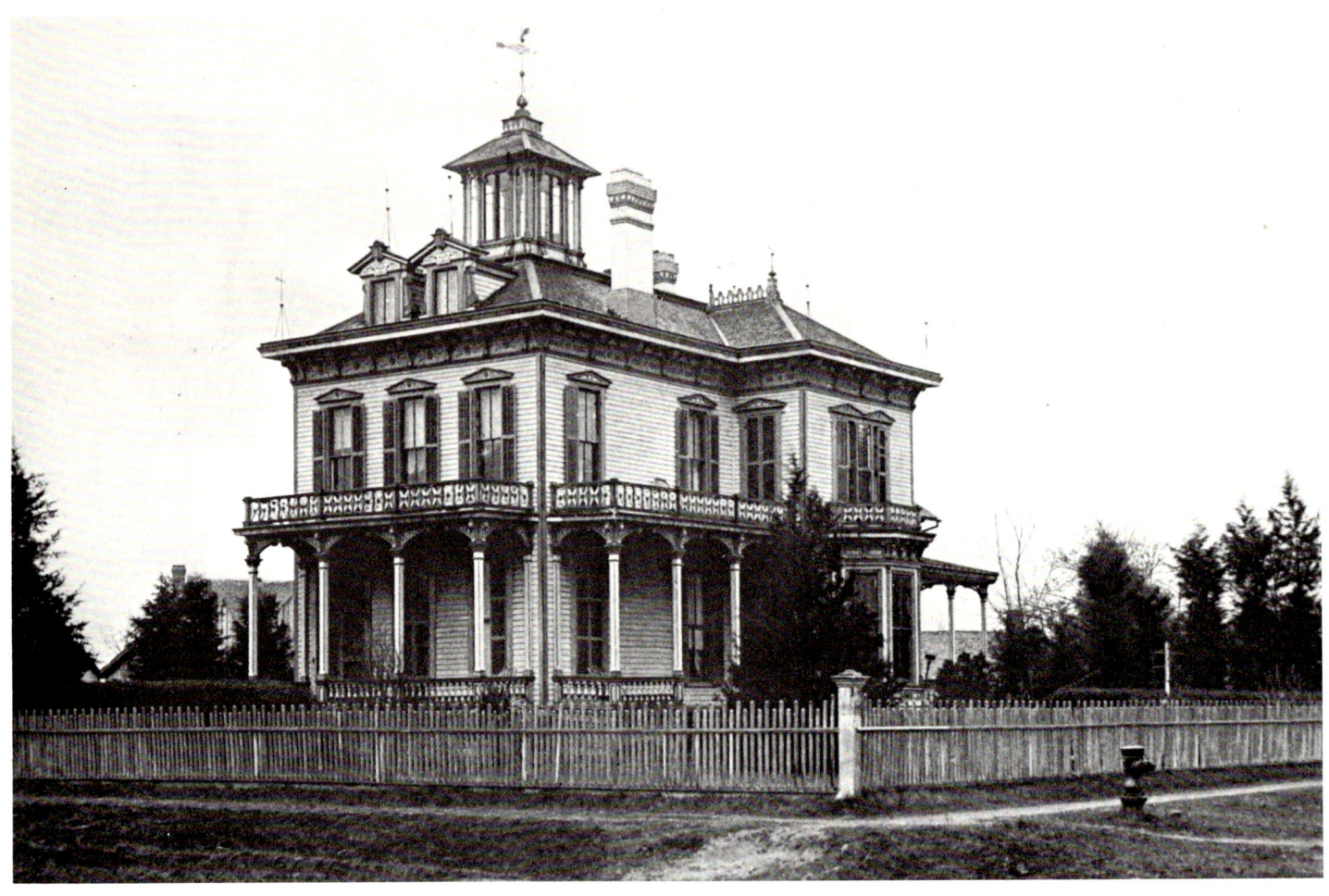

6. A residence at Denison.

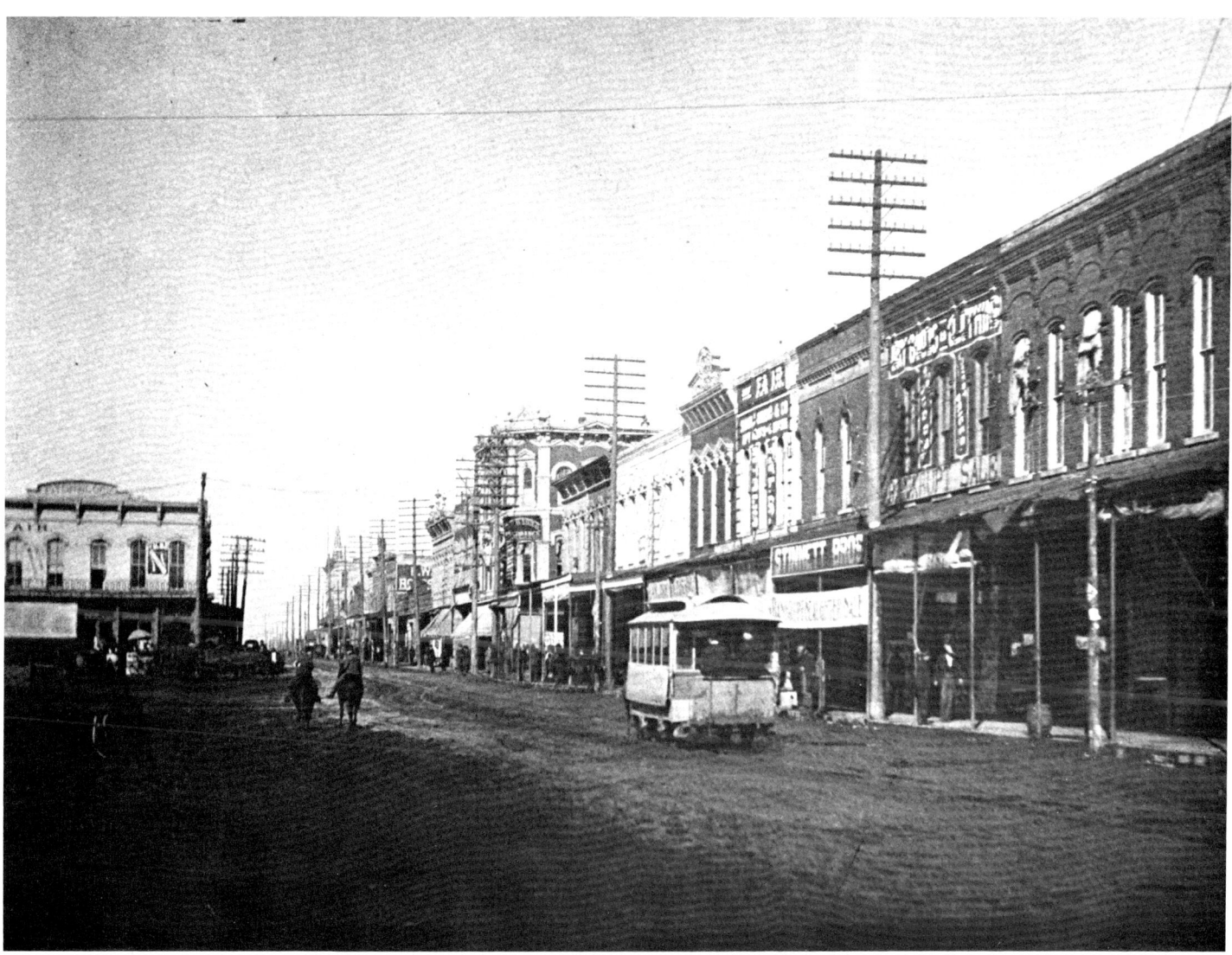

7. Business part of Travis Street, Sherman.

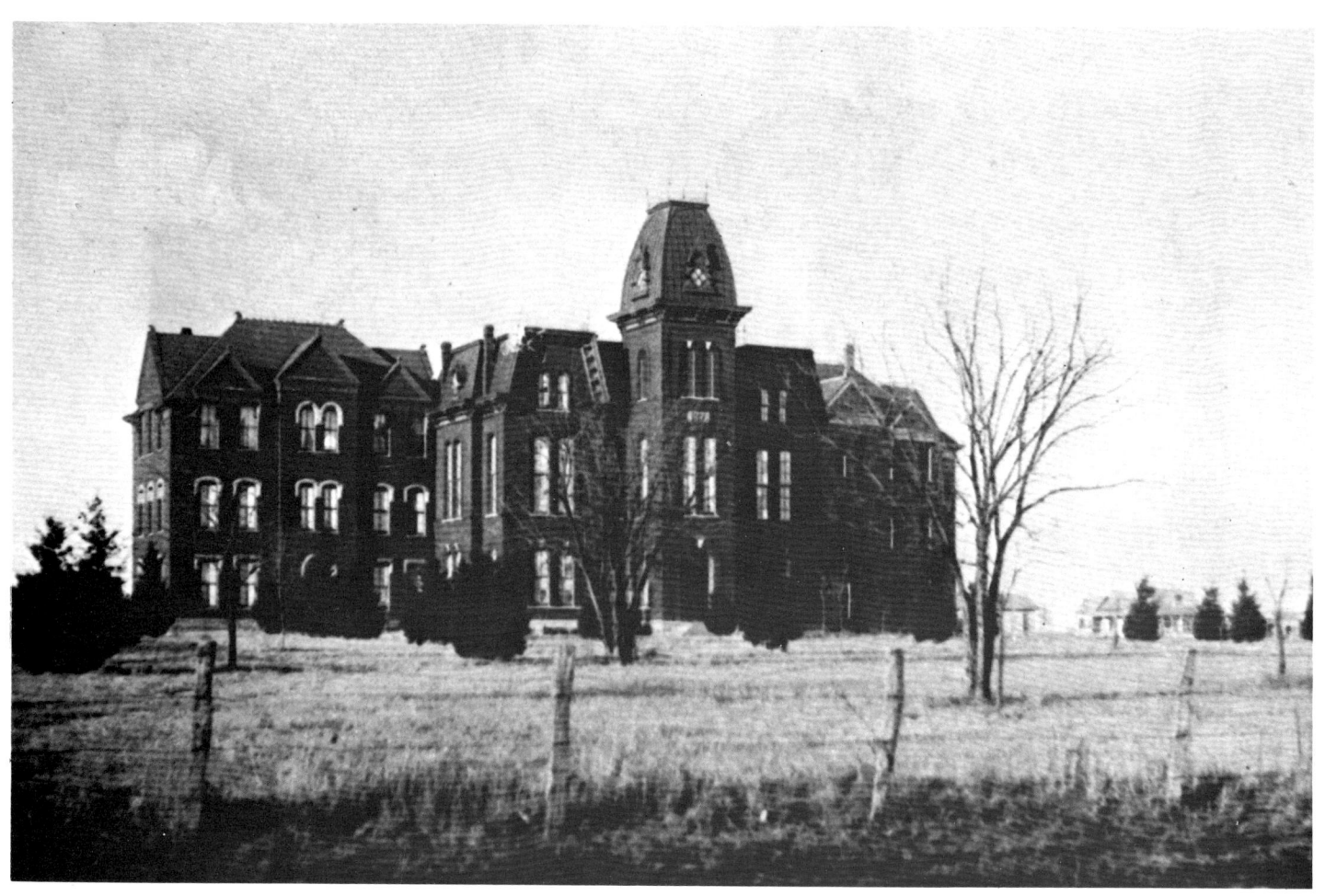

8. Austin College, Sherman. This building burned in 1913.

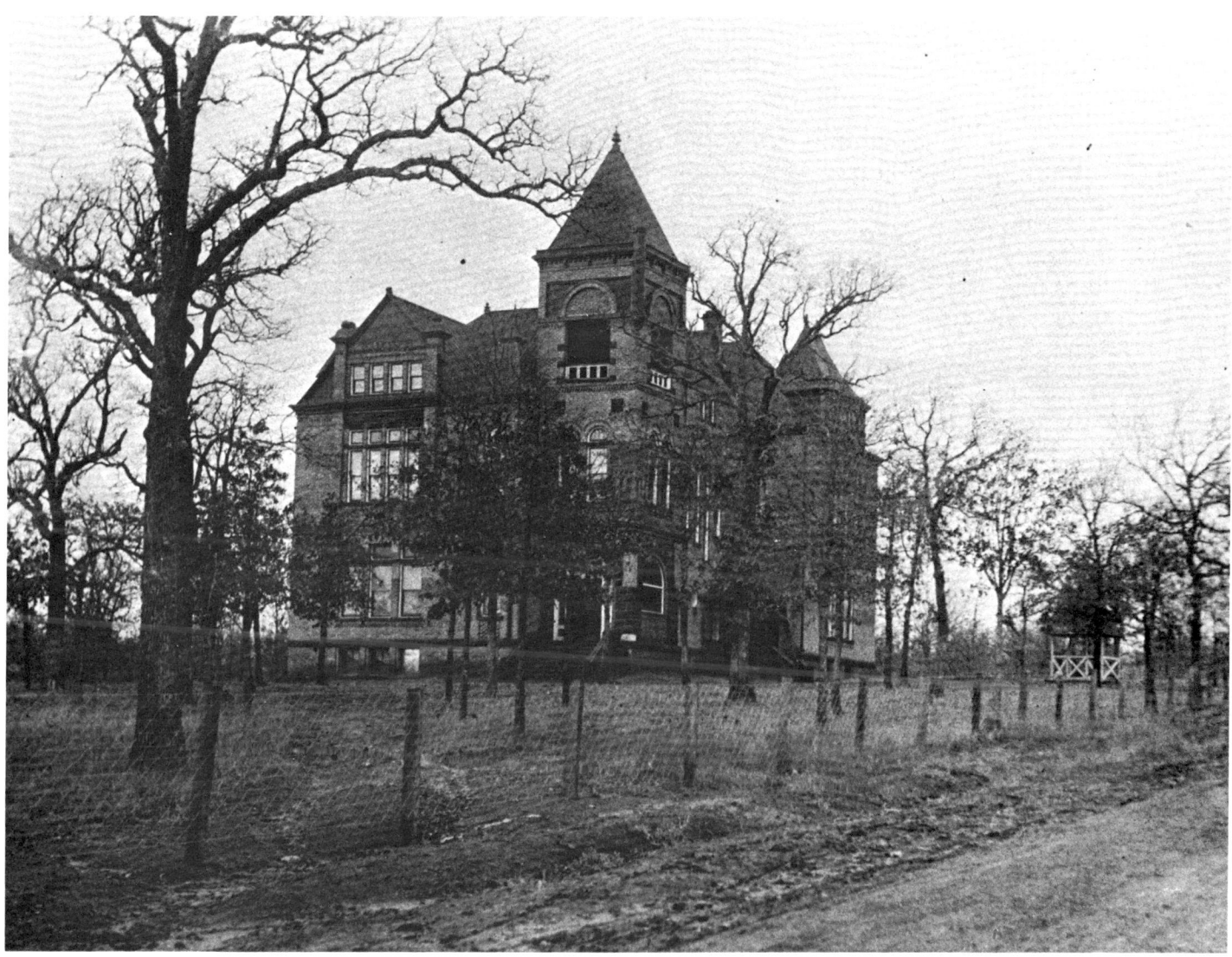

9. North Texas State Normal, Denton.

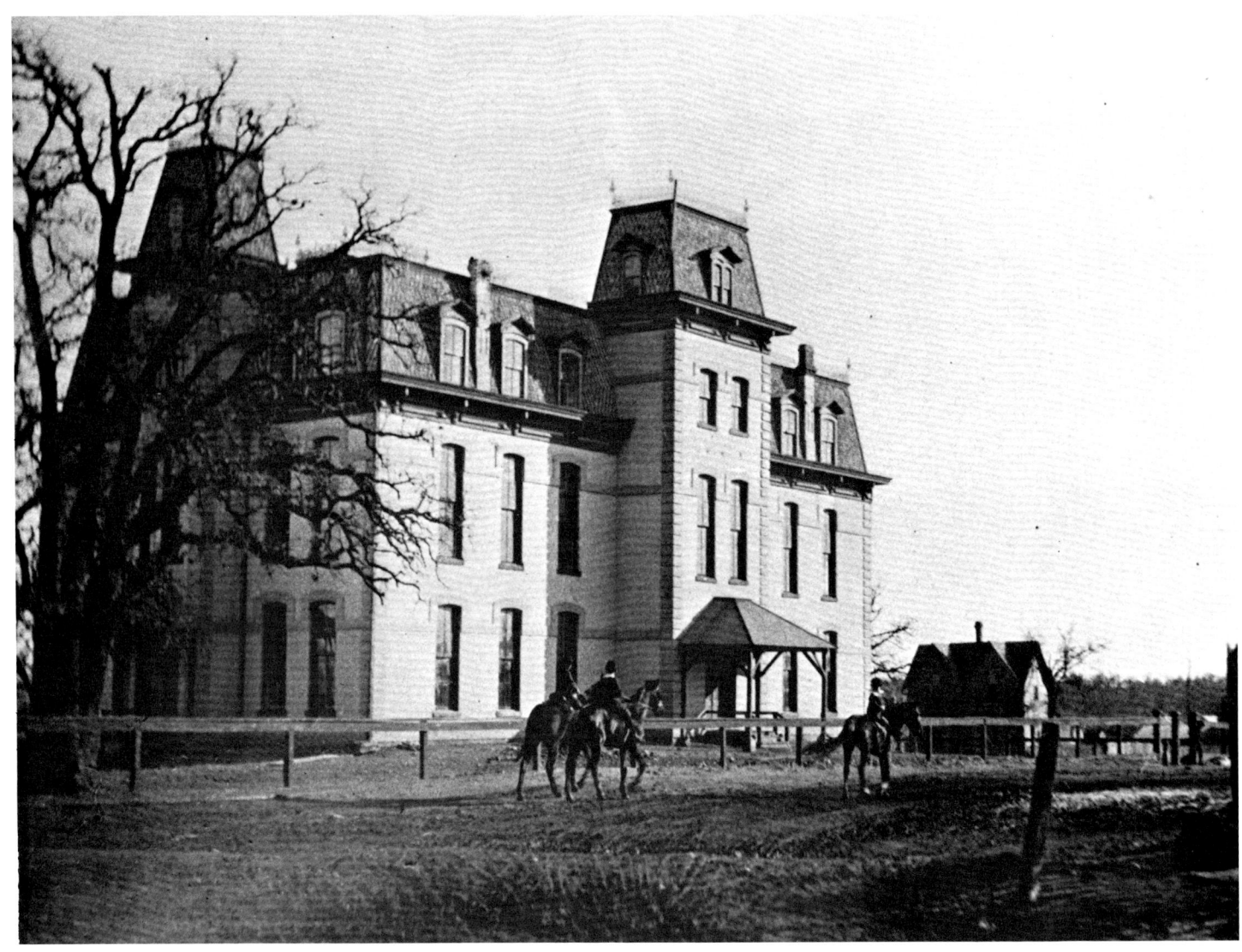

10. Public School, Denton.

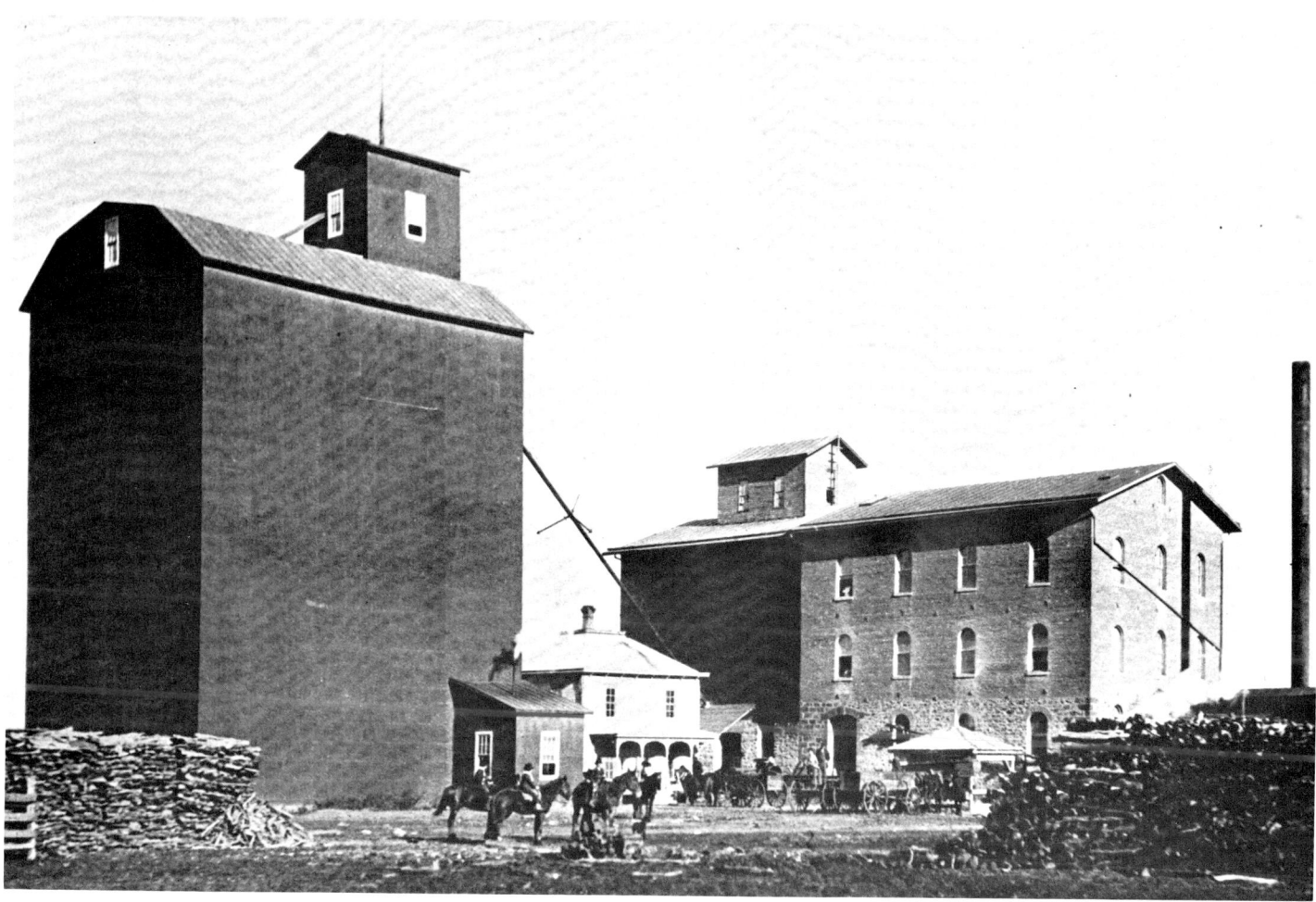

11. Alliance Milling Co., Denton.

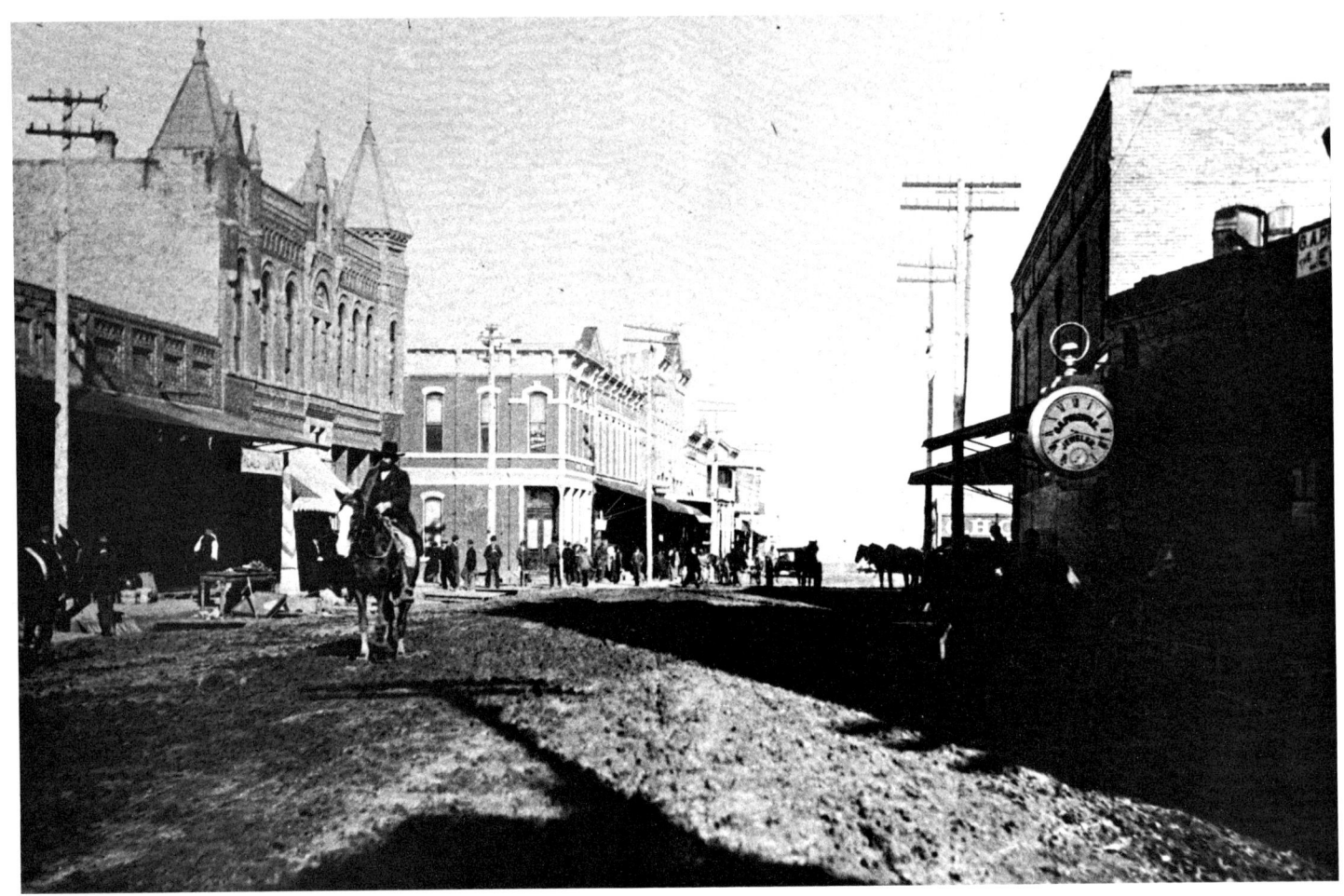

12. A Greenville street scene.

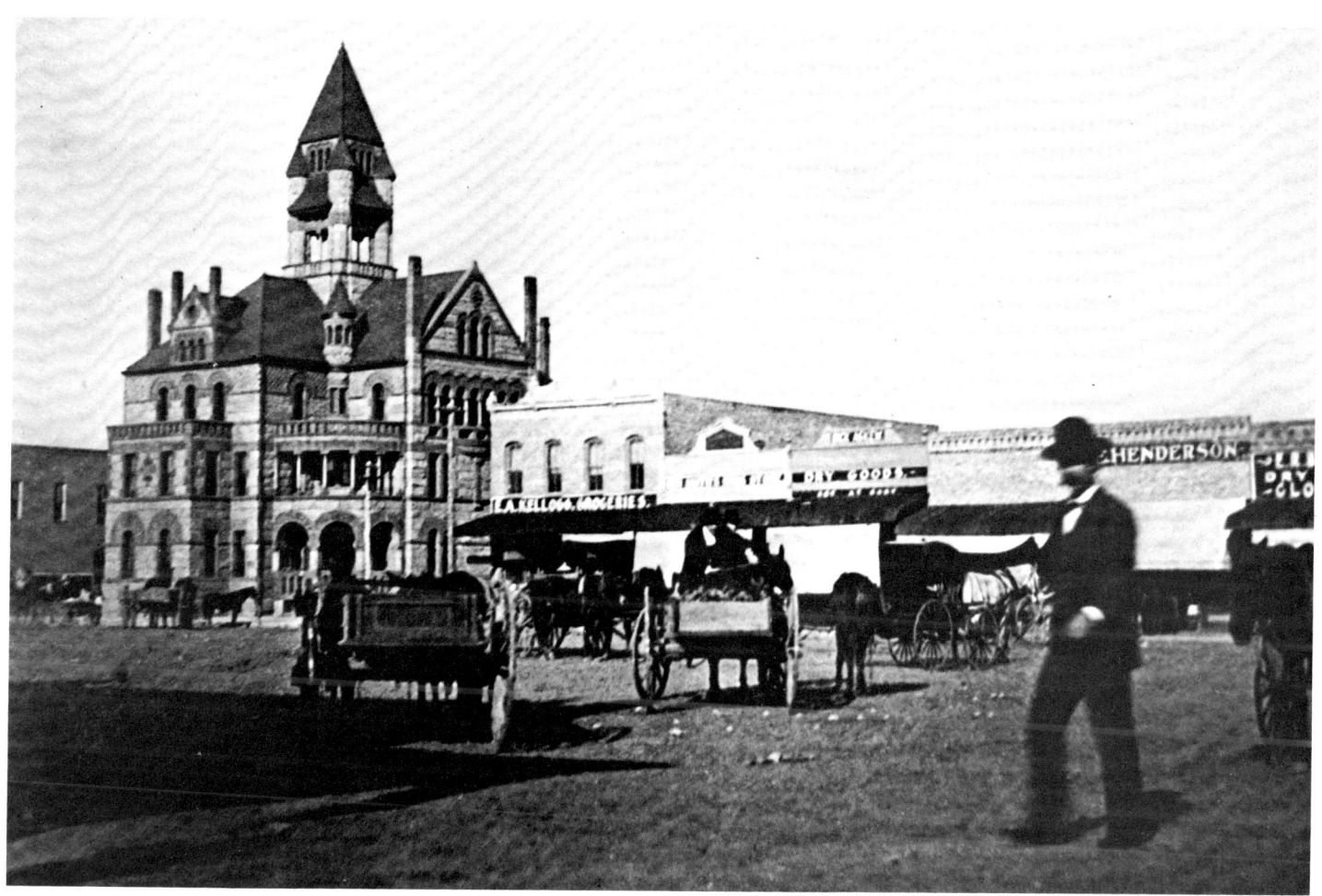

13. Hopkins County Courthouse, Sulphur Springs. The town's original name was "Bright Star."

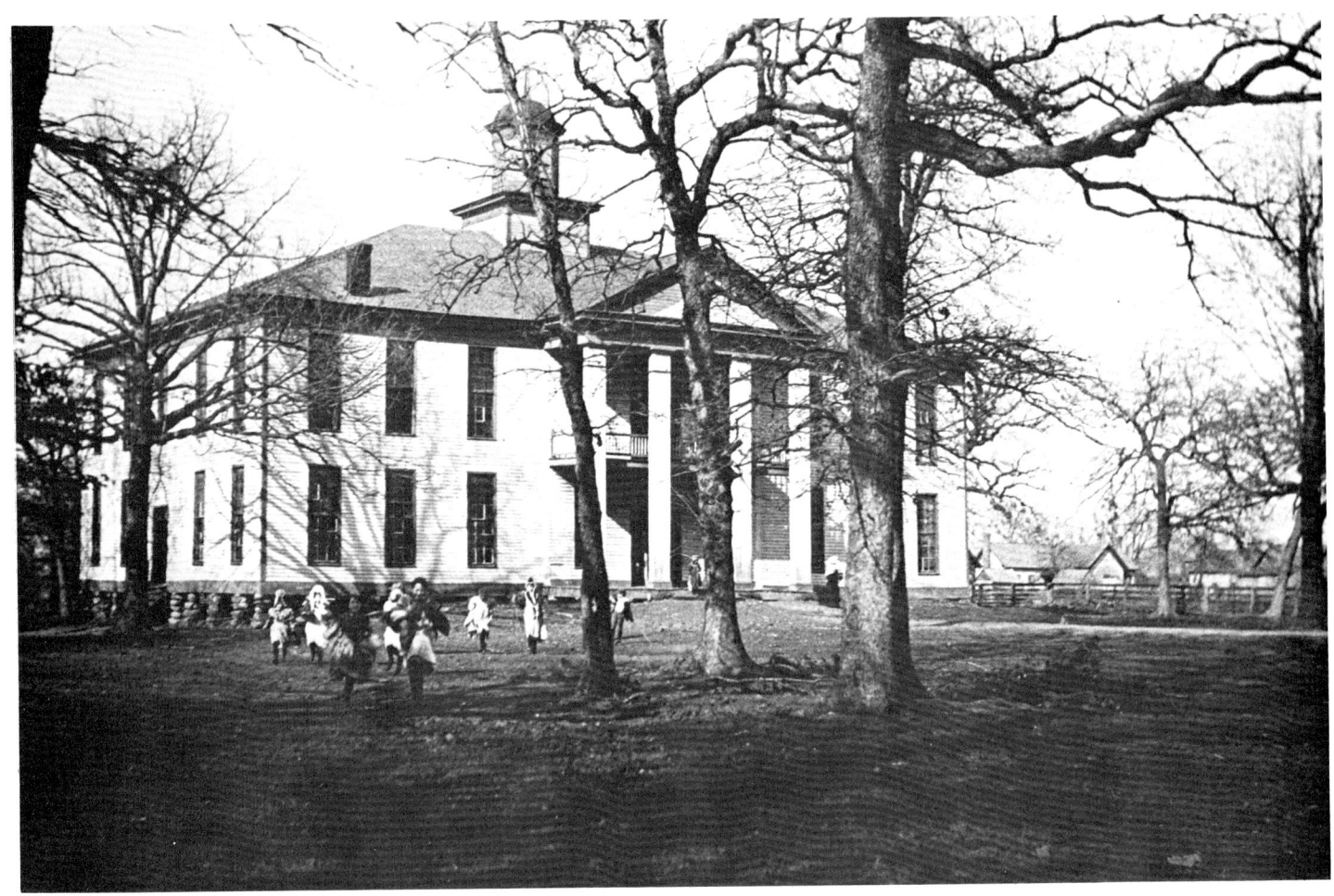

14. School at Sulphur Springs. It was later destroyed by fire.

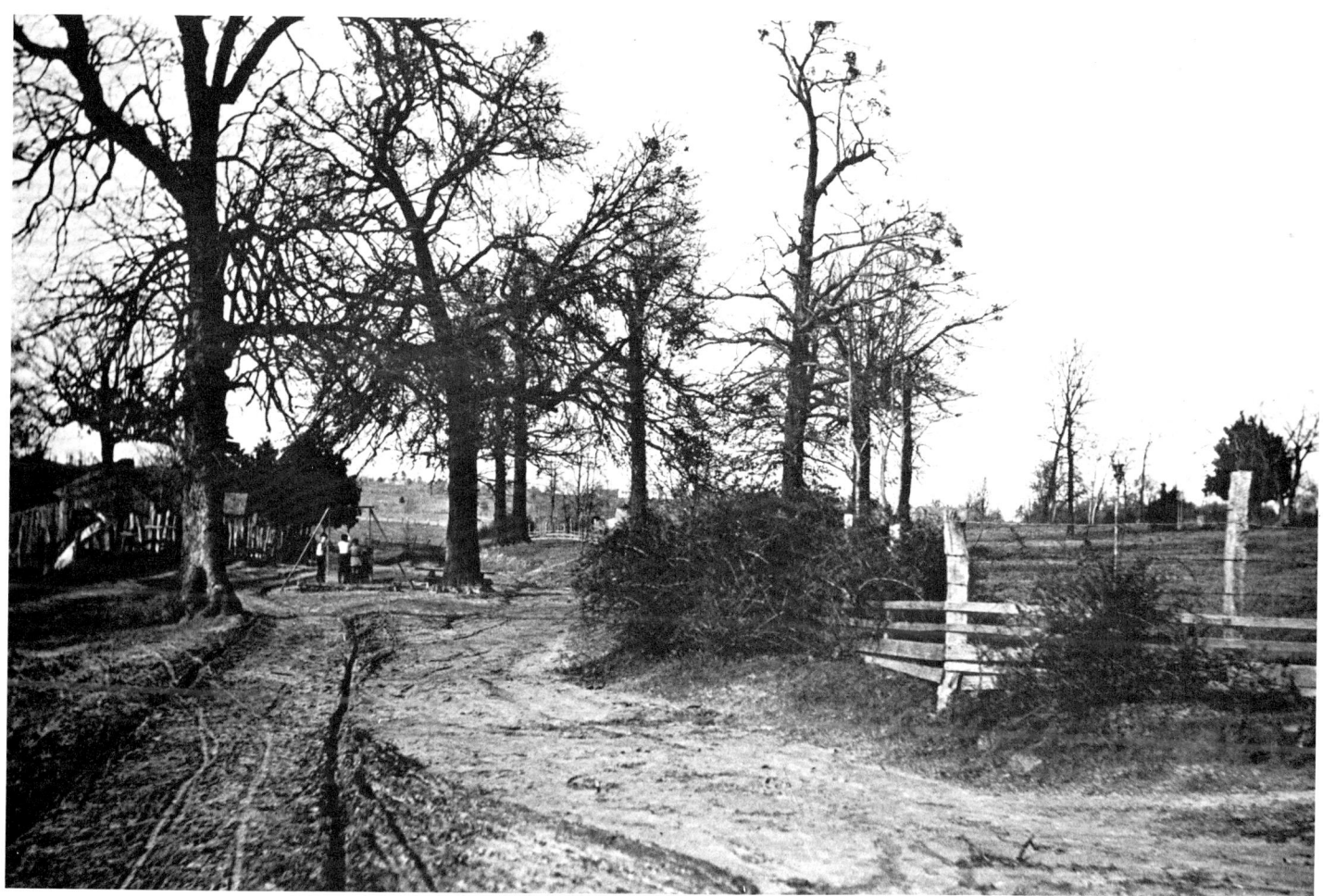

15. A rural road and well in Franklin County.

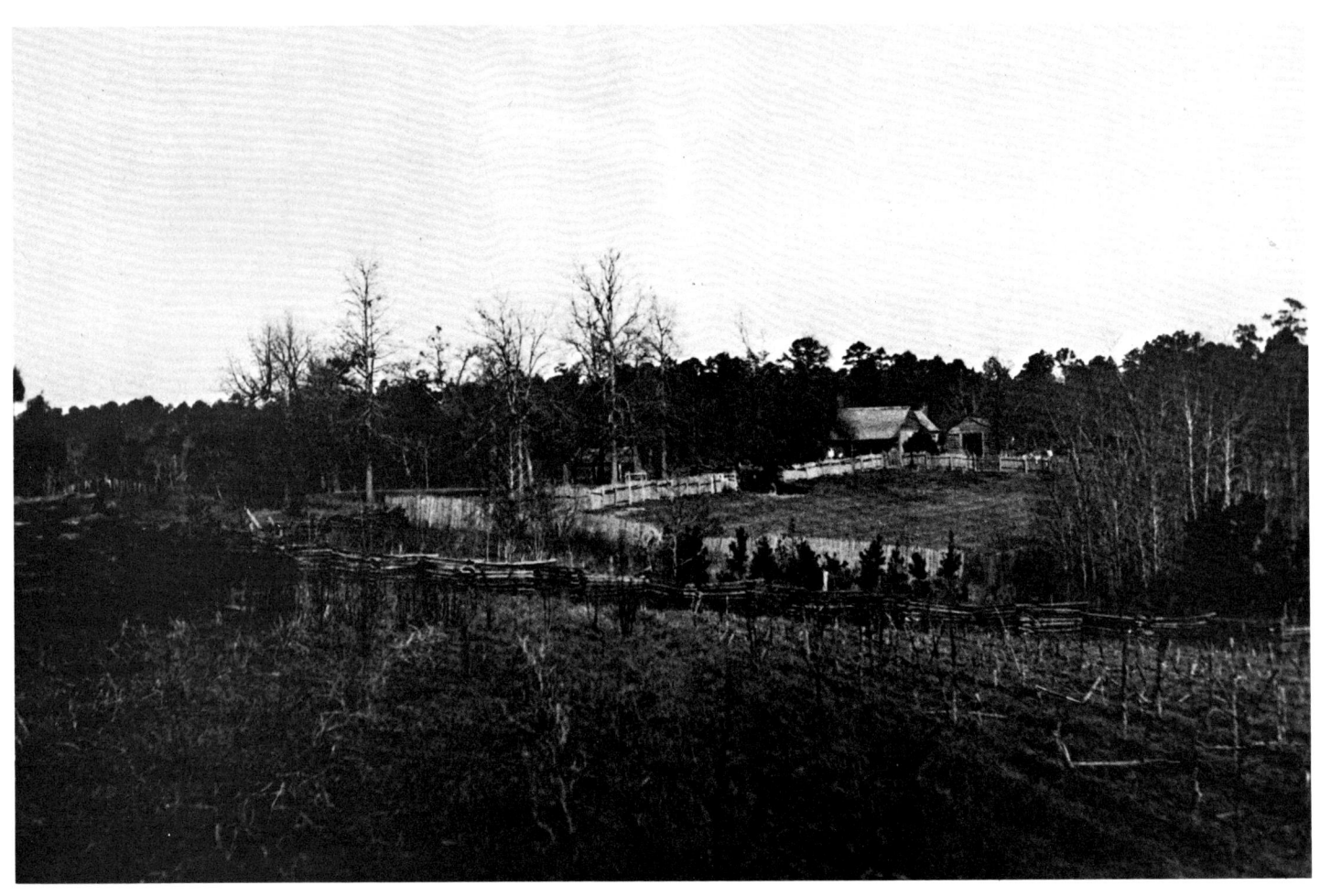

16. A farm in Camp County, near Pittsburg.

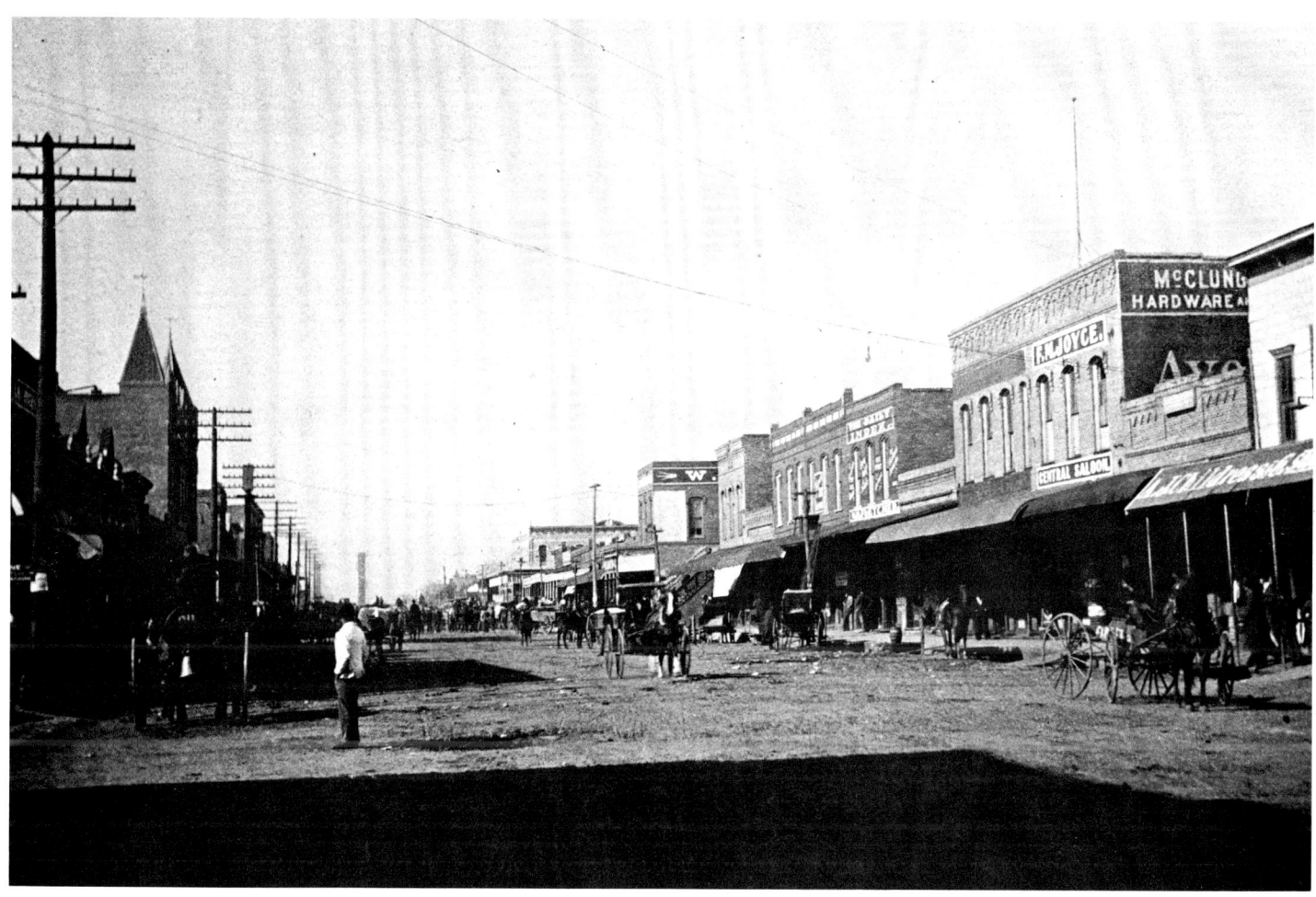

17. A scene in Terrell. The sign at the left reads, "$10 Fine For Leaving Your Team or Horse Untied."

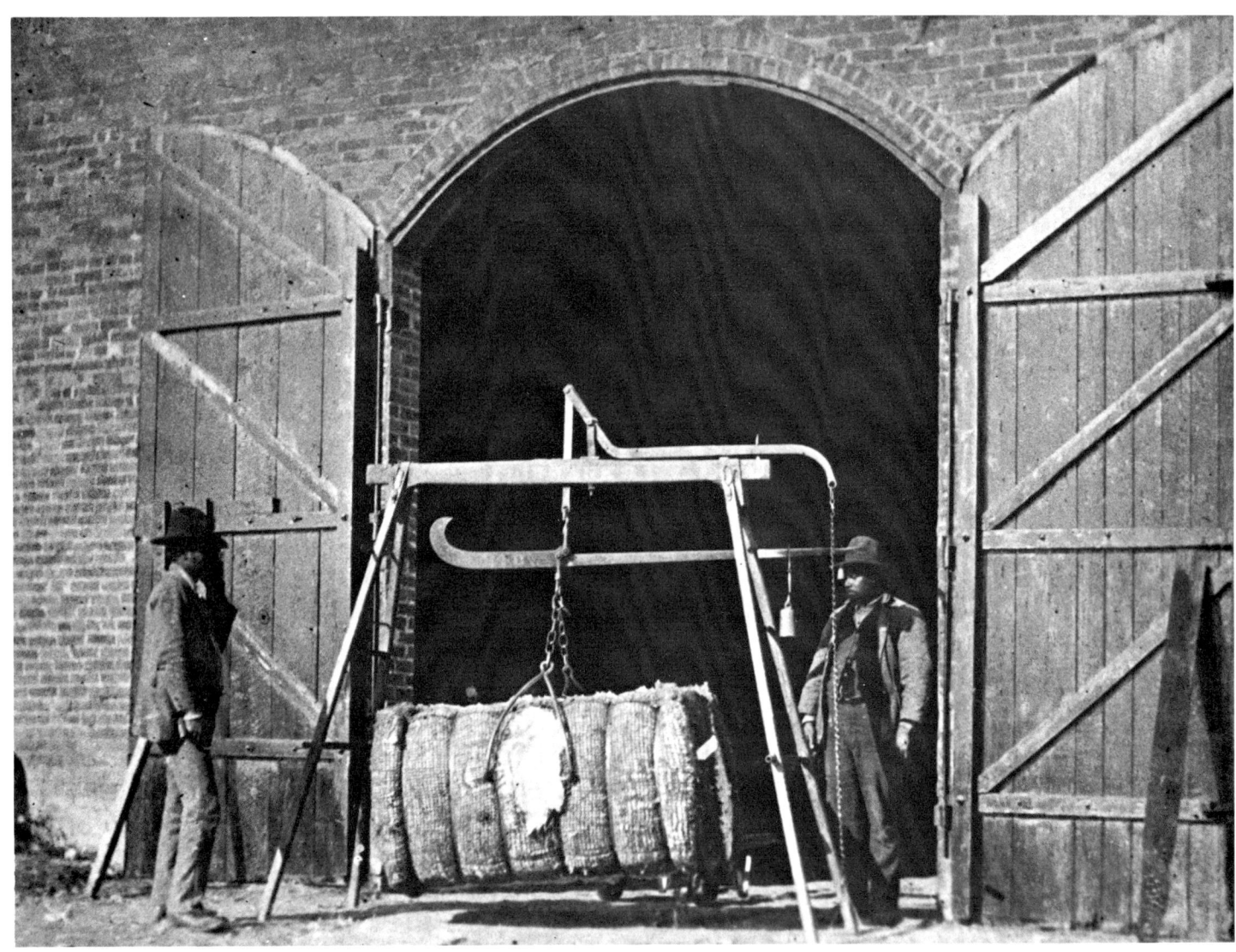

18. Compress at Terrell.

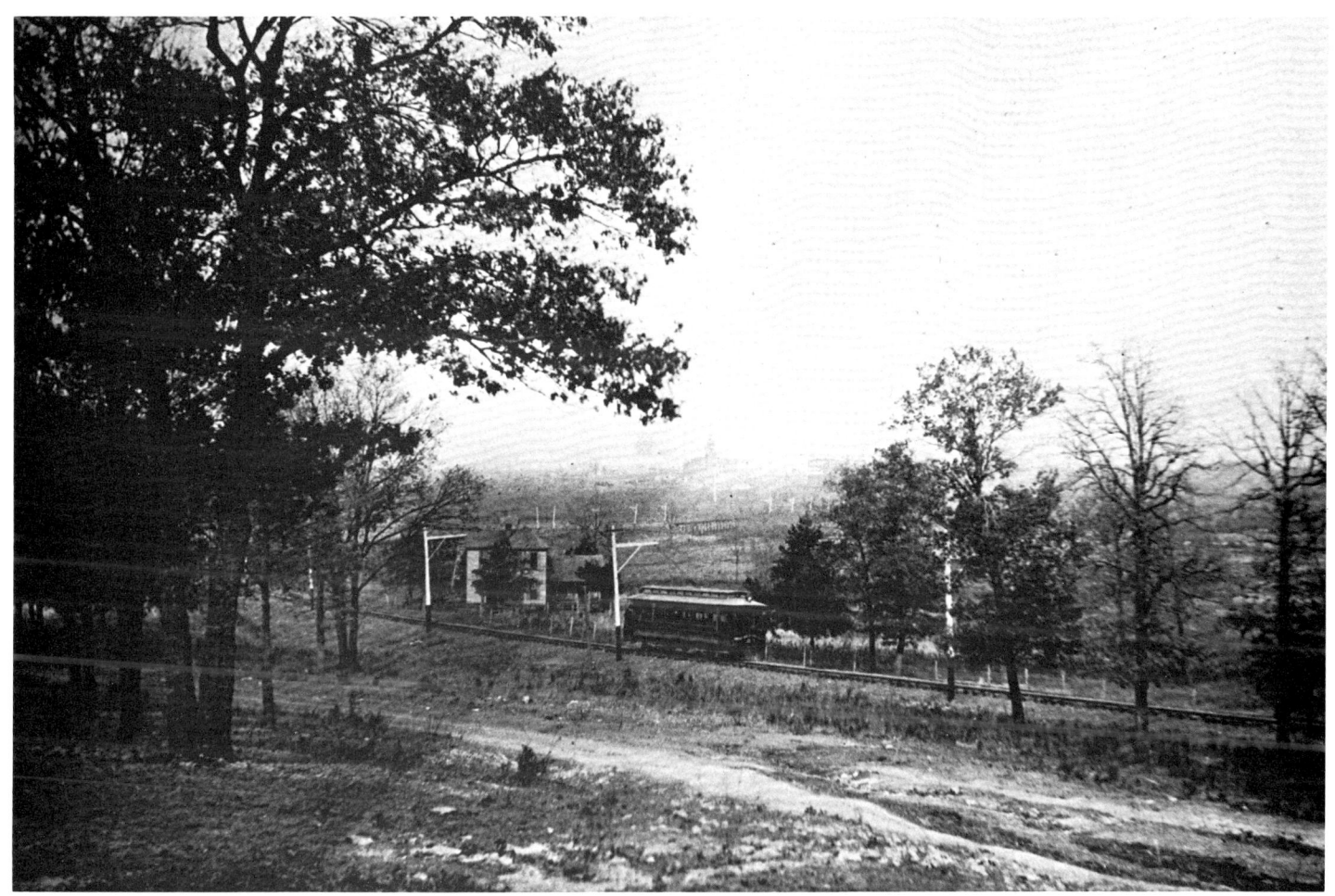

19. Looking toward Dallas from Oak Cliff.

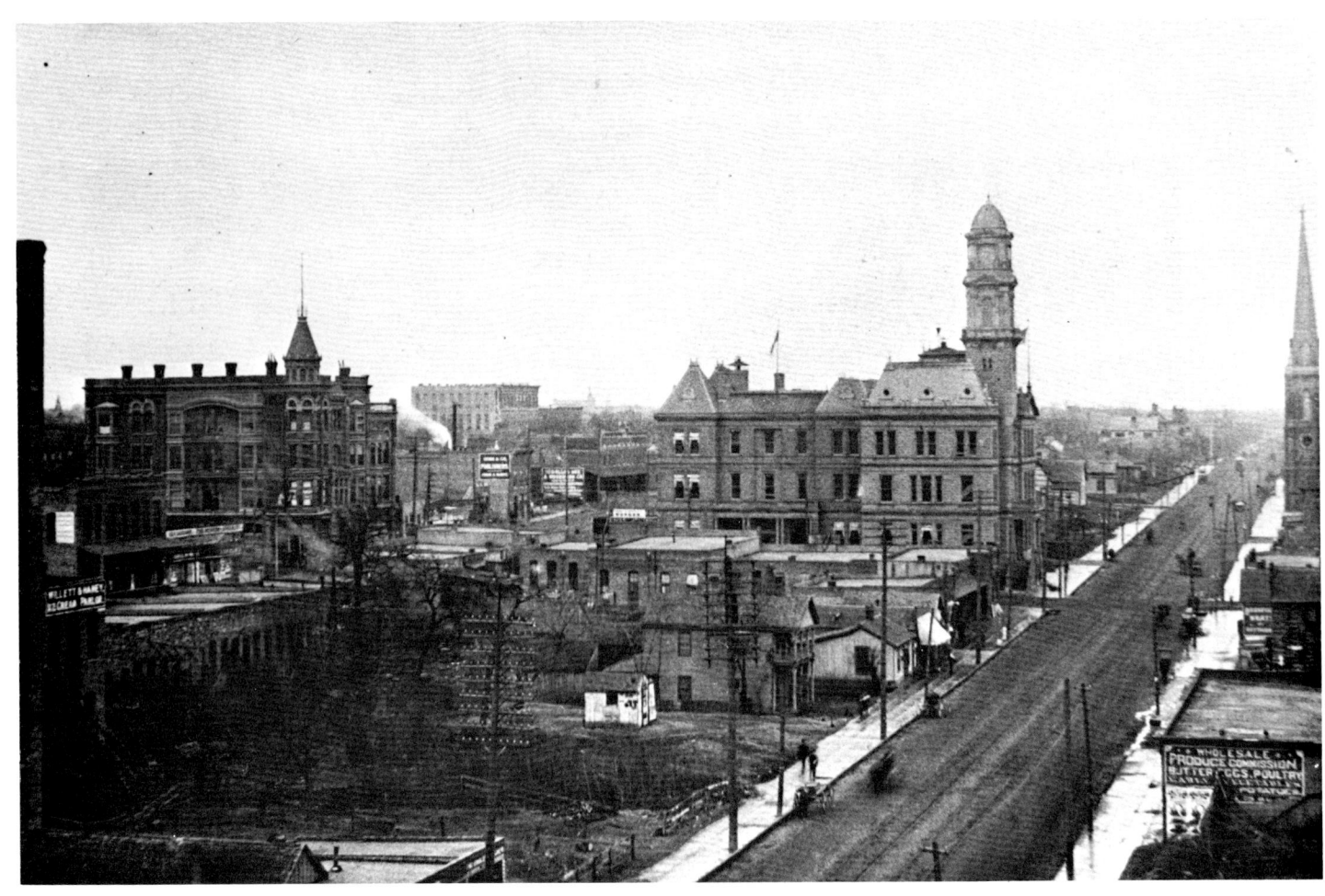

20. Looking east from the Oriental Hotel, Dallas. The large building in the center is the Post Office at Ervay and Commerce Streets.

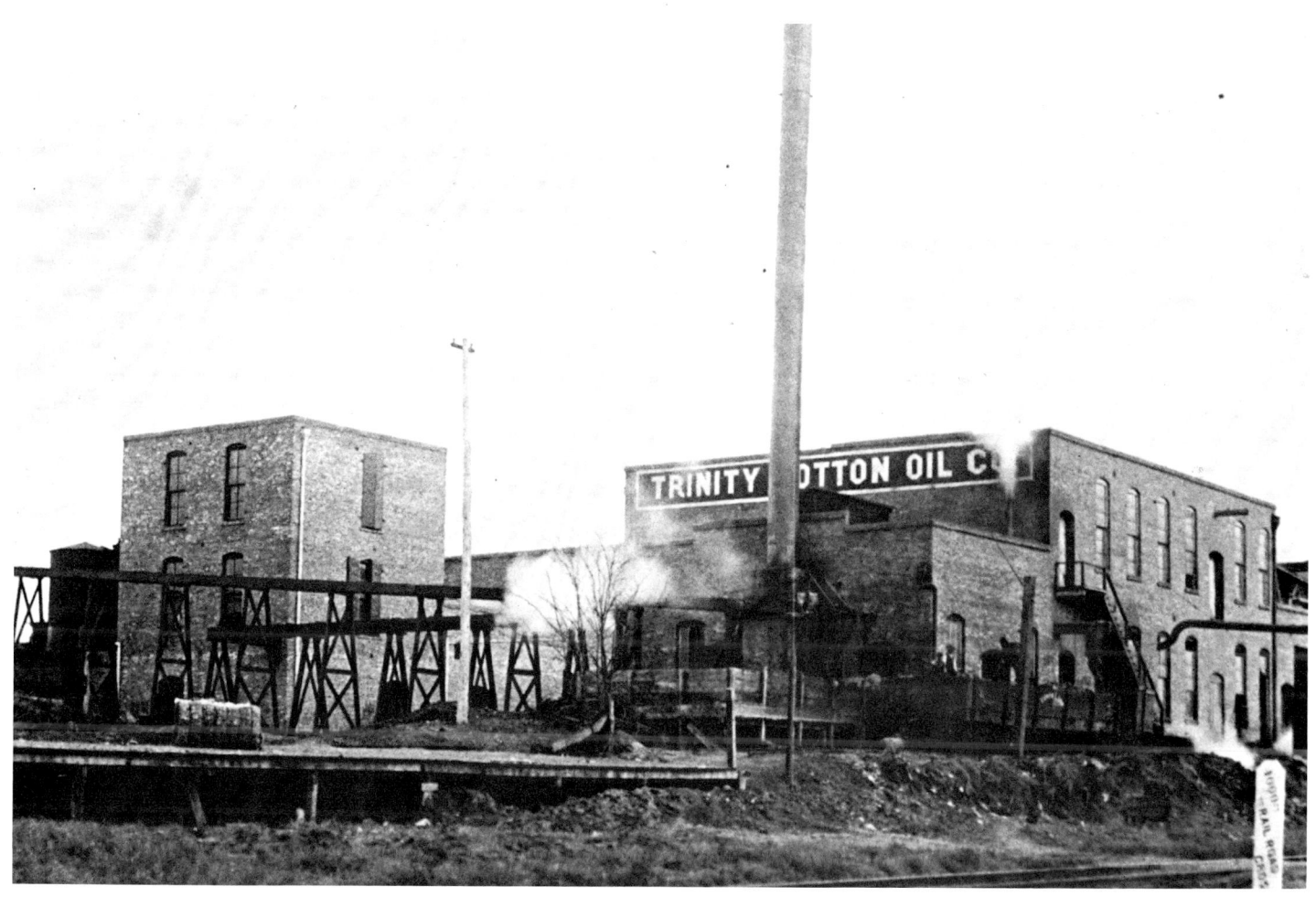

21. Trinity Oil Company, Dallas.

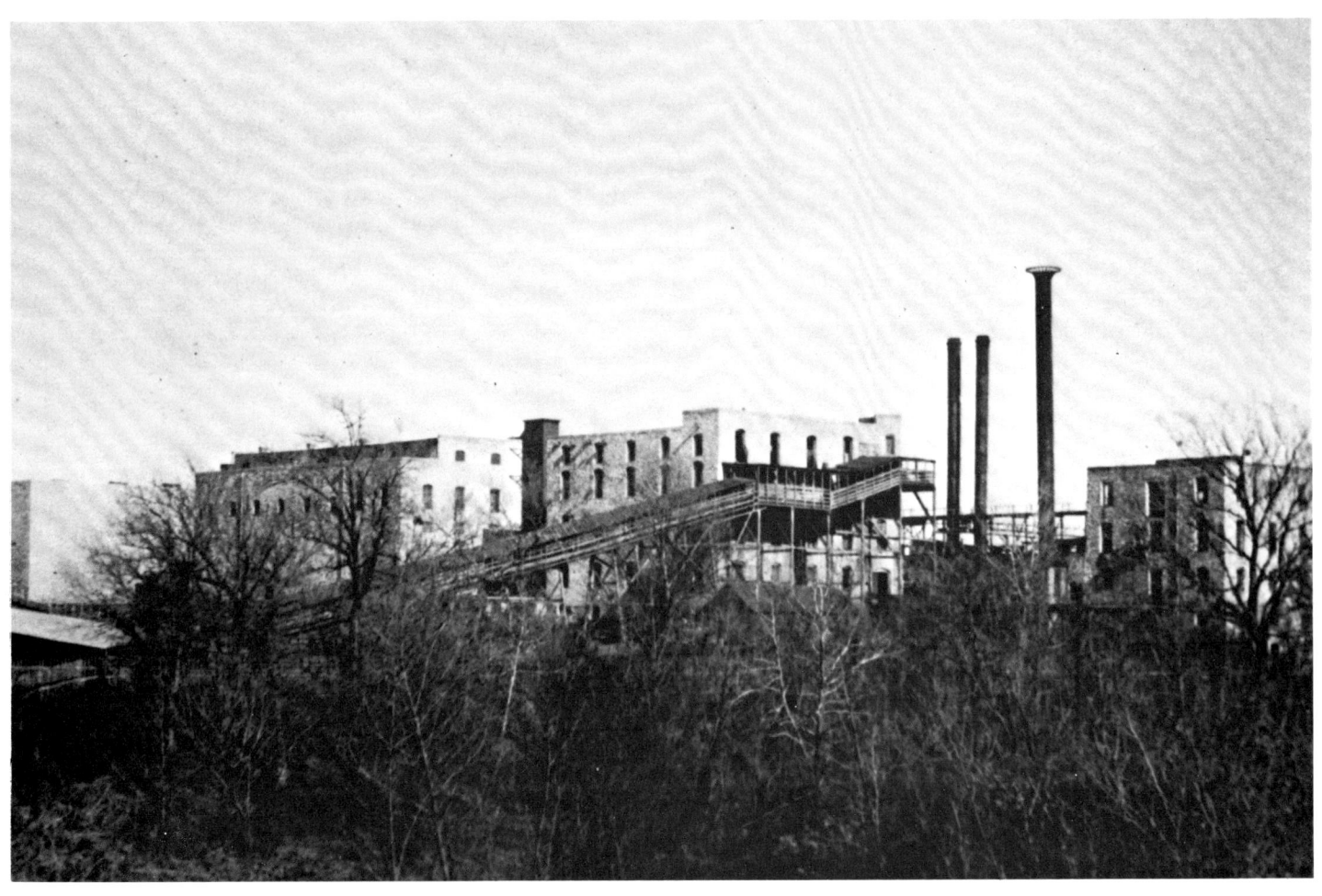

22. Fort Worth Dressed Meat and Packing Co.

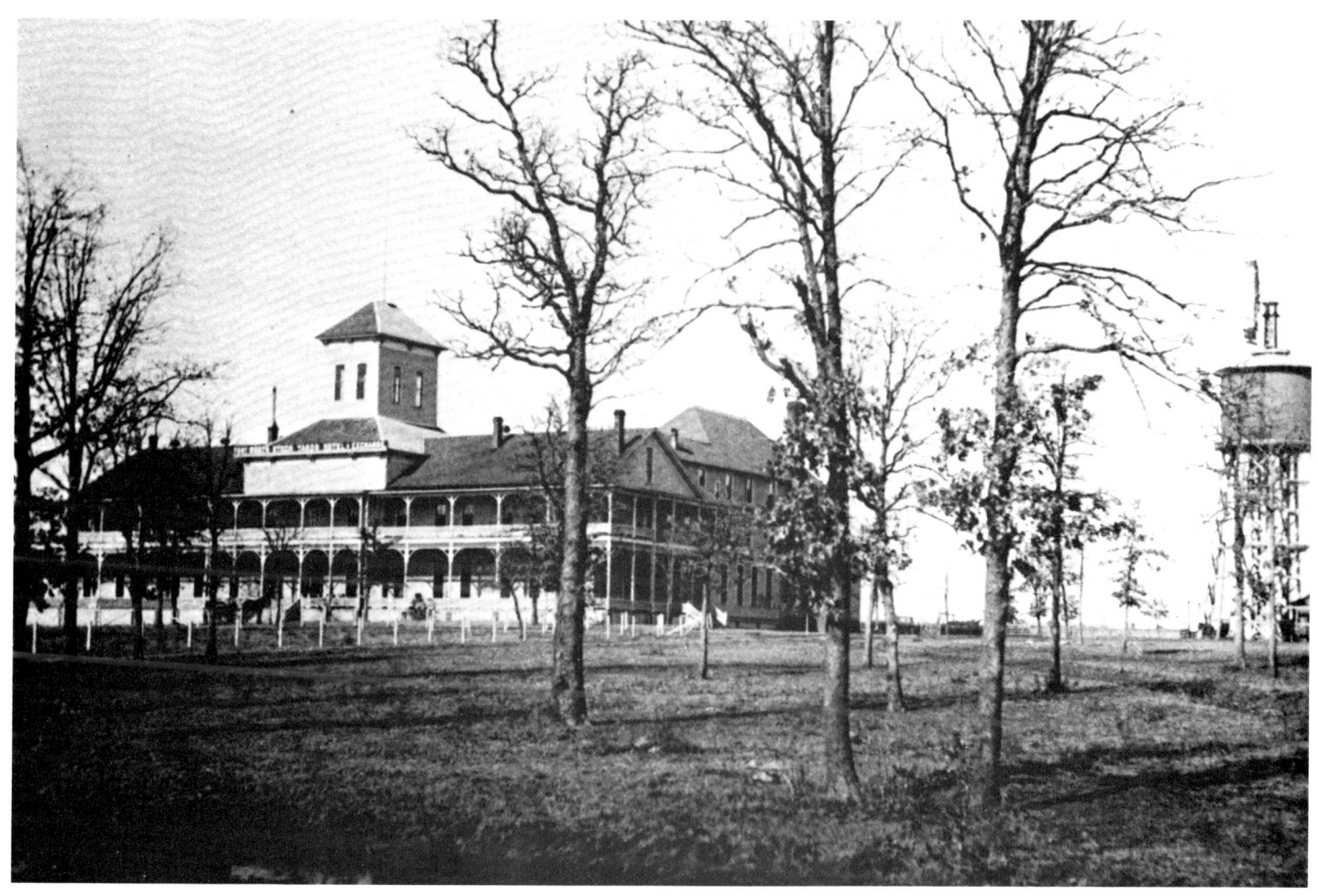

23. Stockyards Hotel & Exchange, Fort Worth.

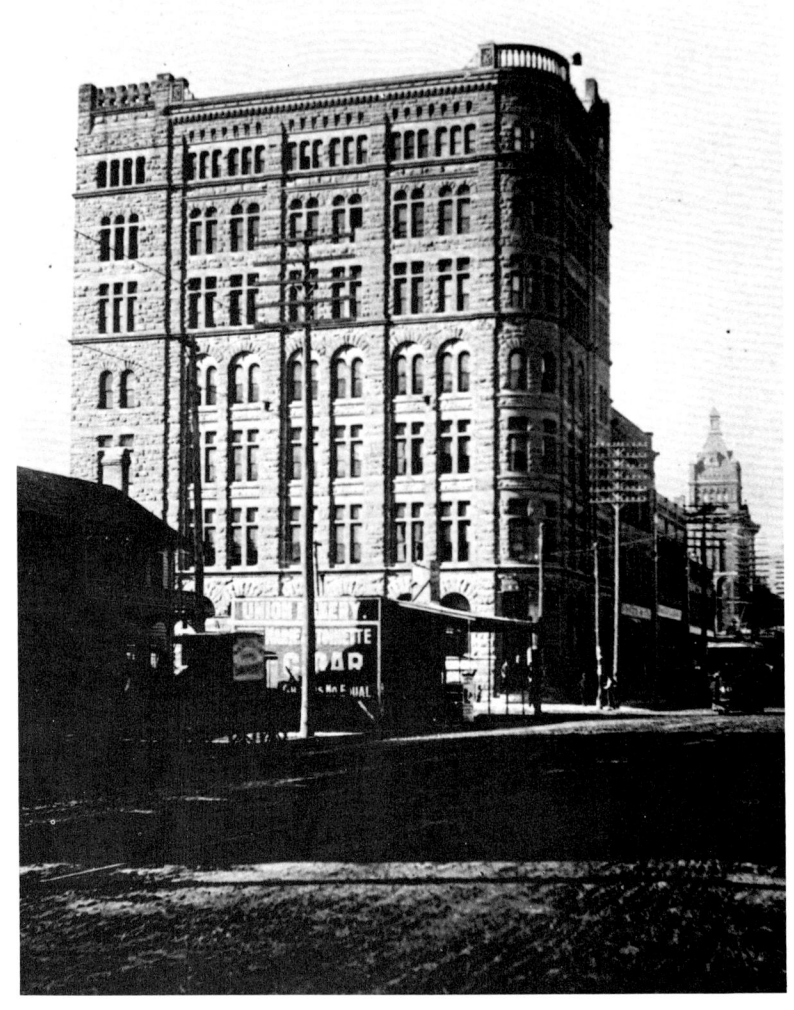

24. Hurley Office Building, South Main, Fort Worth. It was later destroyed by fire.

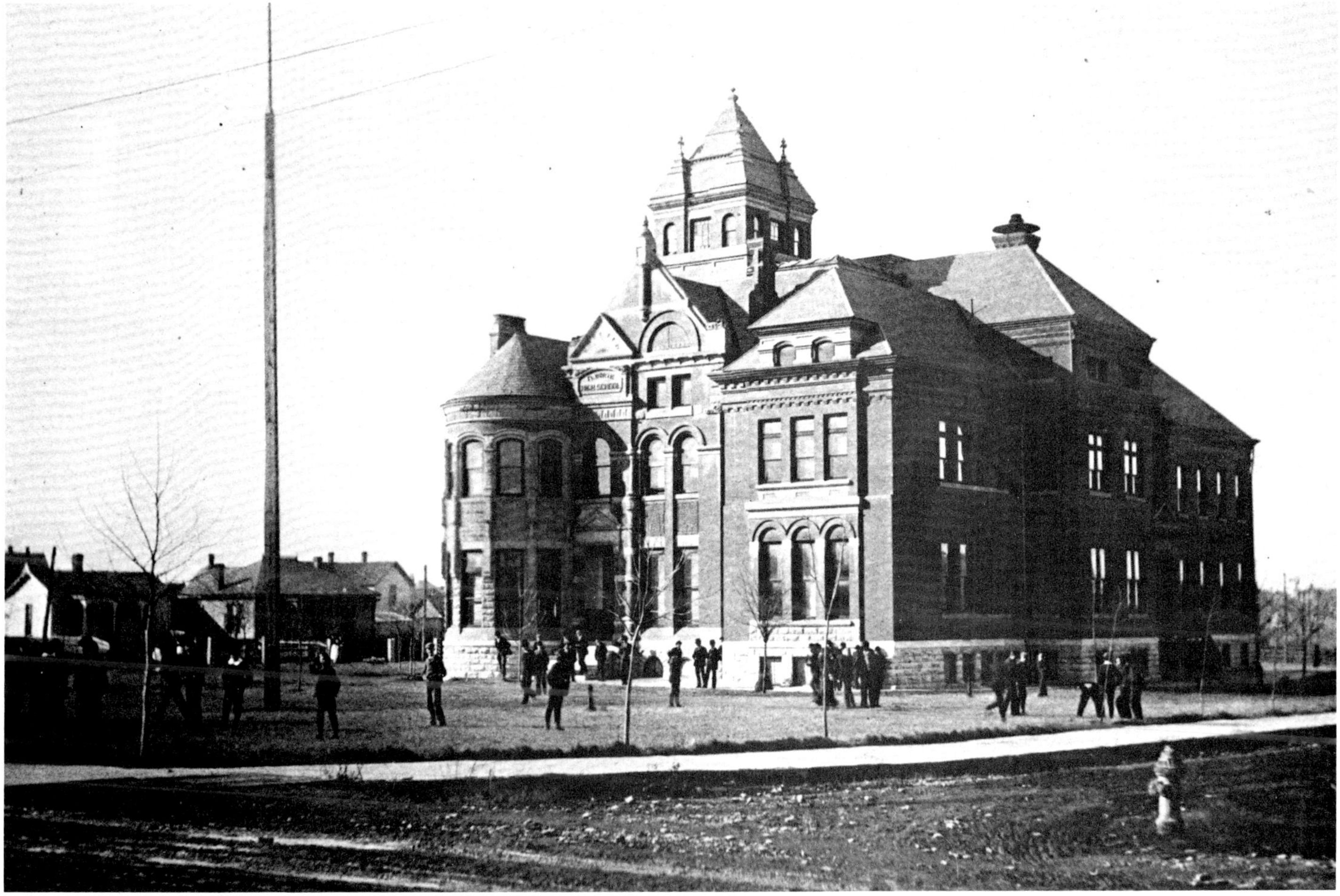

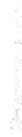

25. Fort Worth High School, Jennings and Daggett Streets. It burned in 1910.

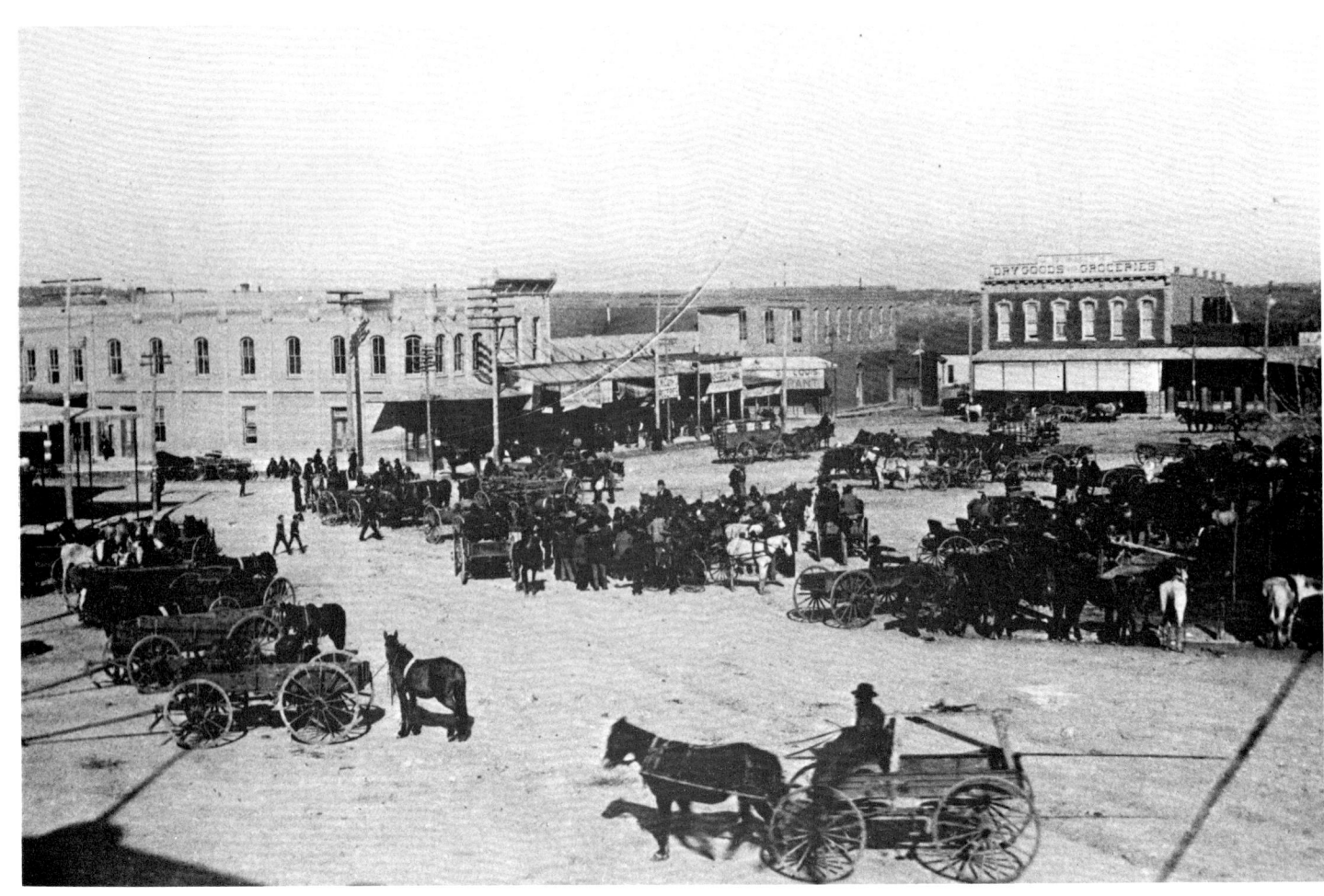

26. Saturday afternoon on the north side of the square, Weatherford.

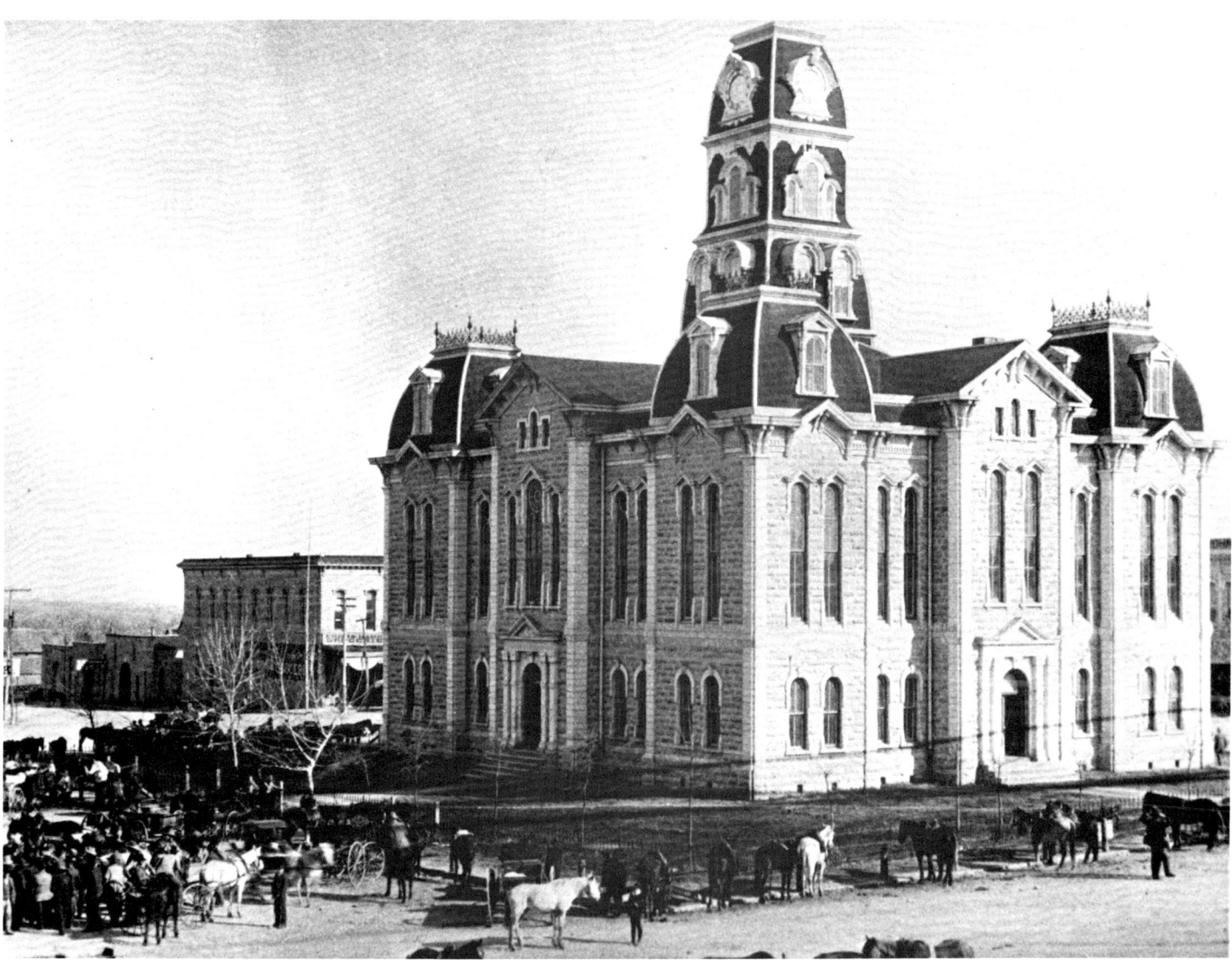

27. Parker County Courthouse, Weatherford. It is still standing.

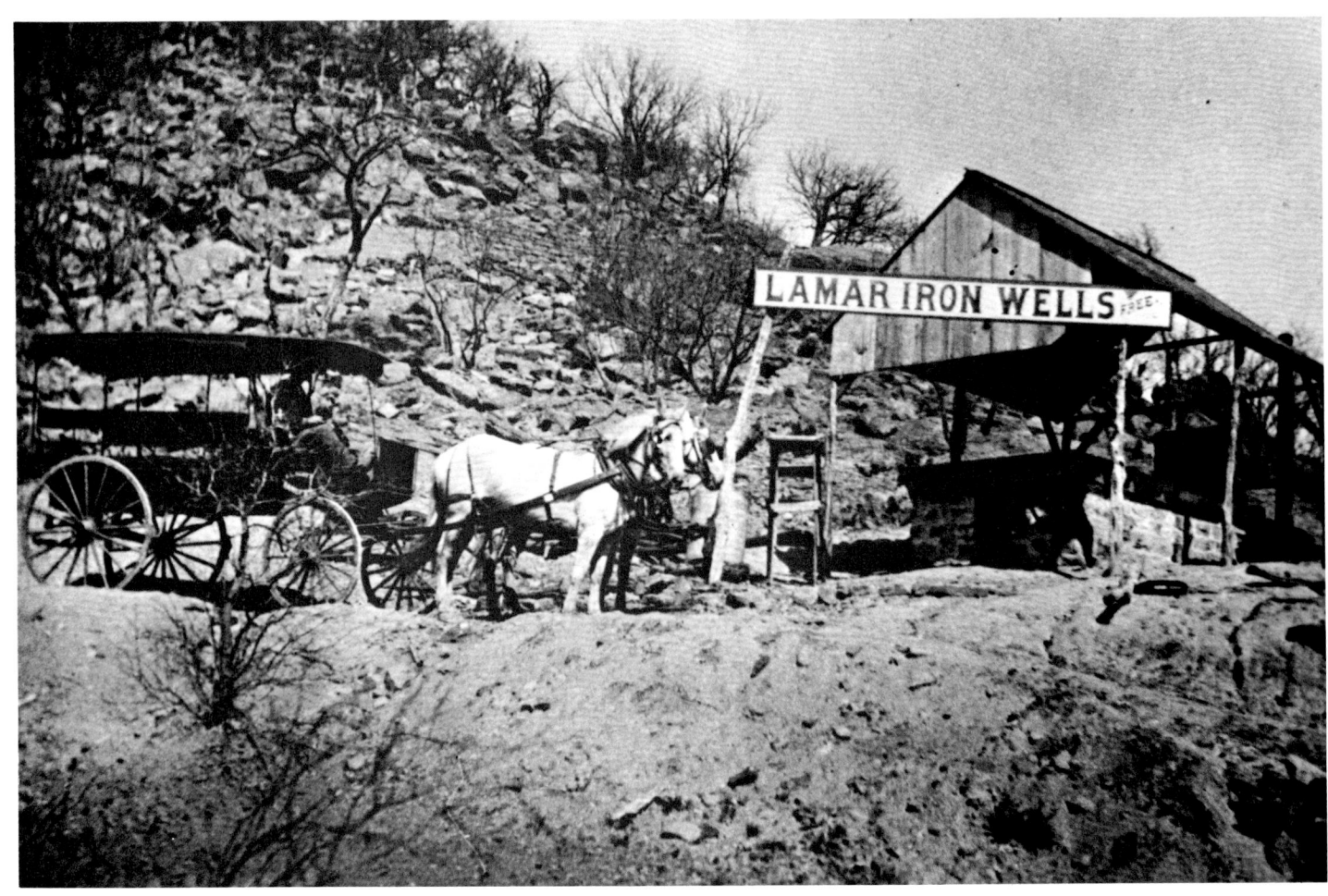

28. A livery hack at the Lamar Mineral Well, Palo Pinto County, near Mineral Wells.

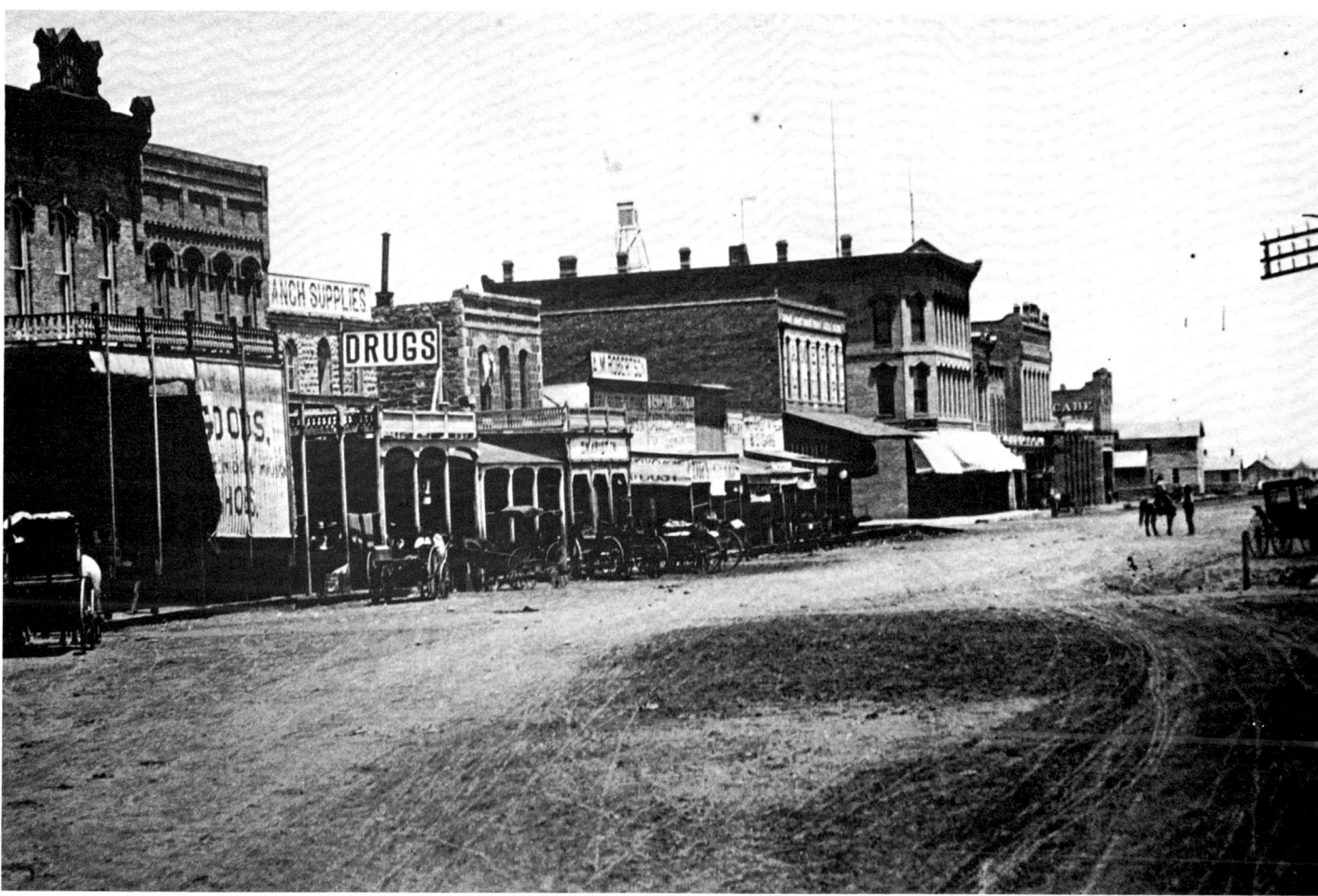

29. A street scene in Abilene.

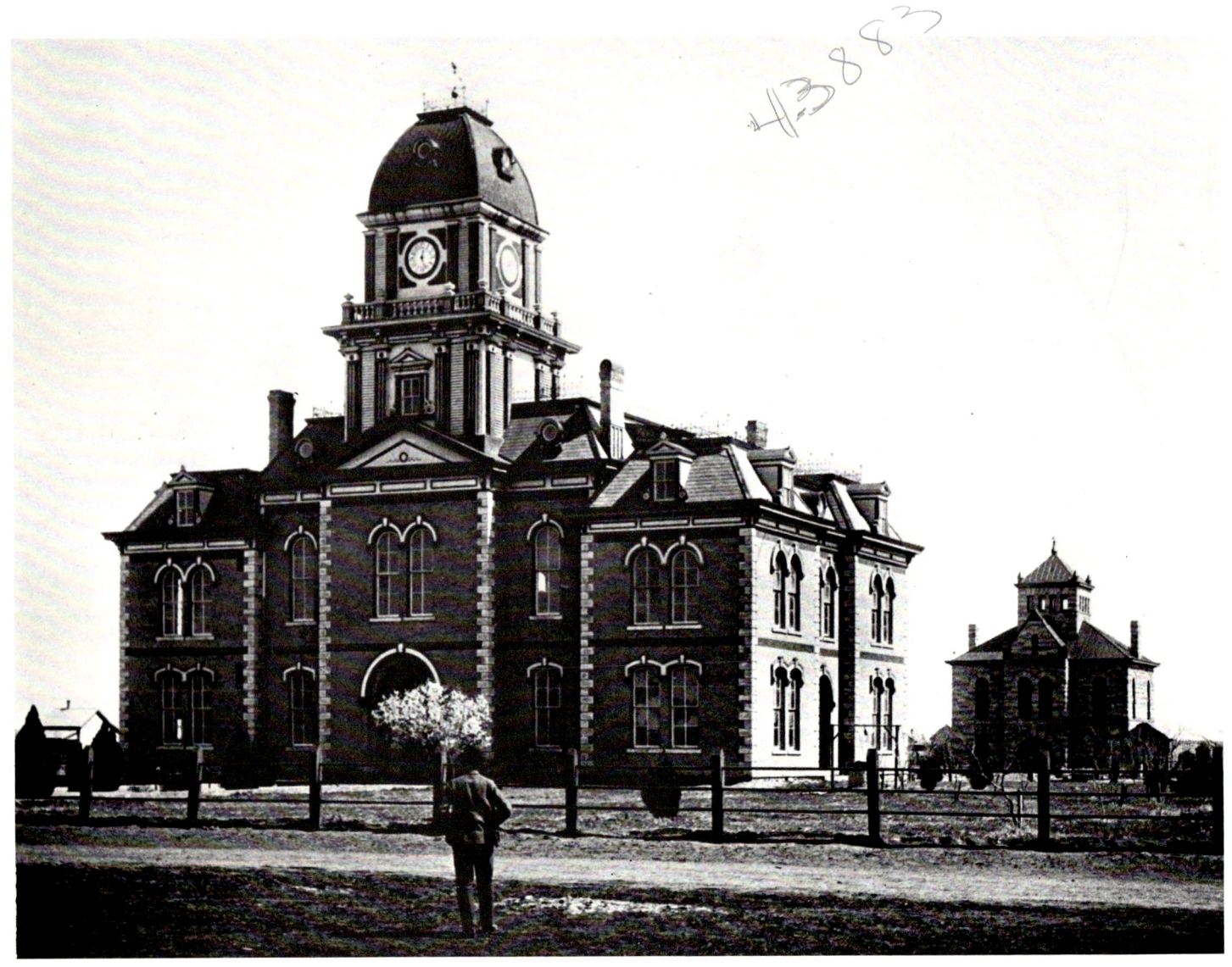

30. Taylor County Courthouse, Abilene. It was torn down in 1914, but the jail (at rear) stood until the 1930s.

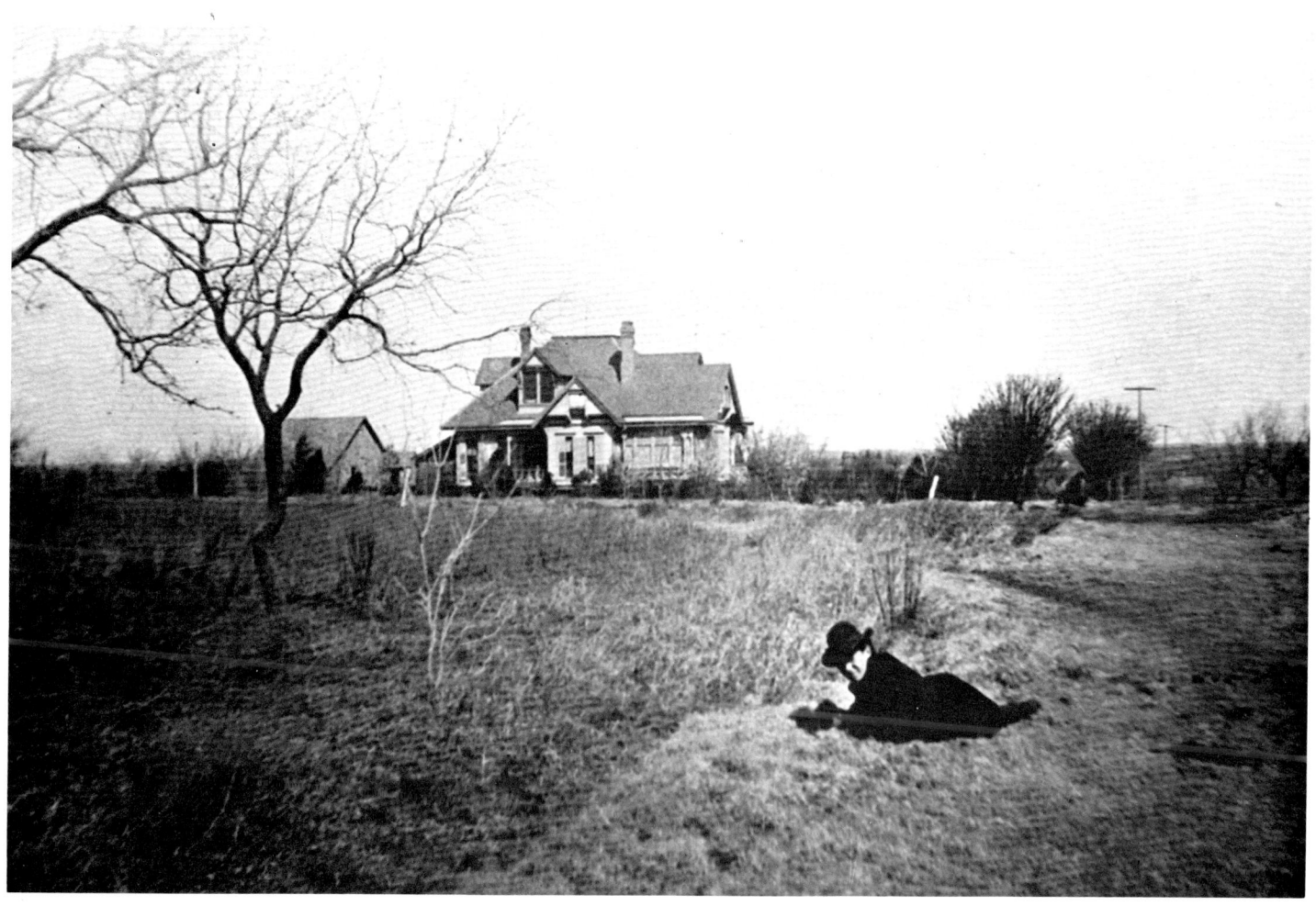

31. A scene near Abilene.

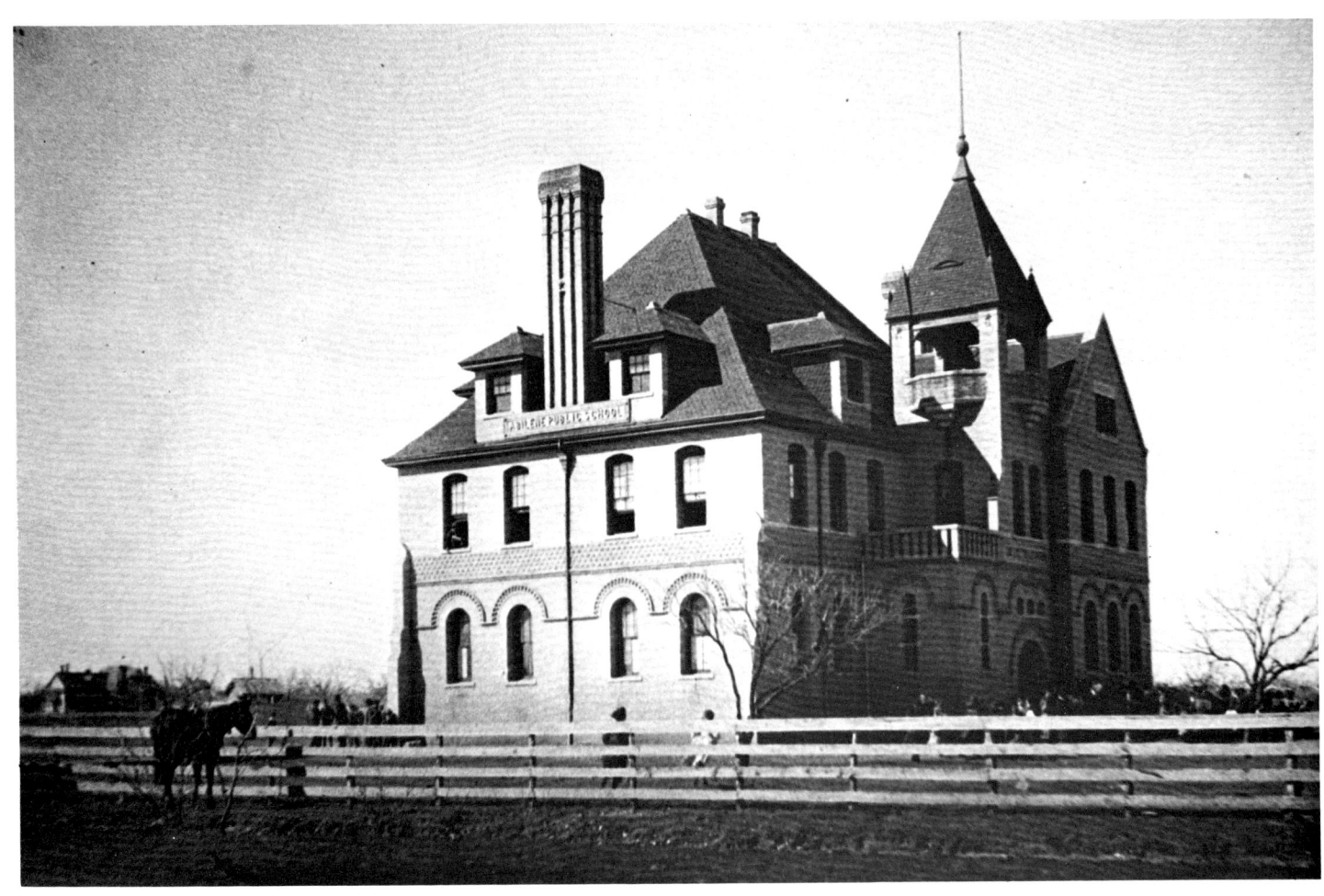
32. Abilene High School.

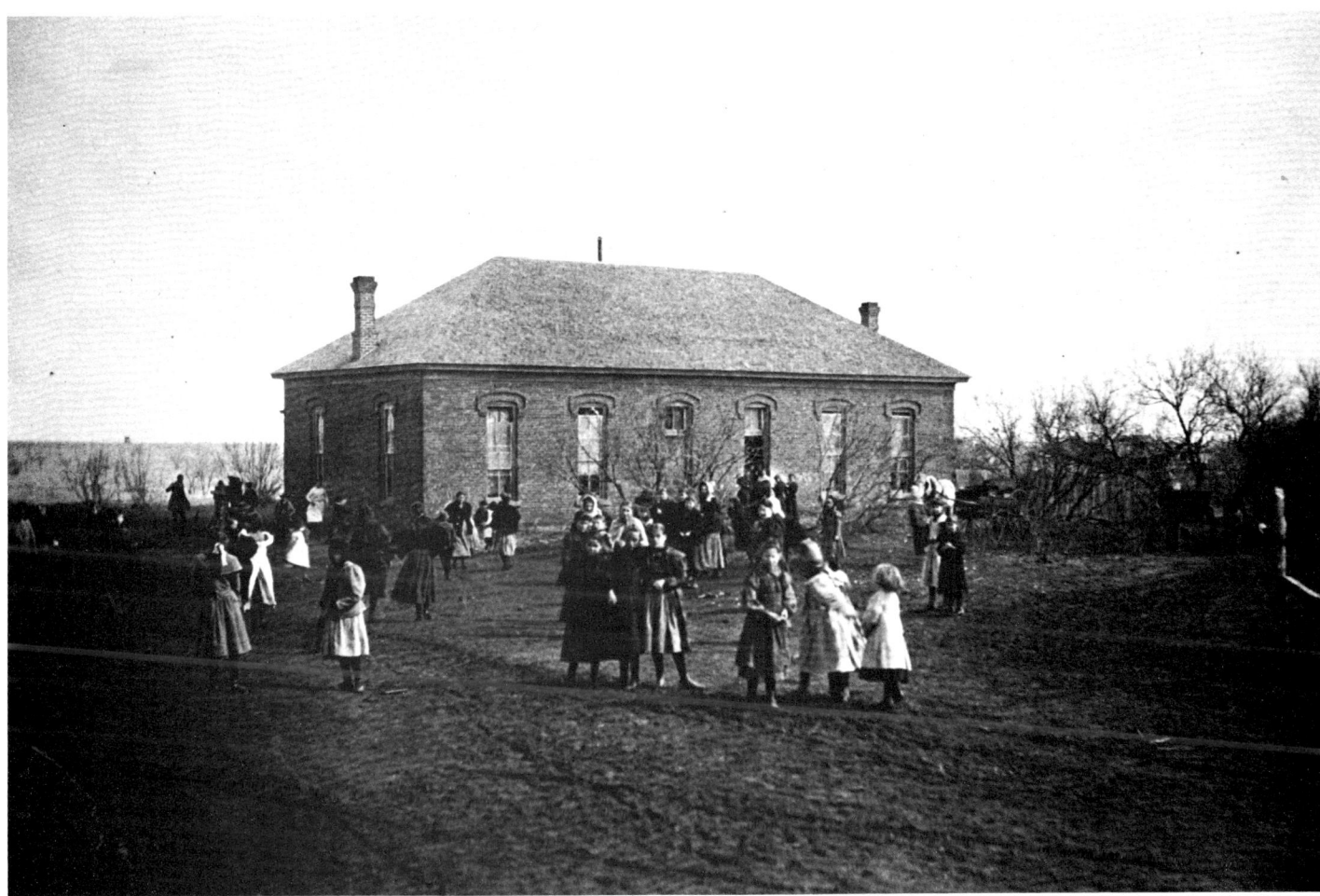

33. School at Colorado City.

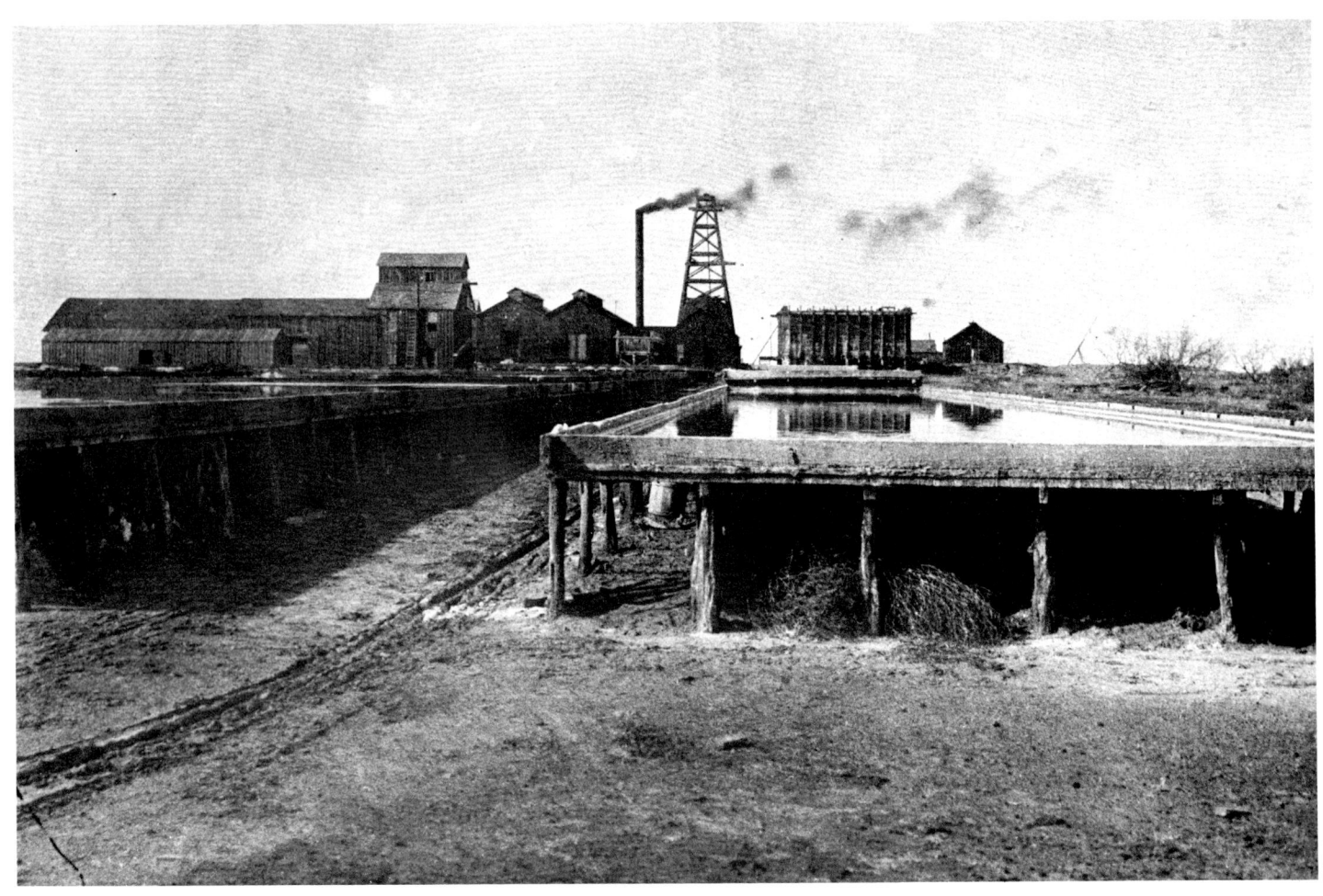

34. Salt works near Colorado City.

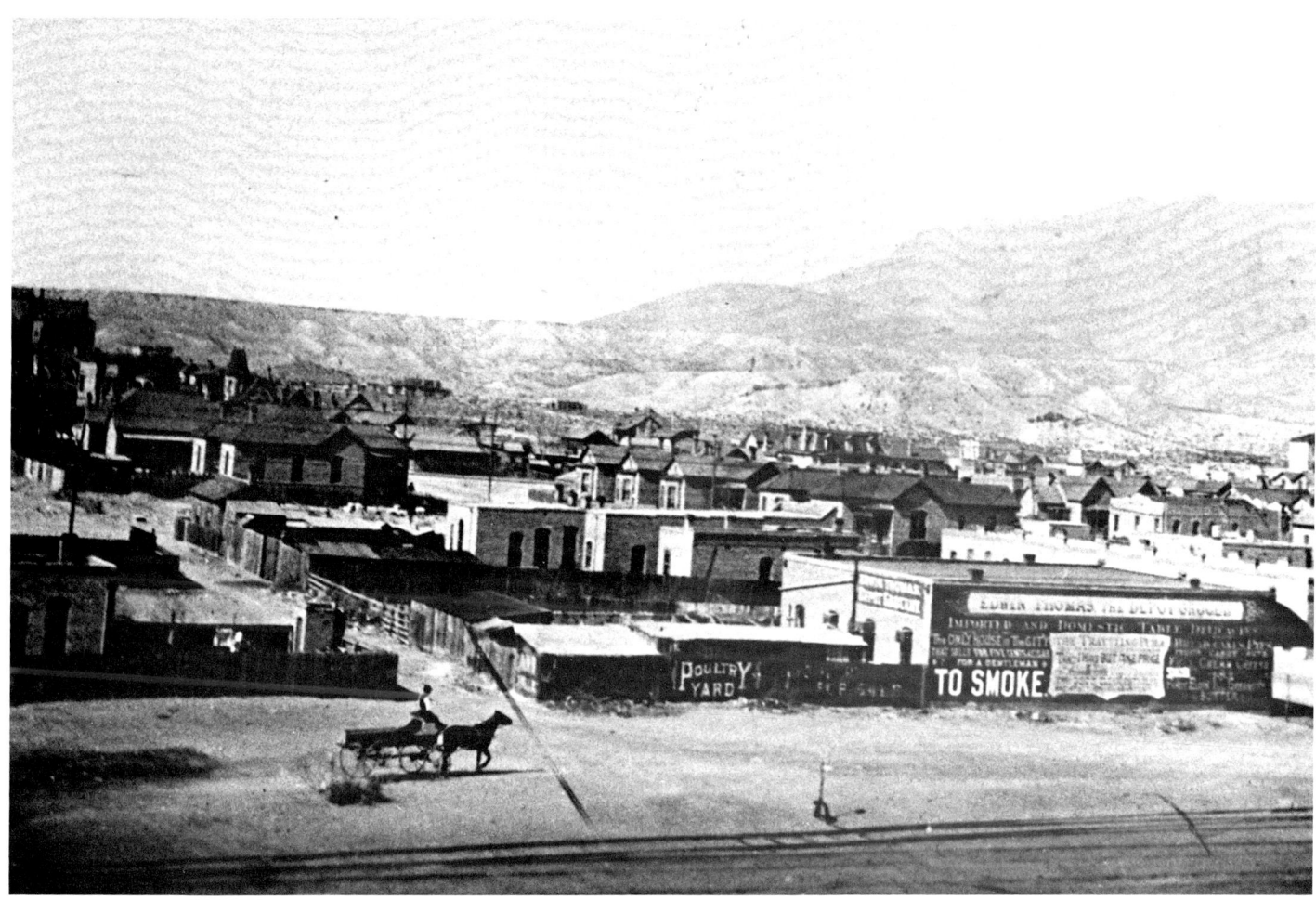

35. El Paso, near the depot.

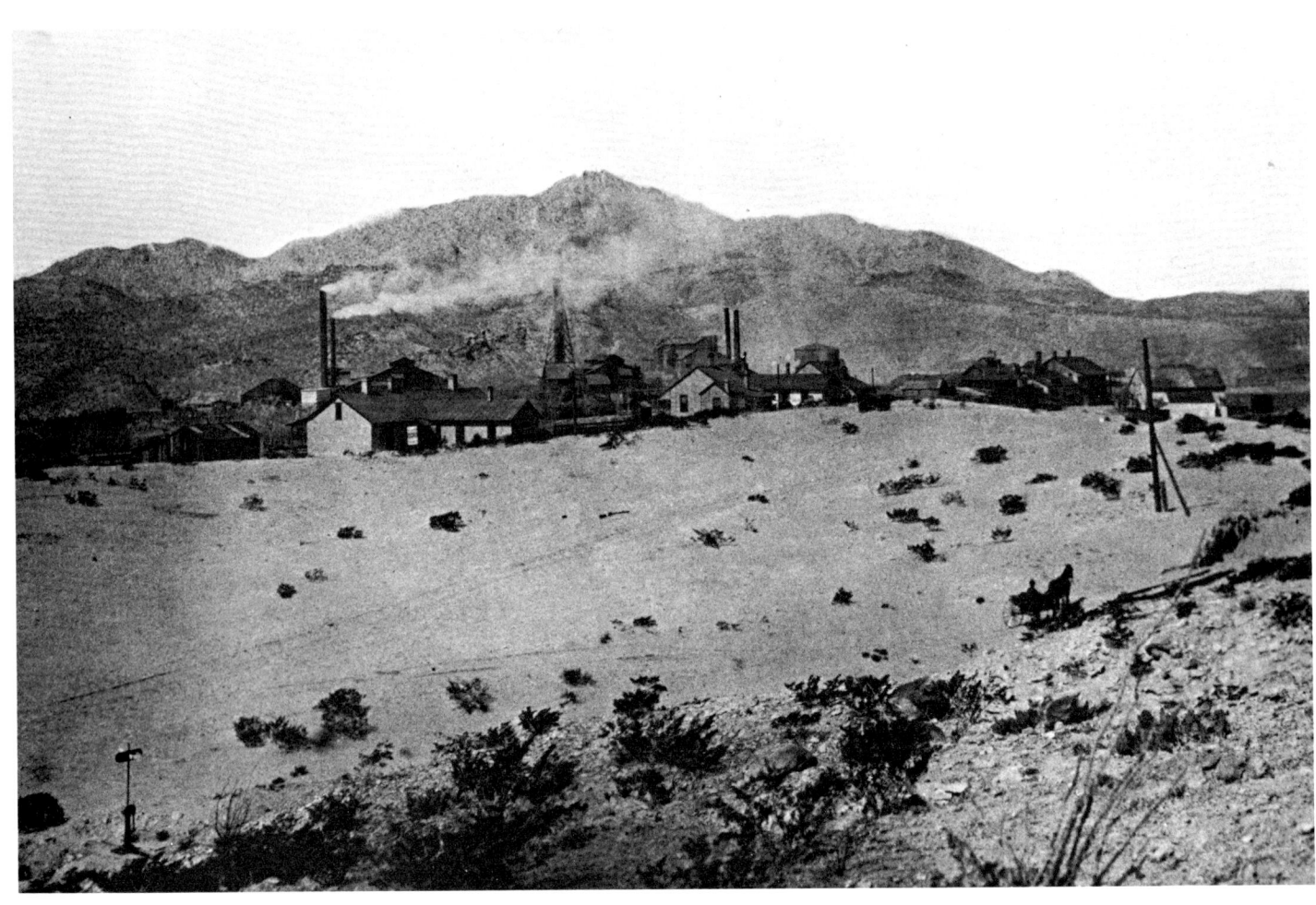

36. Smelter, El Paso.

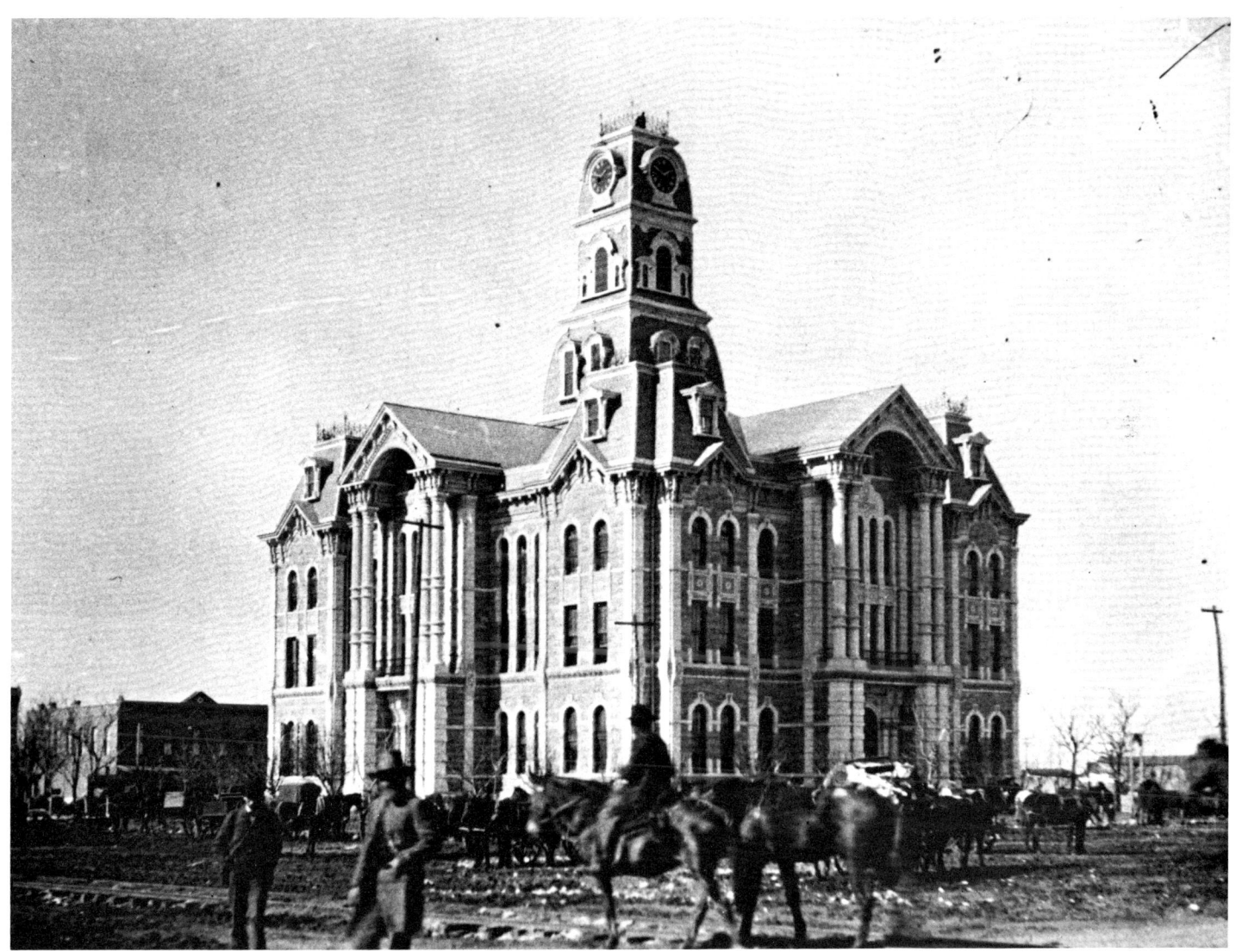
37. Hill County Courthouse, Hillsboro, with mulecar rails in foreground.

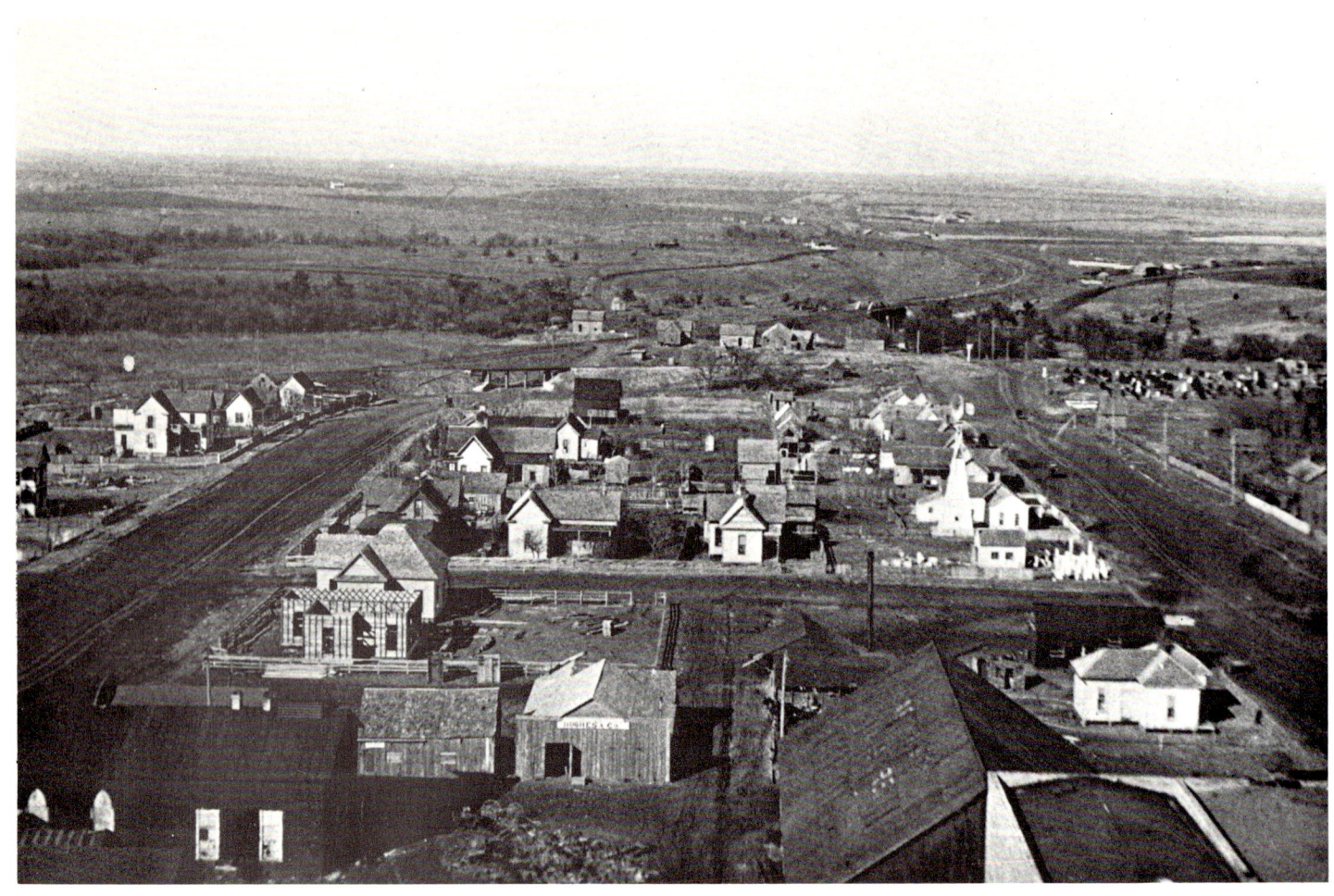

38. Scene from the Courthouse at Hillsboro.

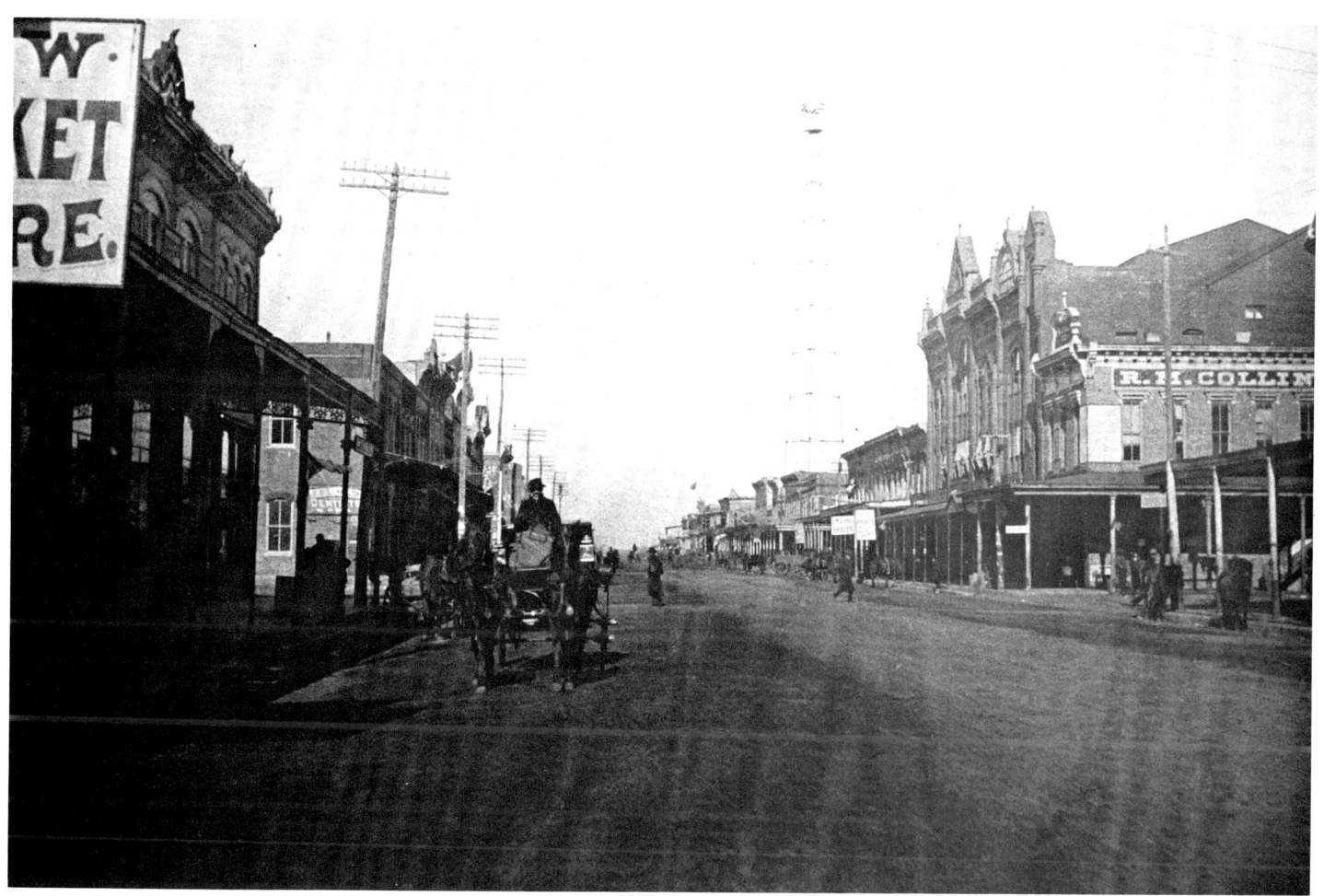

39. Beaton Street from East Sixth, Corsicana. The sixty-foot tower was for illumination at "Kiber and Cobb" corner. The large building on the right is the opera house, which burned in 1912.

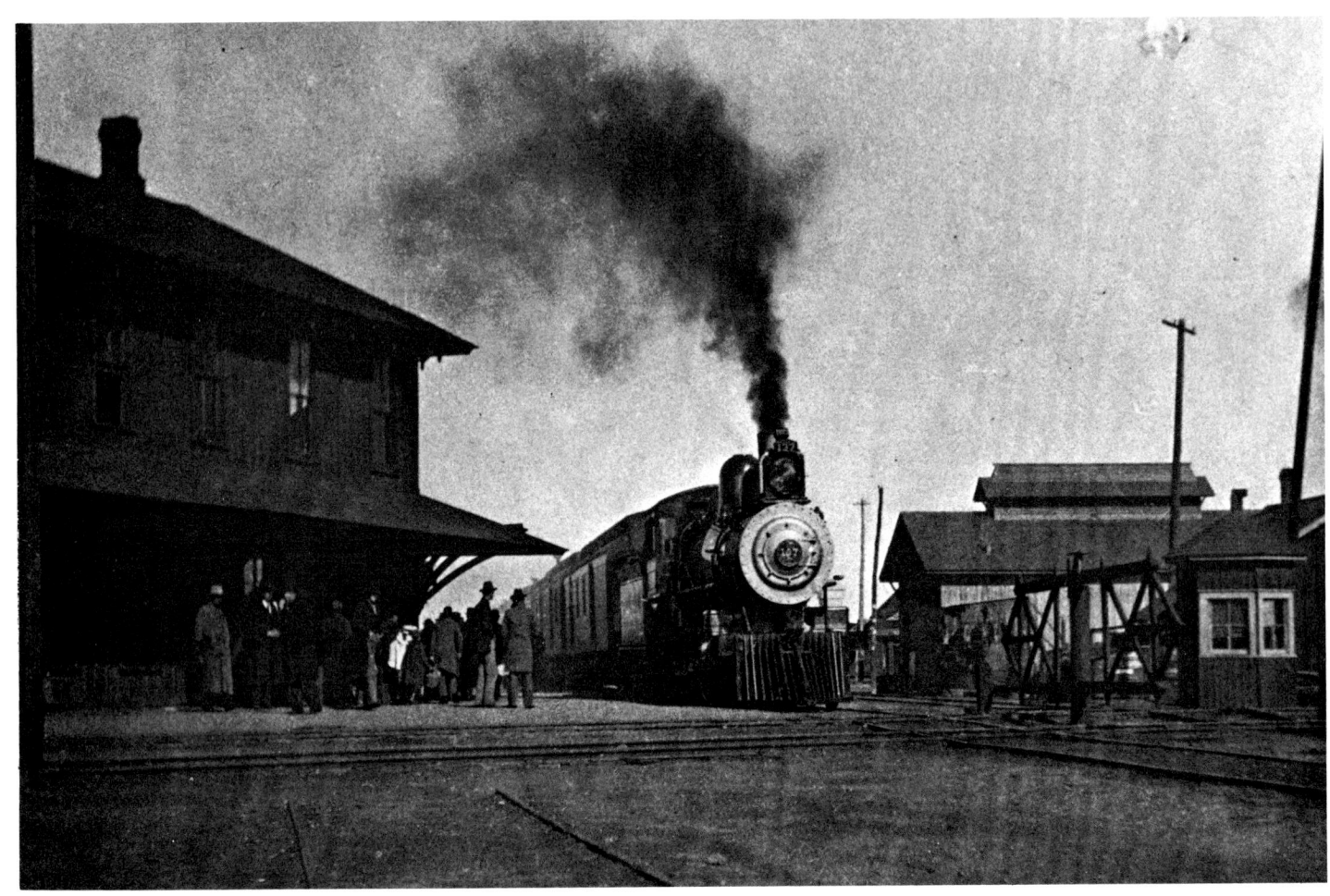

40. Cotton Belt and Houston & Texas Central crossing, Corsicana.

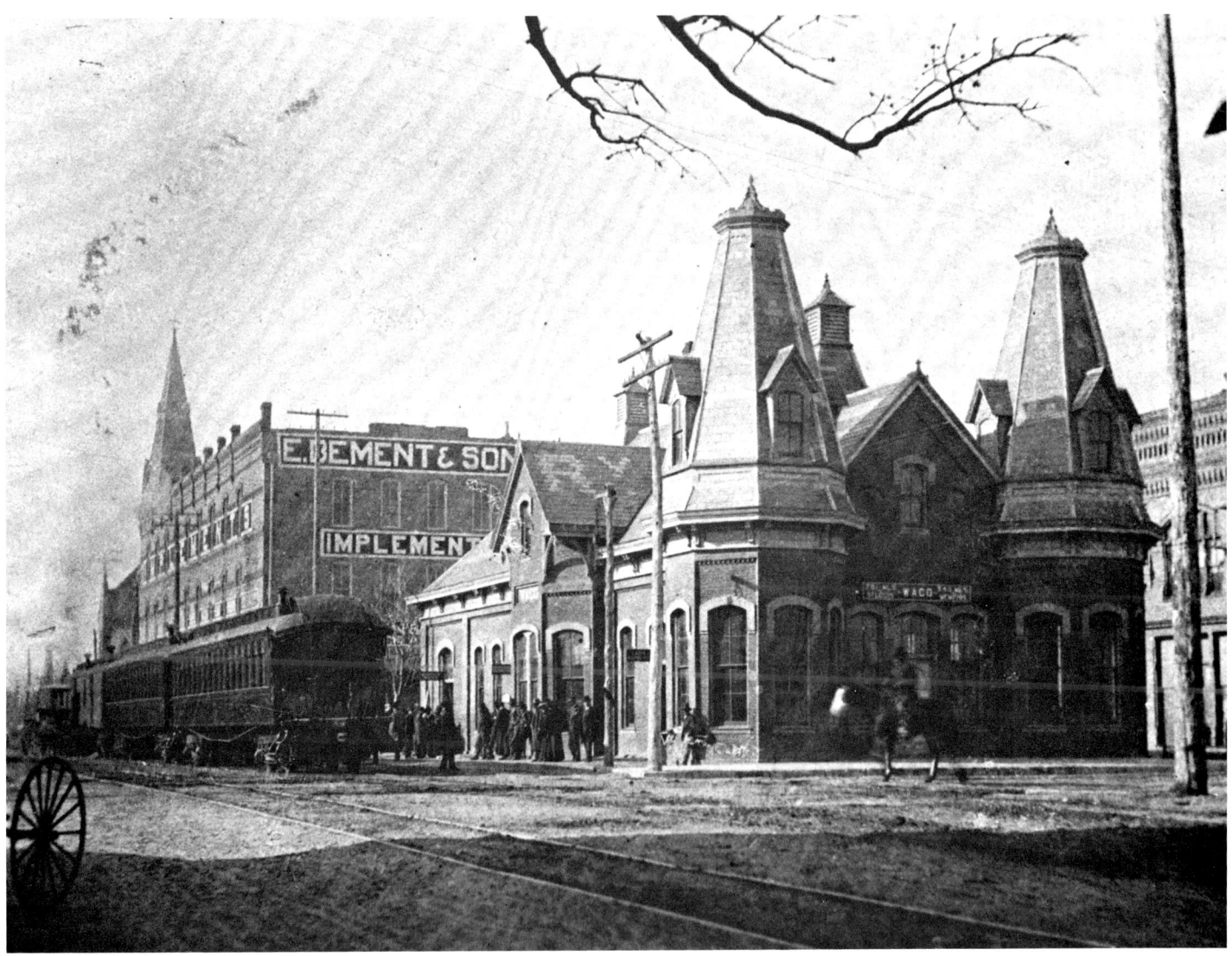

41. Cotton Belt Station, Waco.

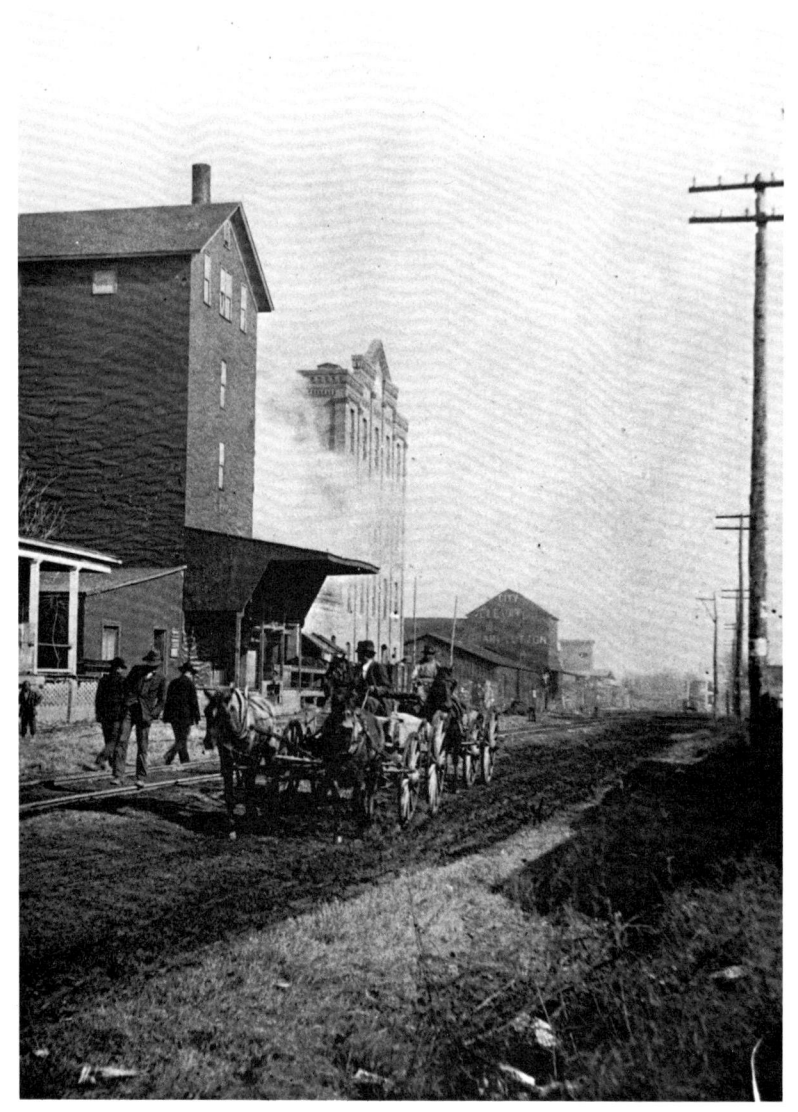

42. Cameron Milling Co., Waco, McLennan County.

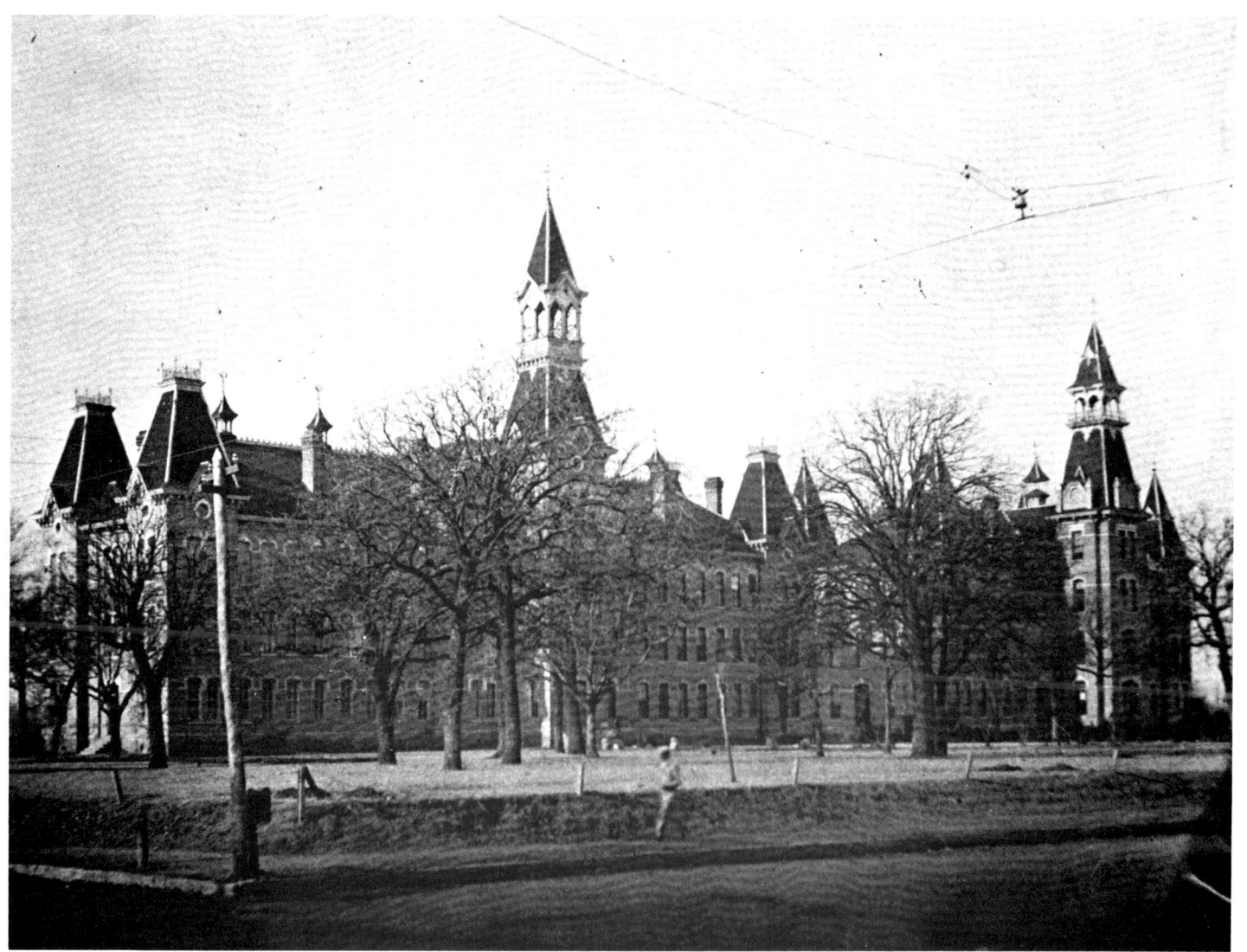

43. Baylor University. It had moved to Waco from Independence in 1887.

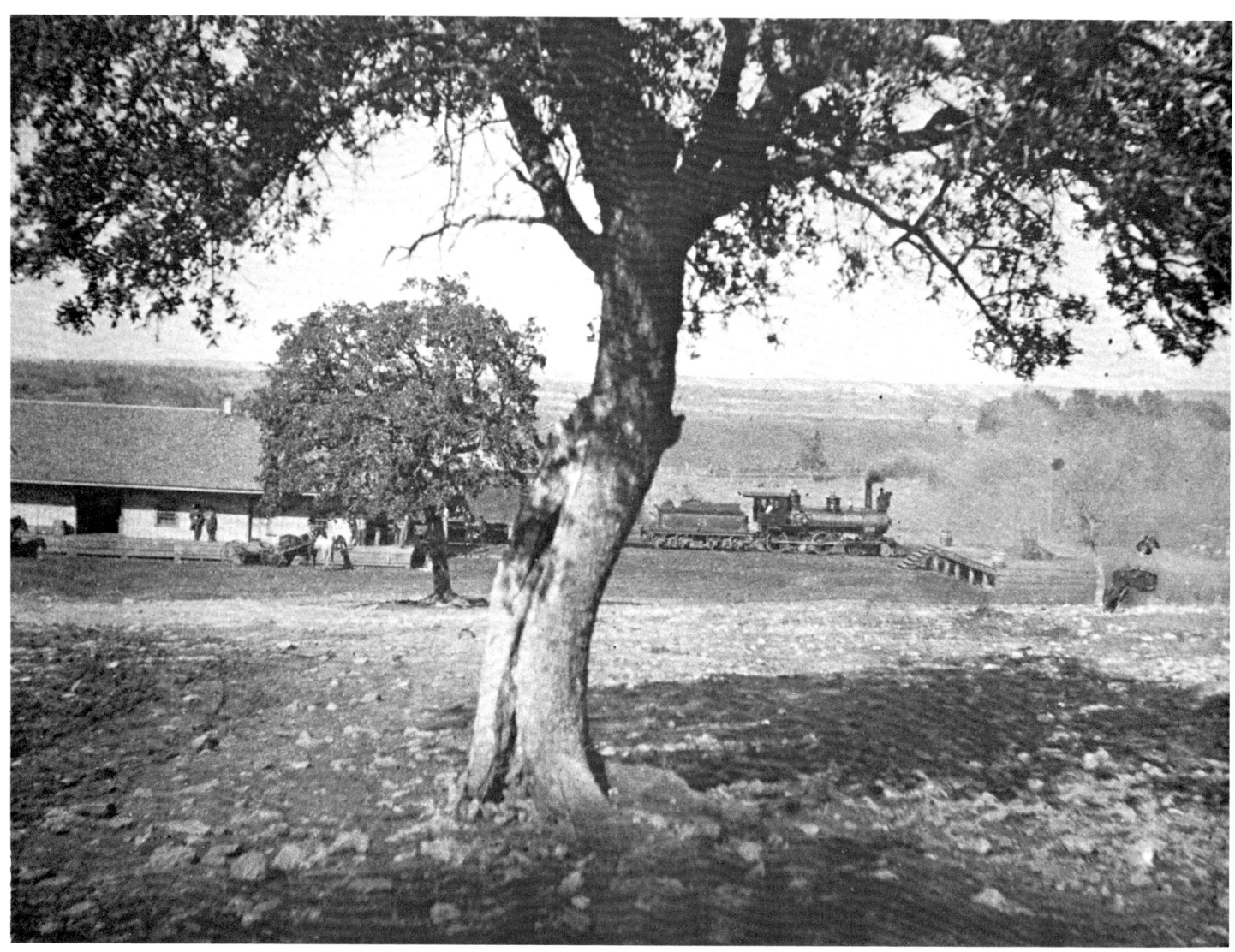

44. Cotton Belt Station, Gatesville.

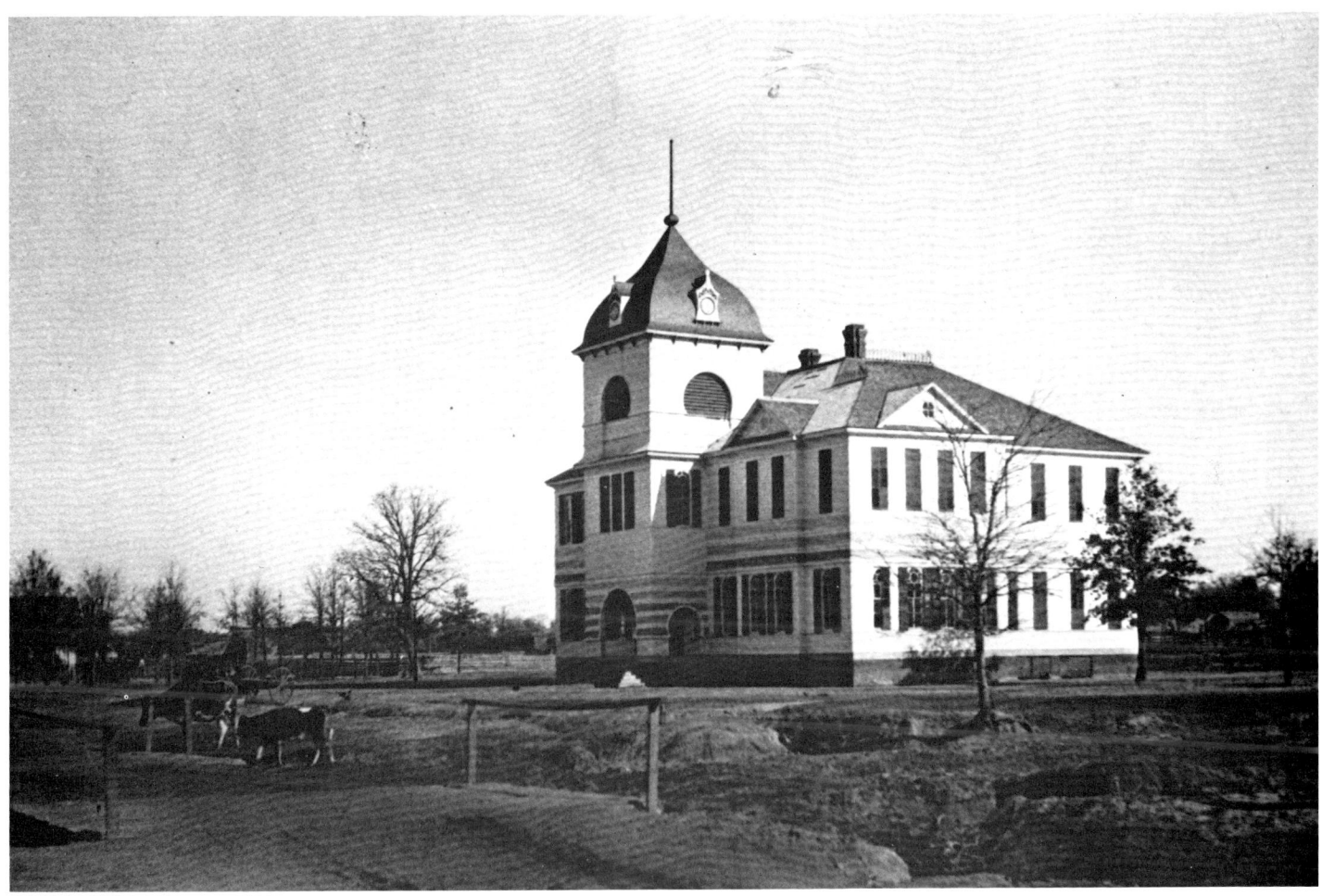

45. School at Hearne.

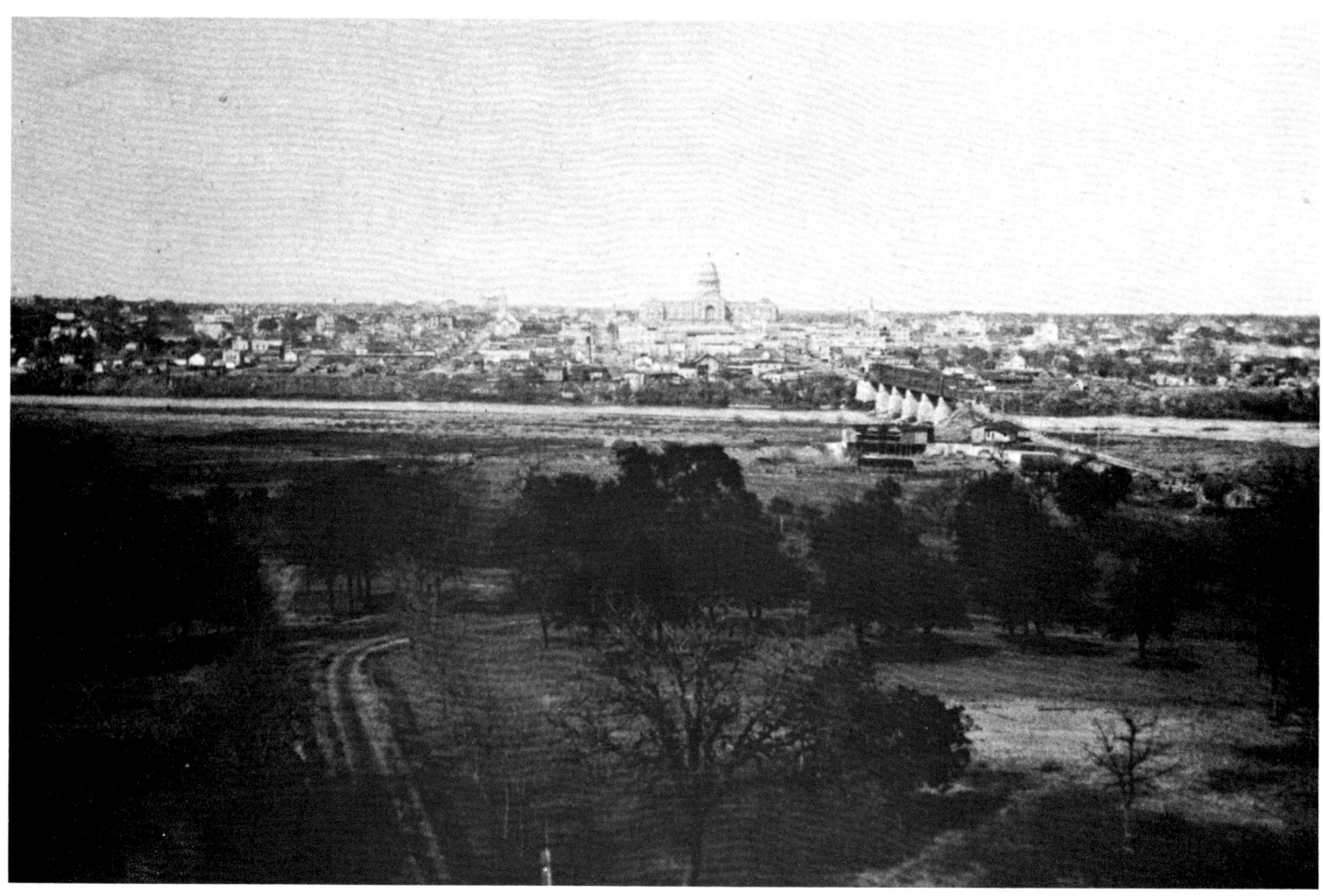

46. Looking north across the Colorado River from south Austin.

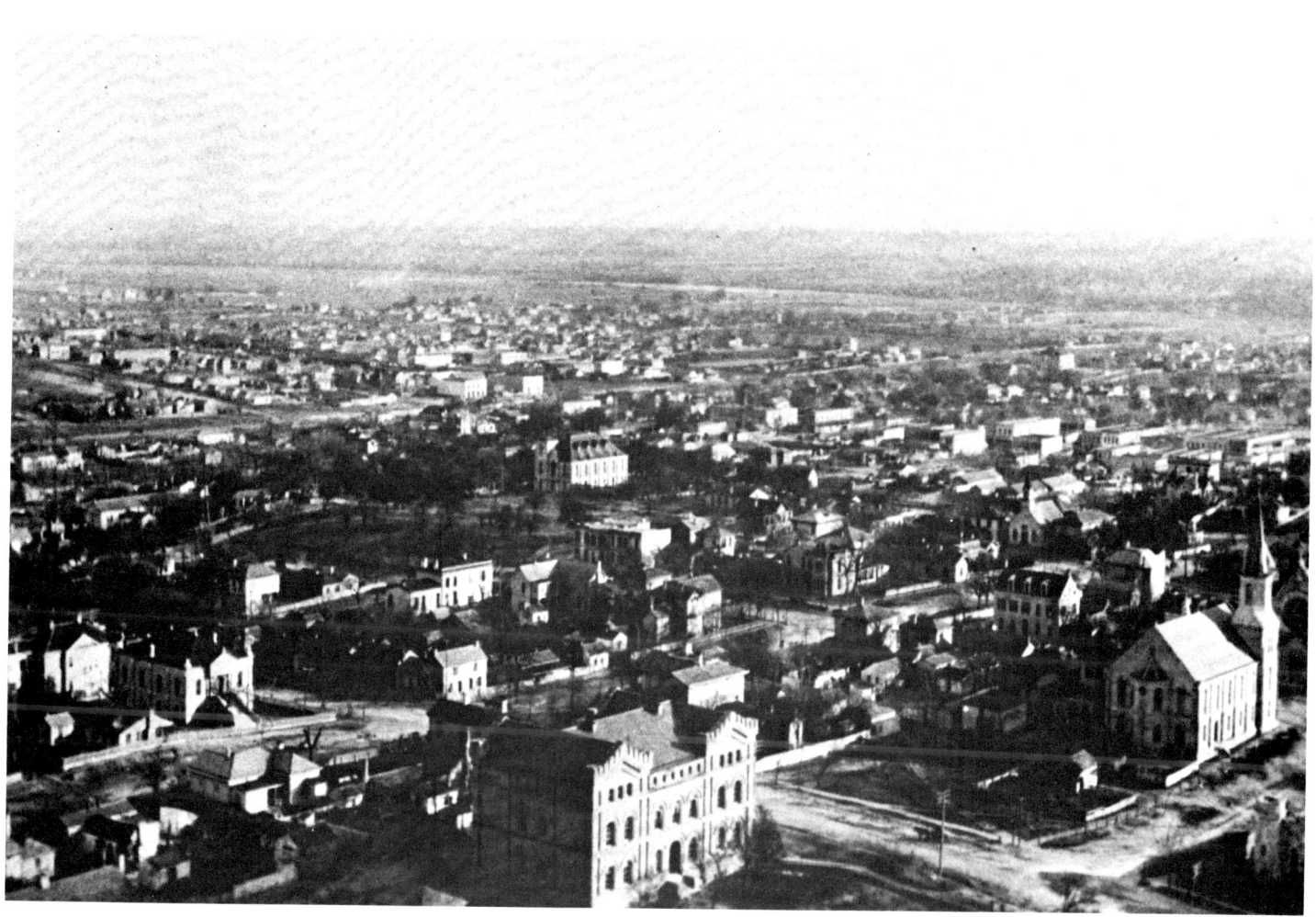

47. Austin, looking southeast from the Capitol dome.

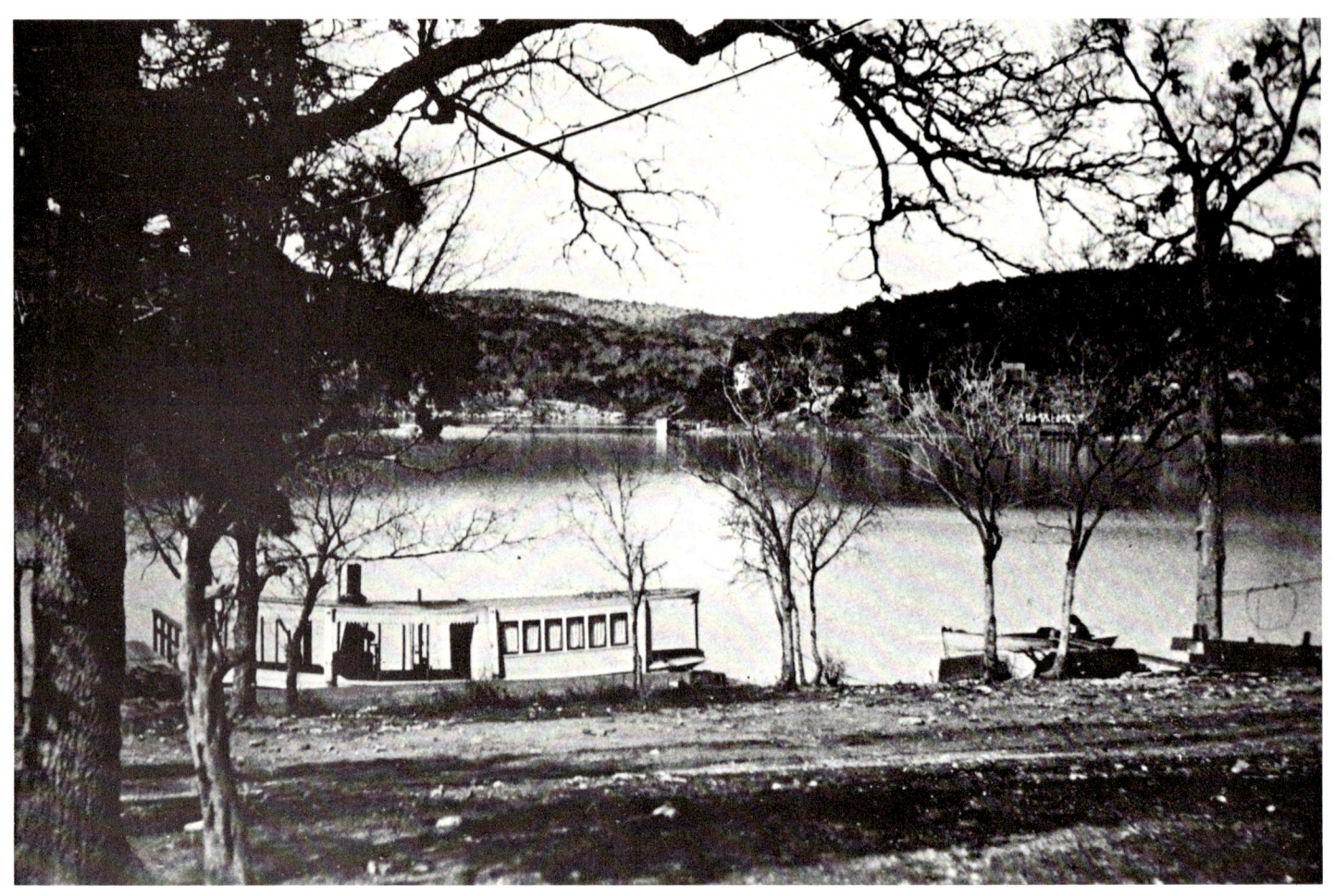

48. Lake McDonald, behind the Austin dam.

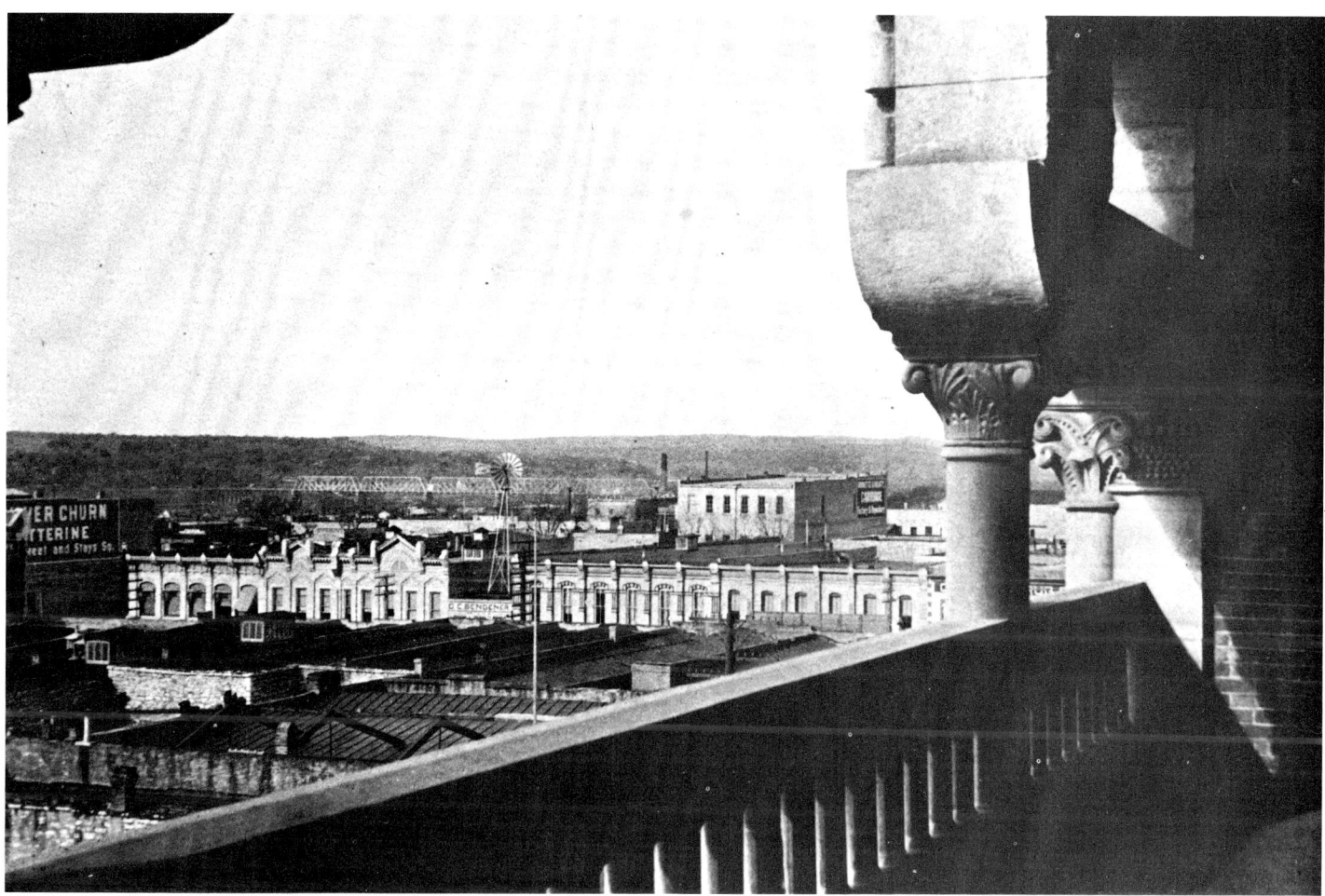

49. Veranda of the Driskill Hotel, Austin, looking southwest toward the Missouri Pacific bridge over the Colorado River.

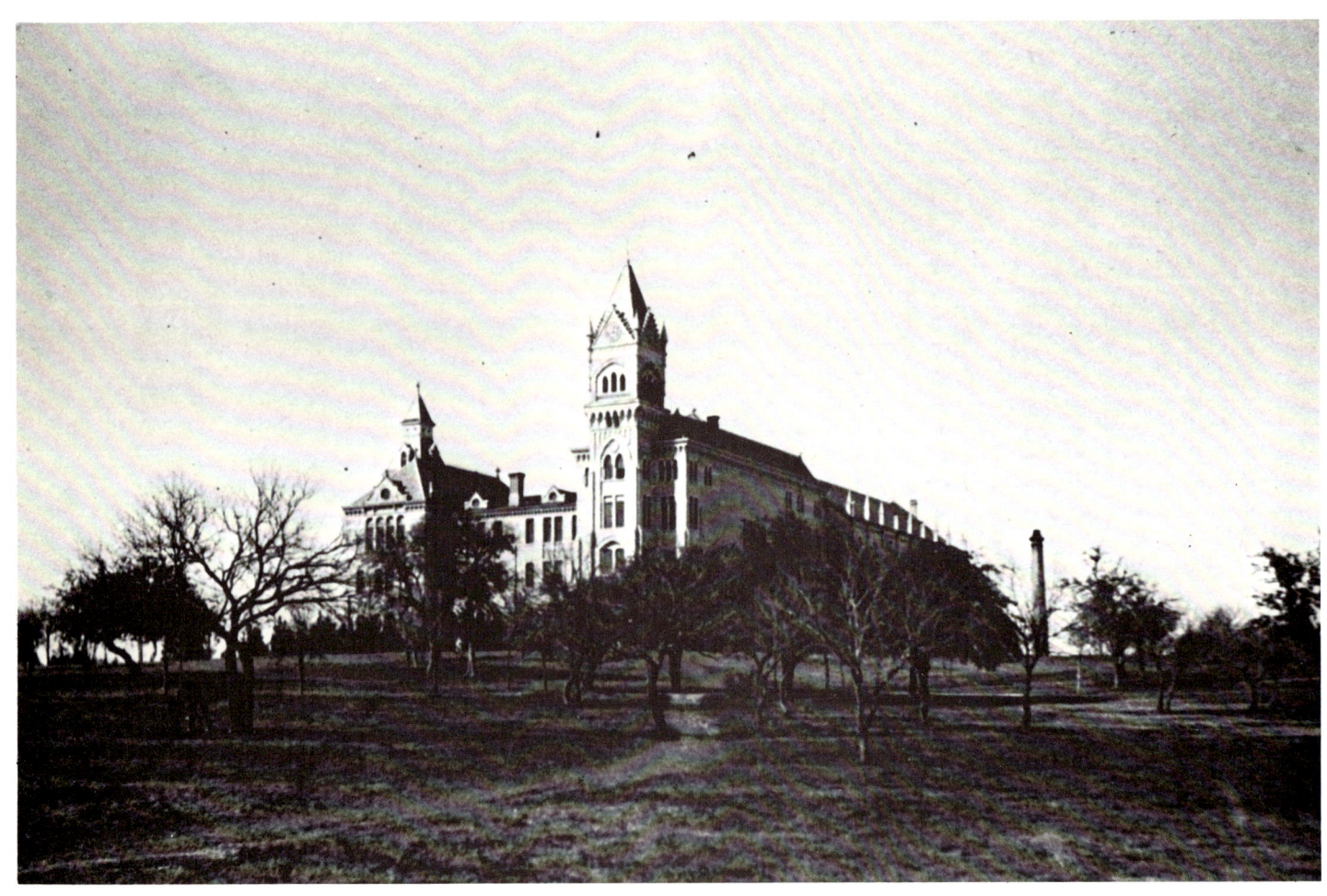

50. University of Texas. This building was torn down in the 1930s and the UT Tower was erected on the site.

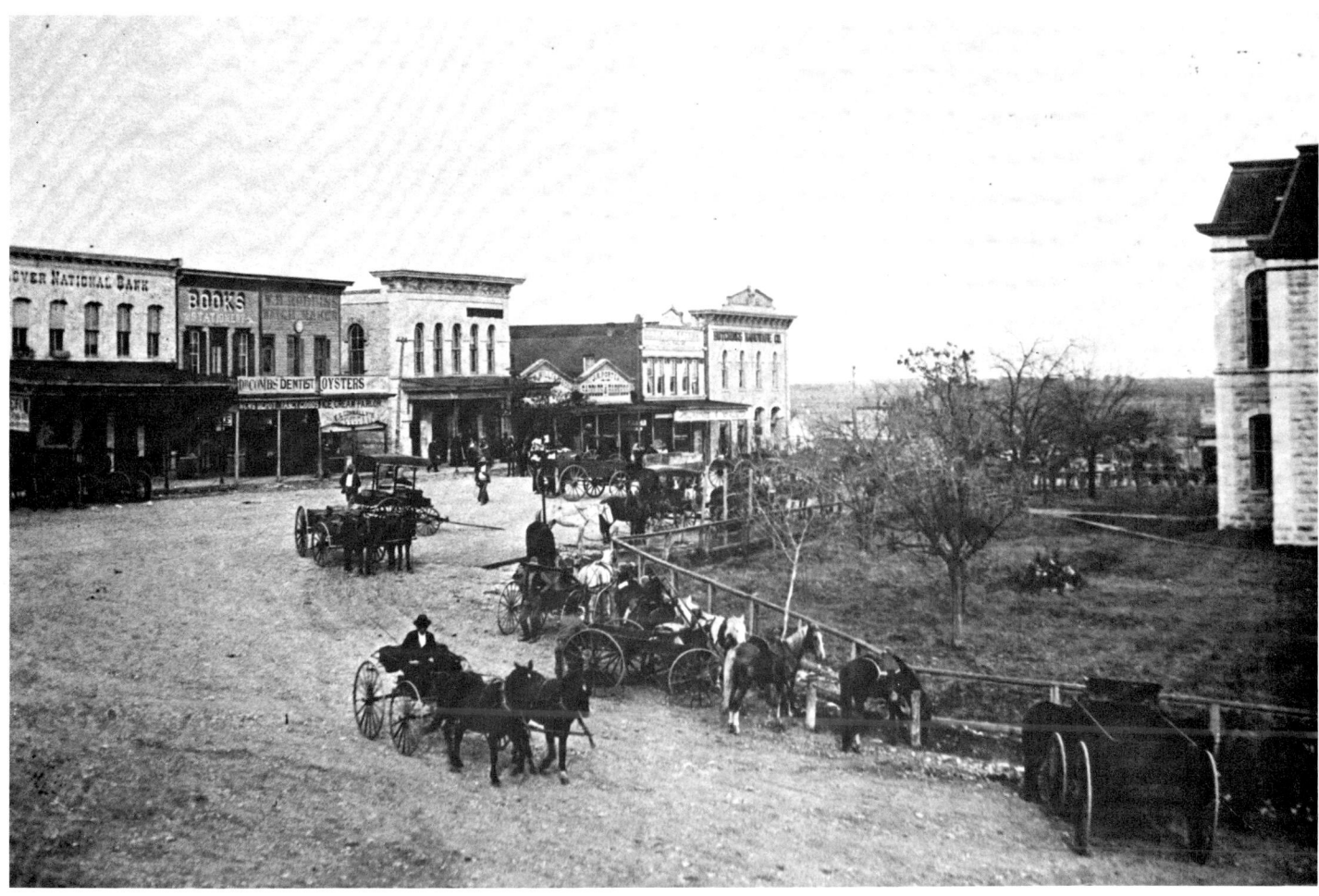

51. Public Square, San Marcos.

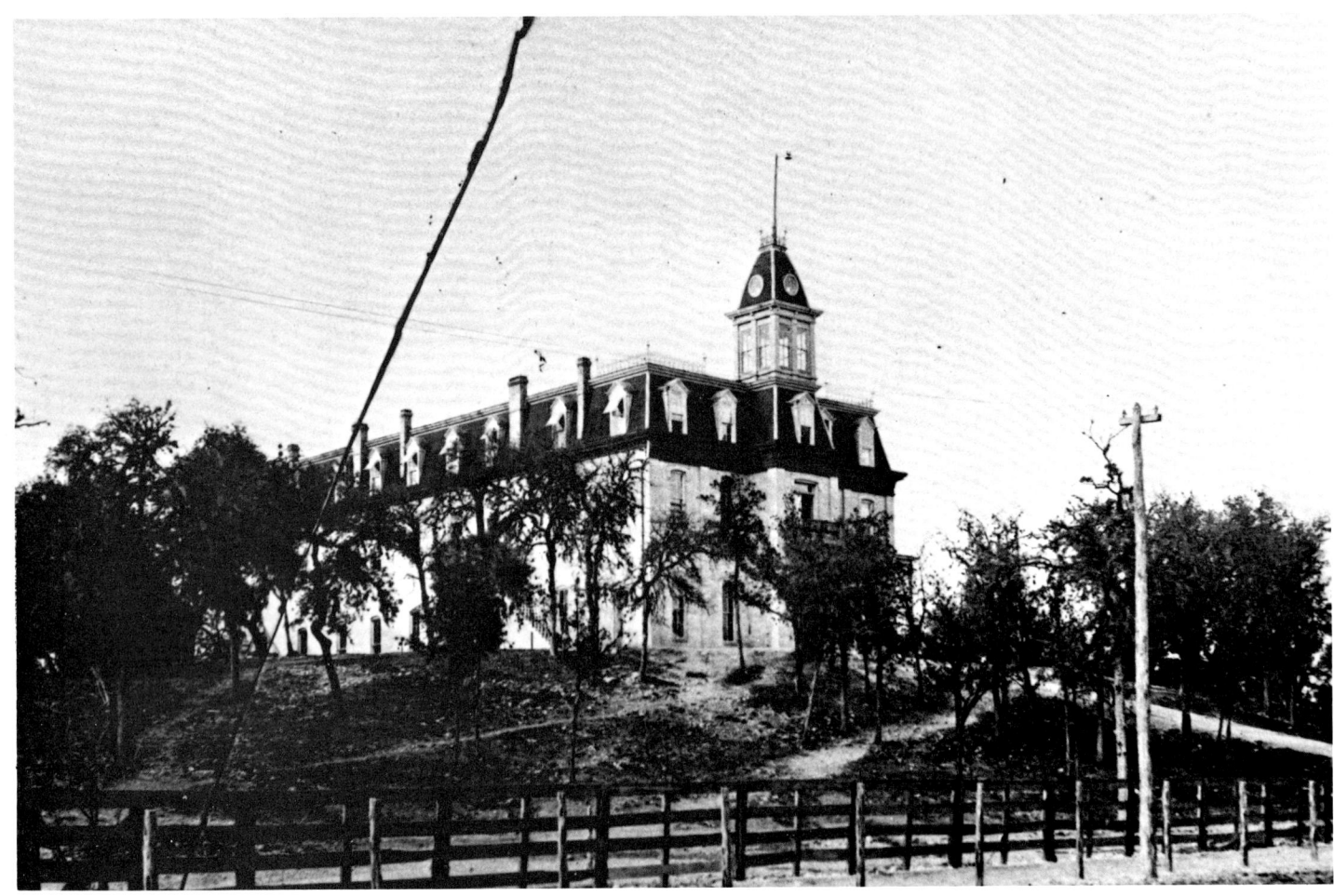

52. Coronal Institute, San Marcos. It was built in 1868 and discontinued in 1917.

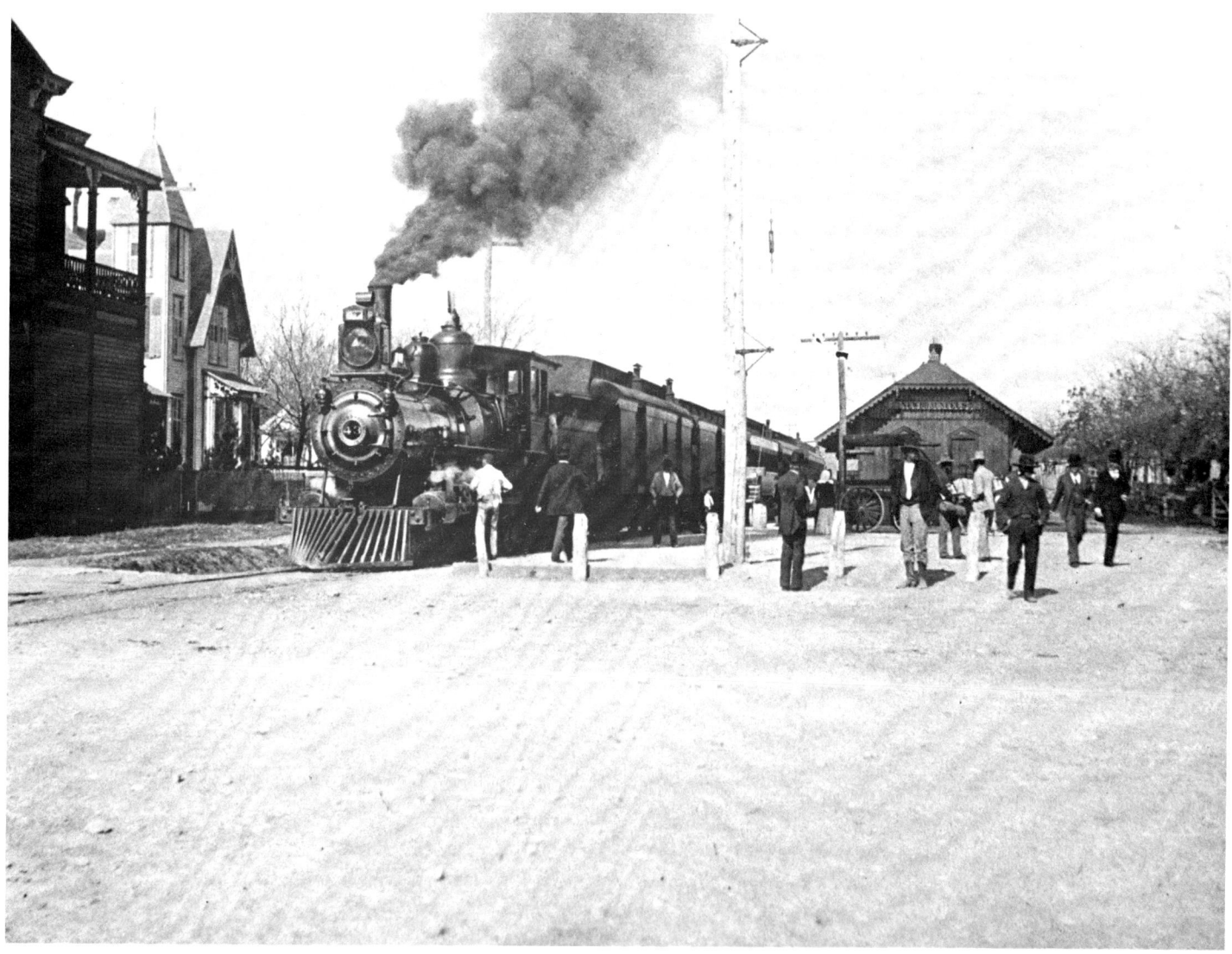

53. Katy Station at New Braunfels.

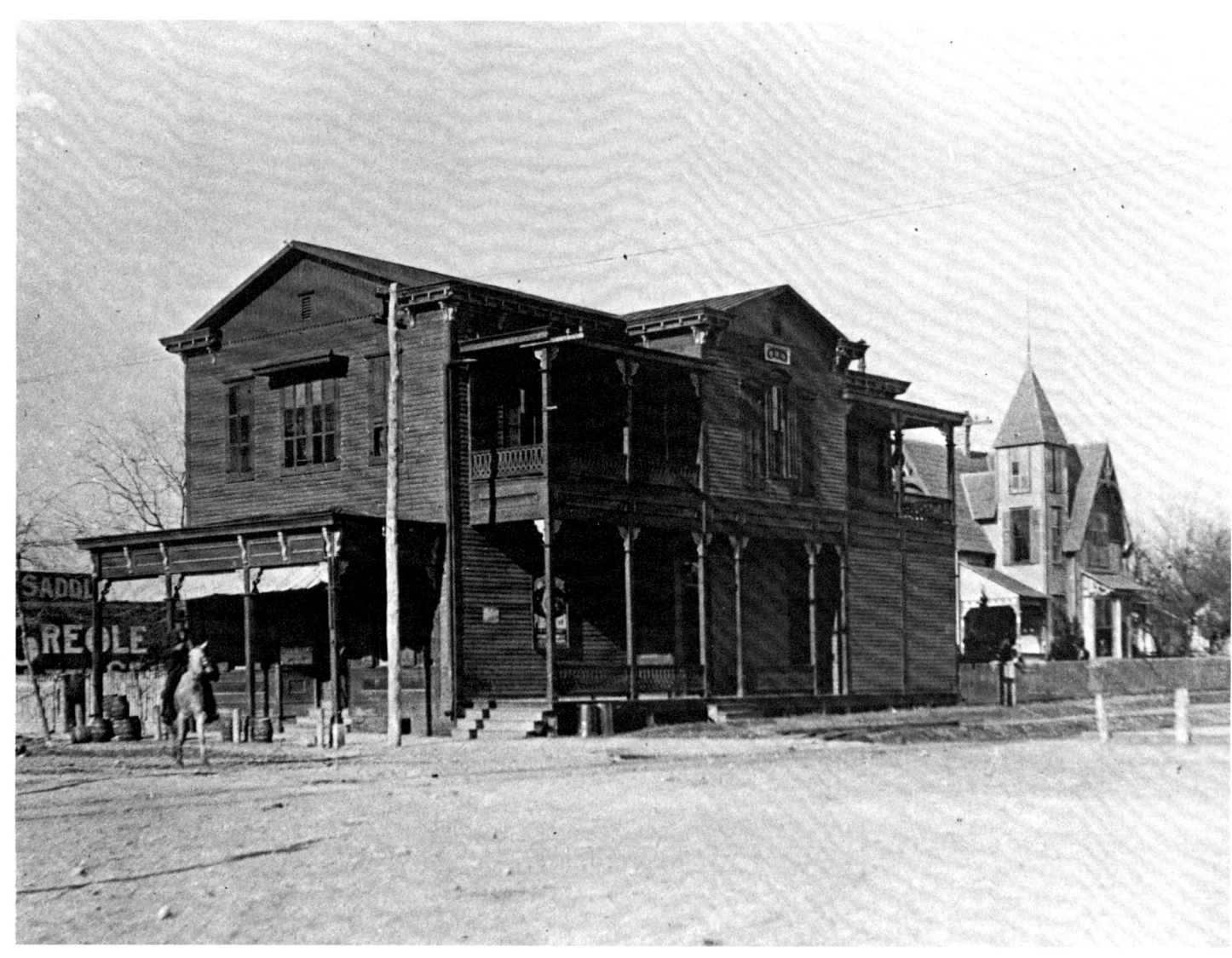
54. Station Hotel, New Braunfels.

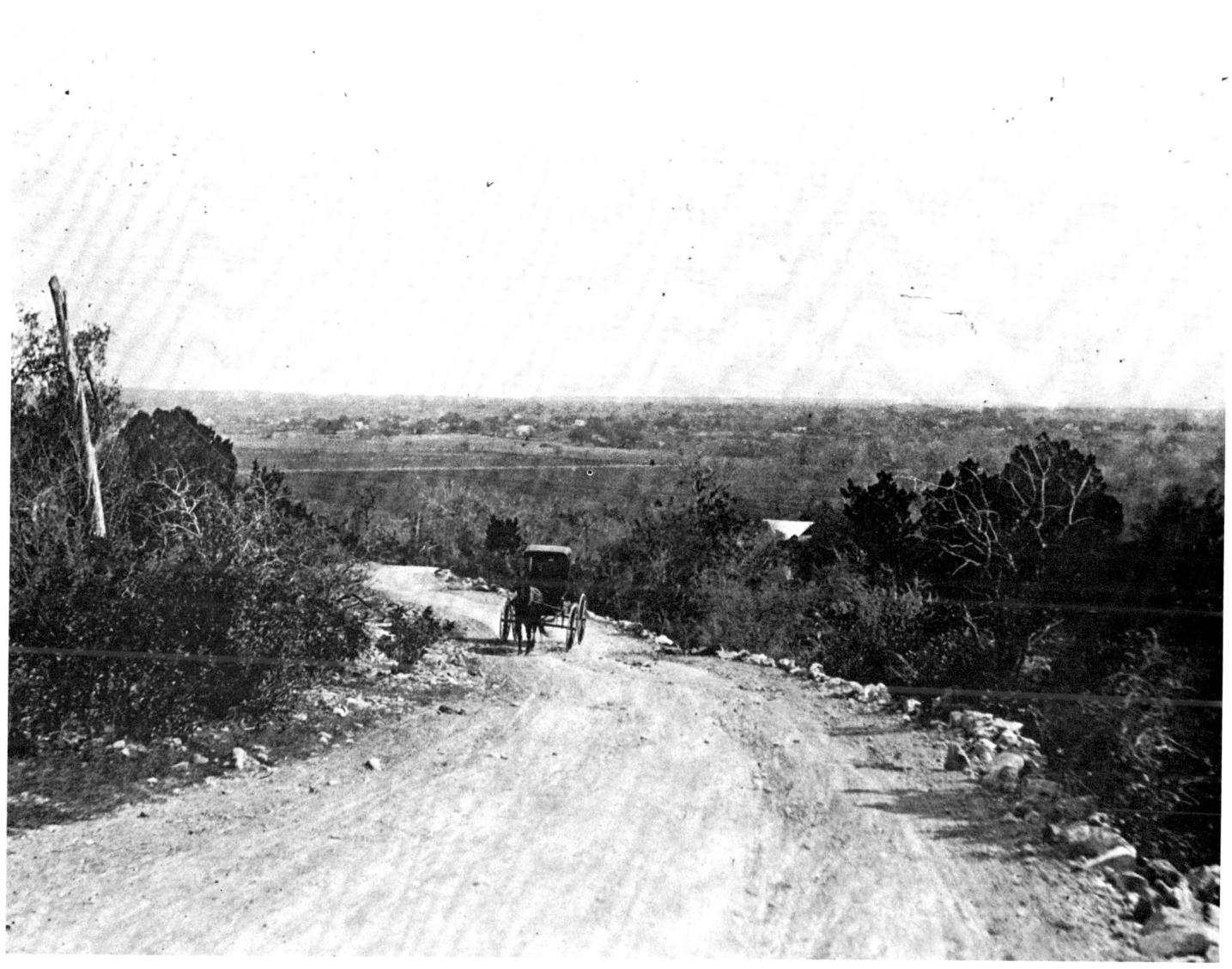

55. On the mountain road, near New Braunfels.

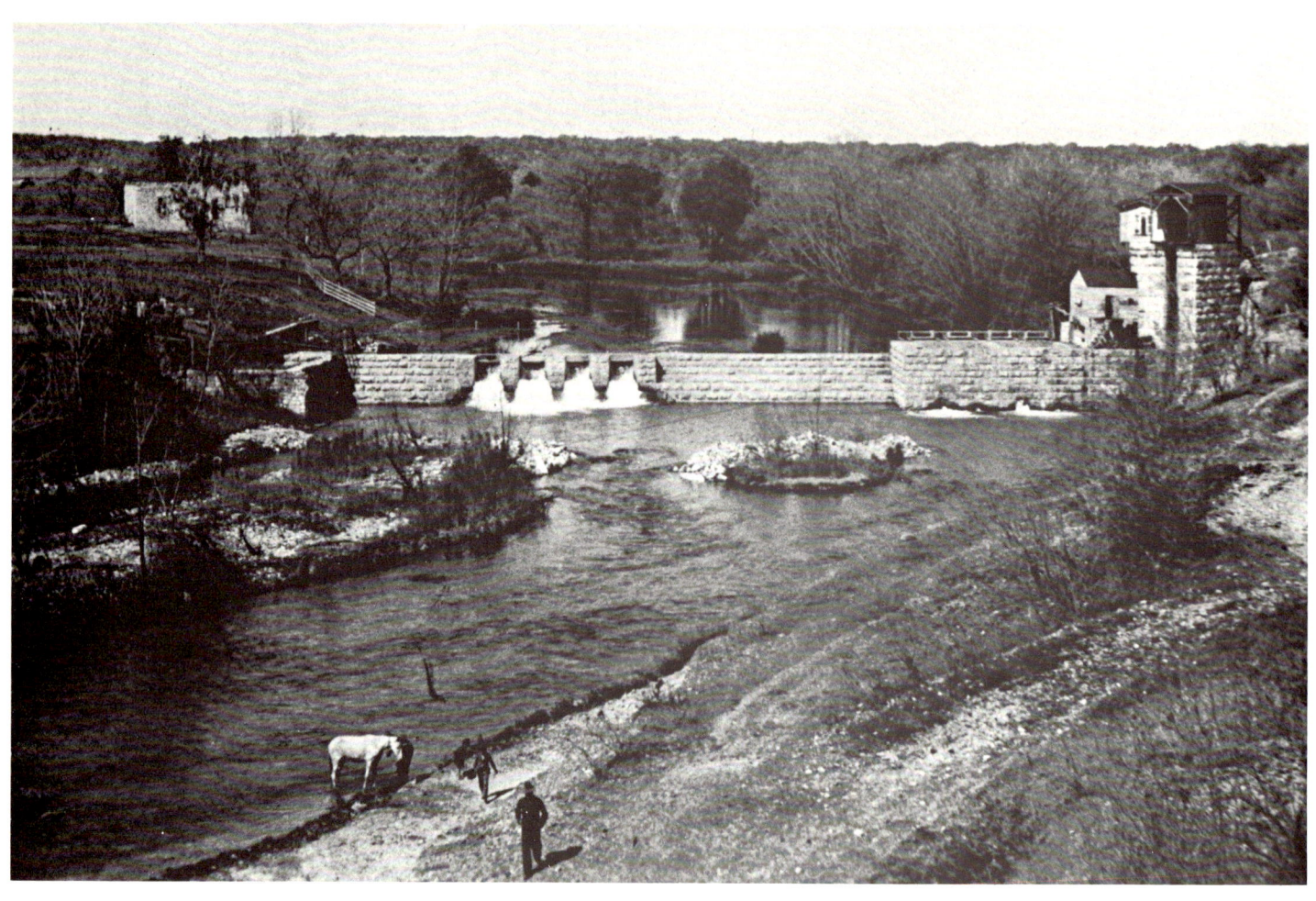

56. A dam on the Comal River, New Braunfels. The gates to the mill race are at right.

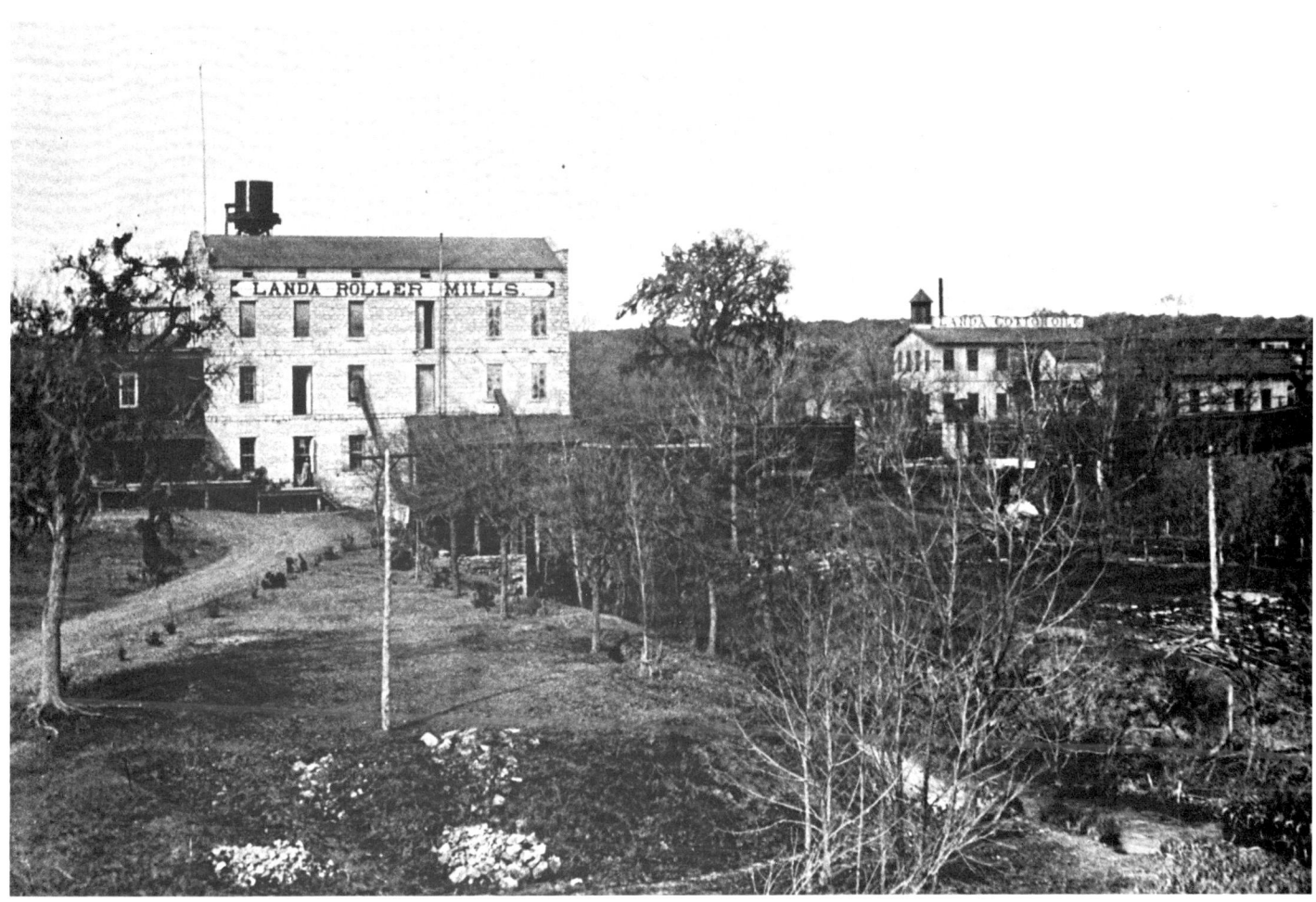

57. Landa Roller Mills, New Braunfels.

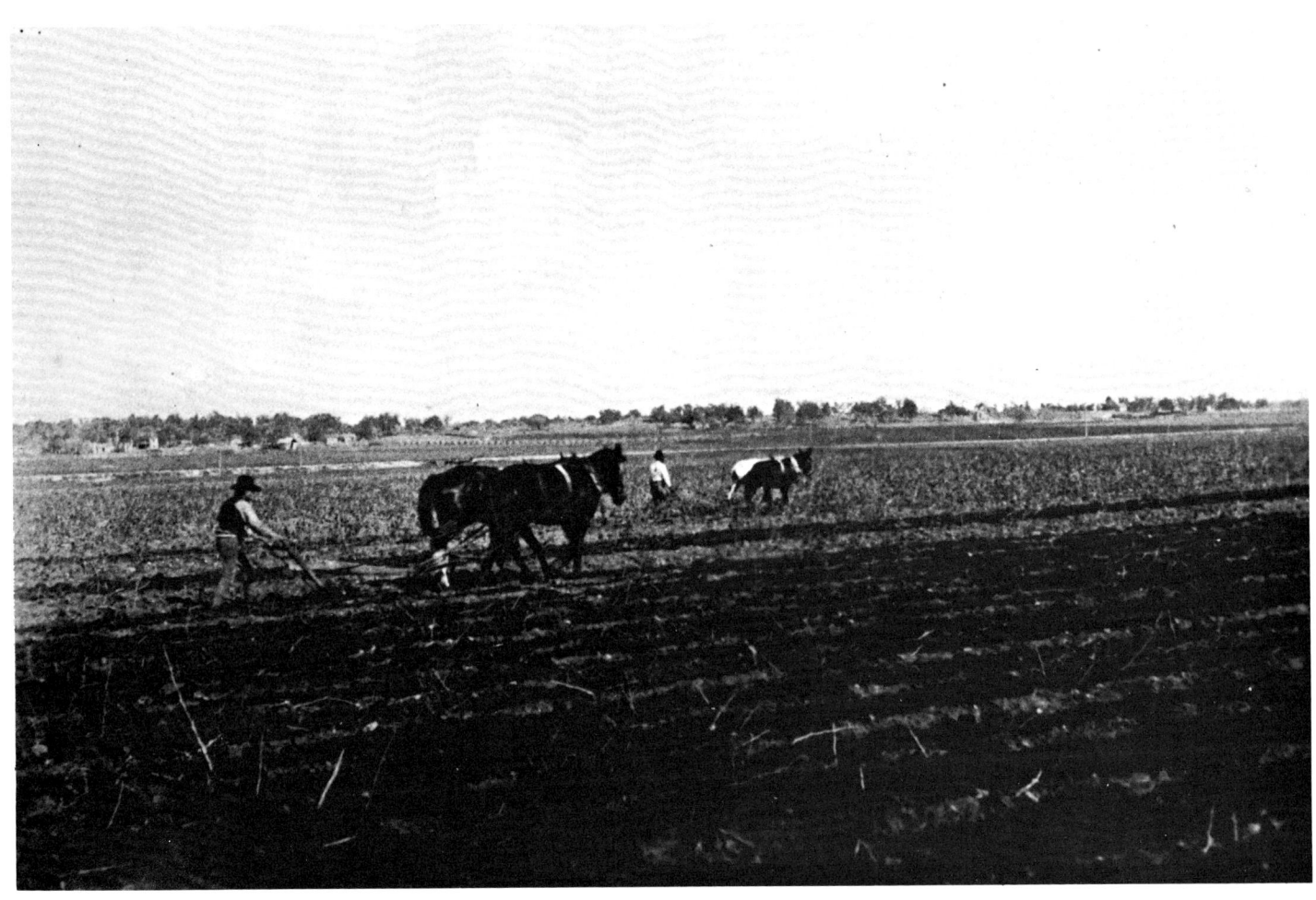

58. A farm in Comal County.

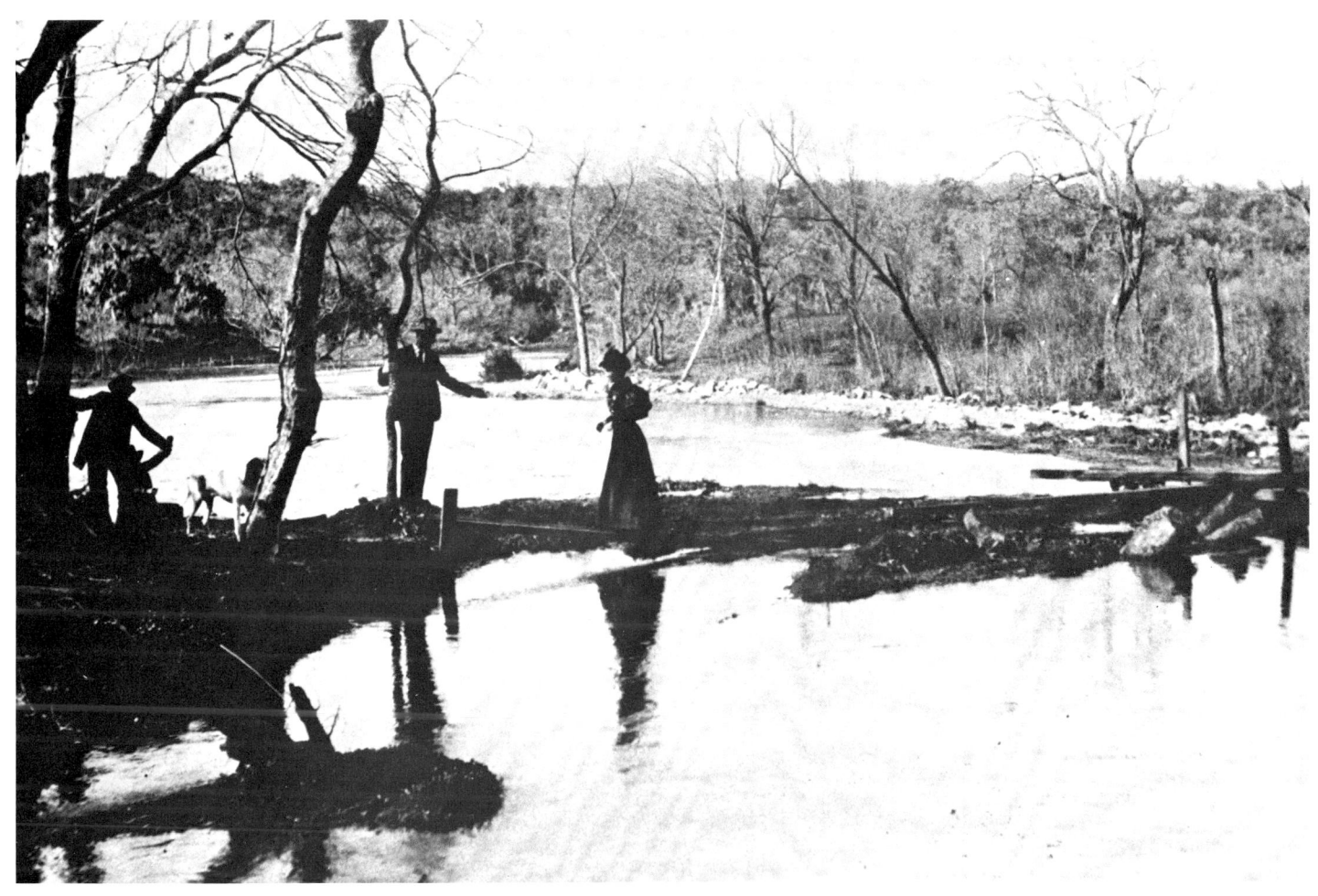

59. A scene on the Comal River.

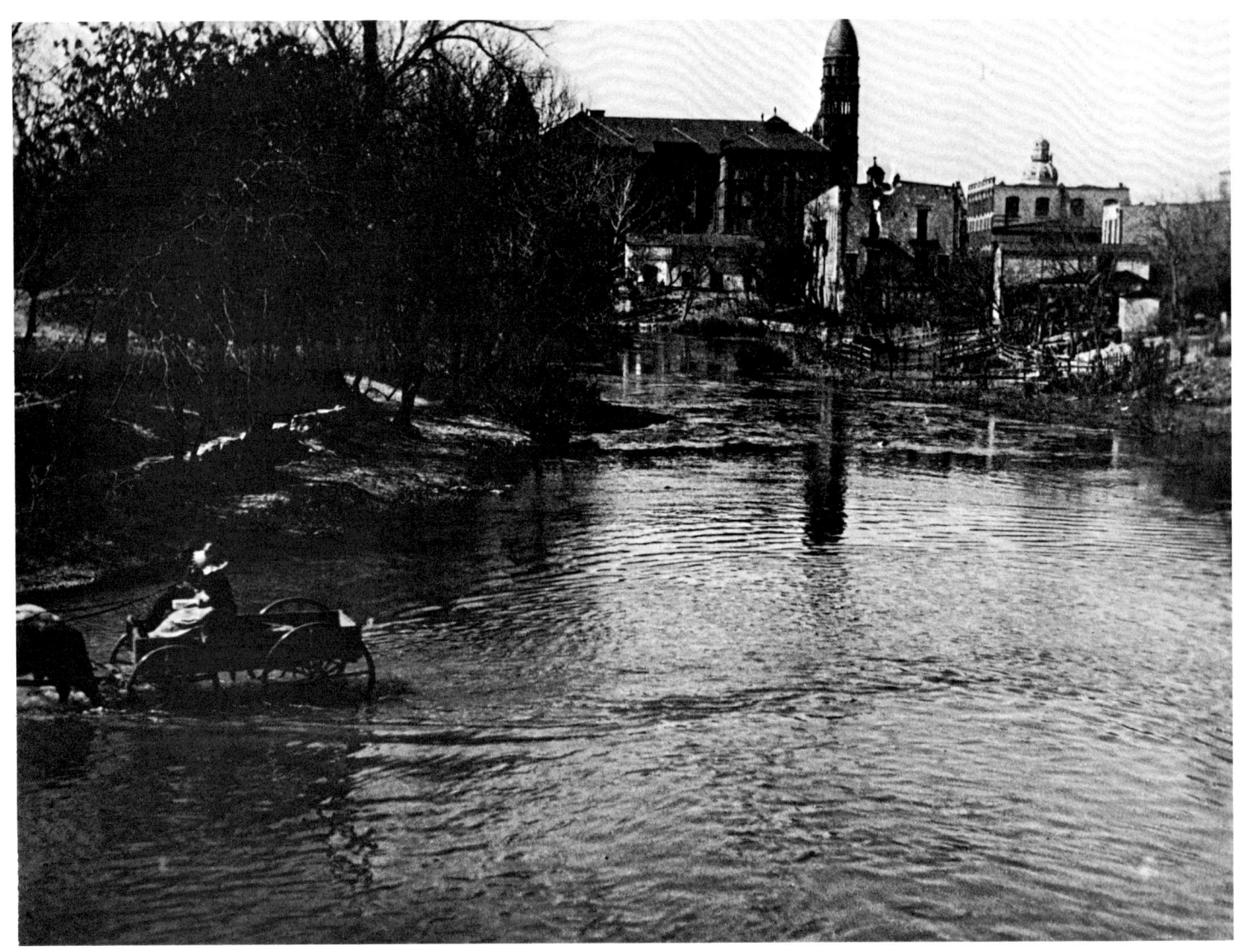

60. A ford on the San Antonio River.

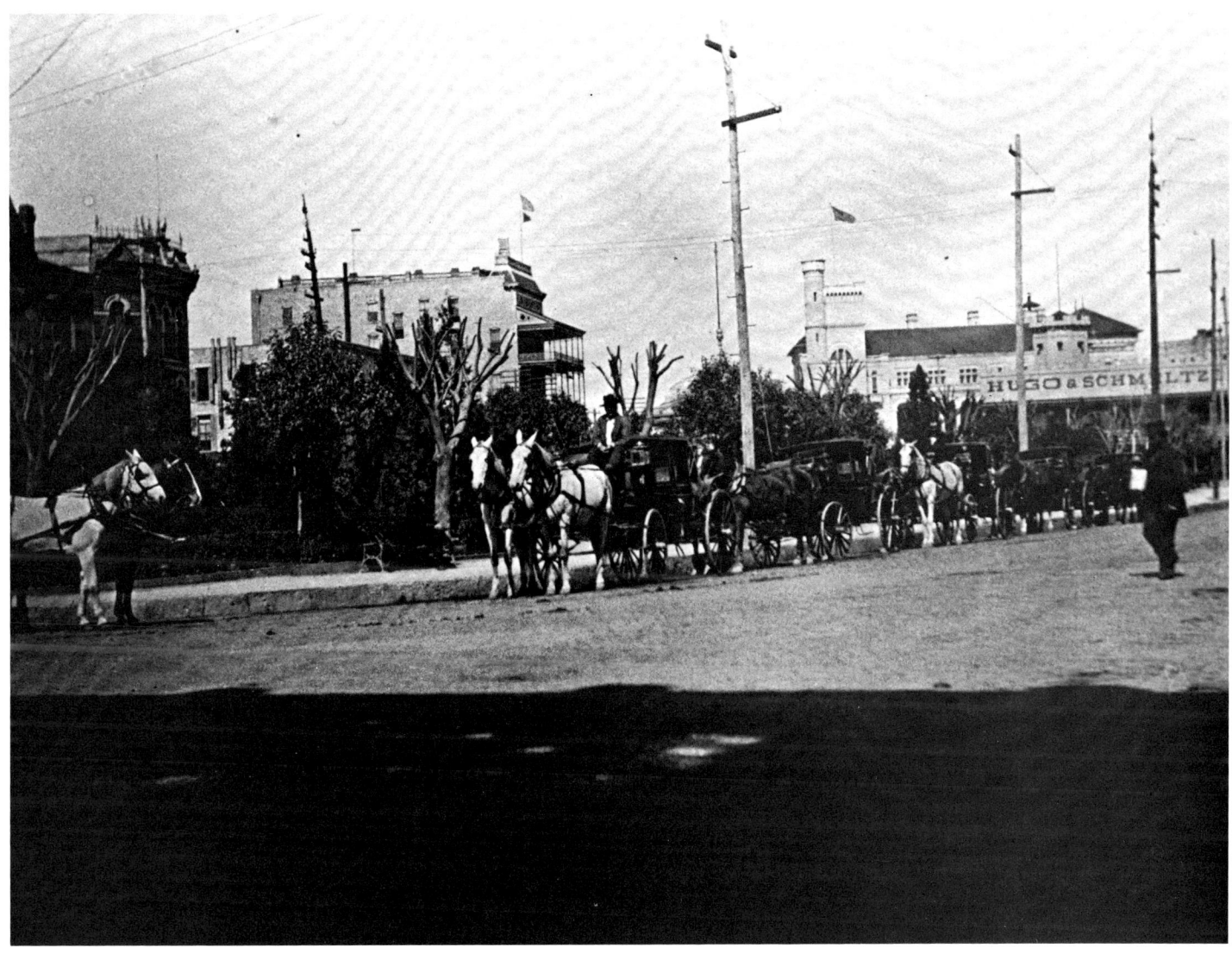

61. Alamo Plaza, San Antonio.

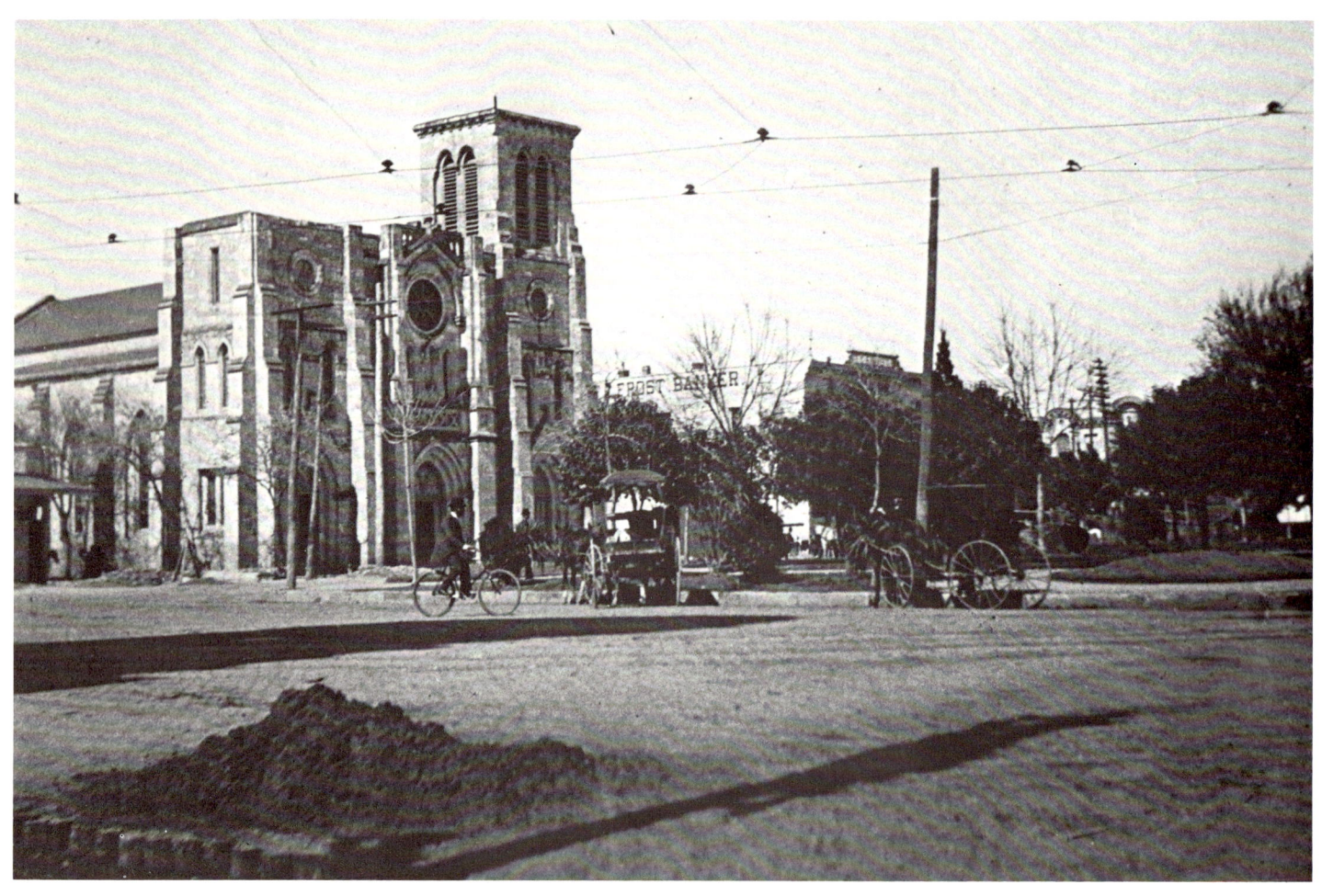

62. San Fernando Cathedral, San Antonio, with the Frost Bank at right. The cathedral is greatly altered today.

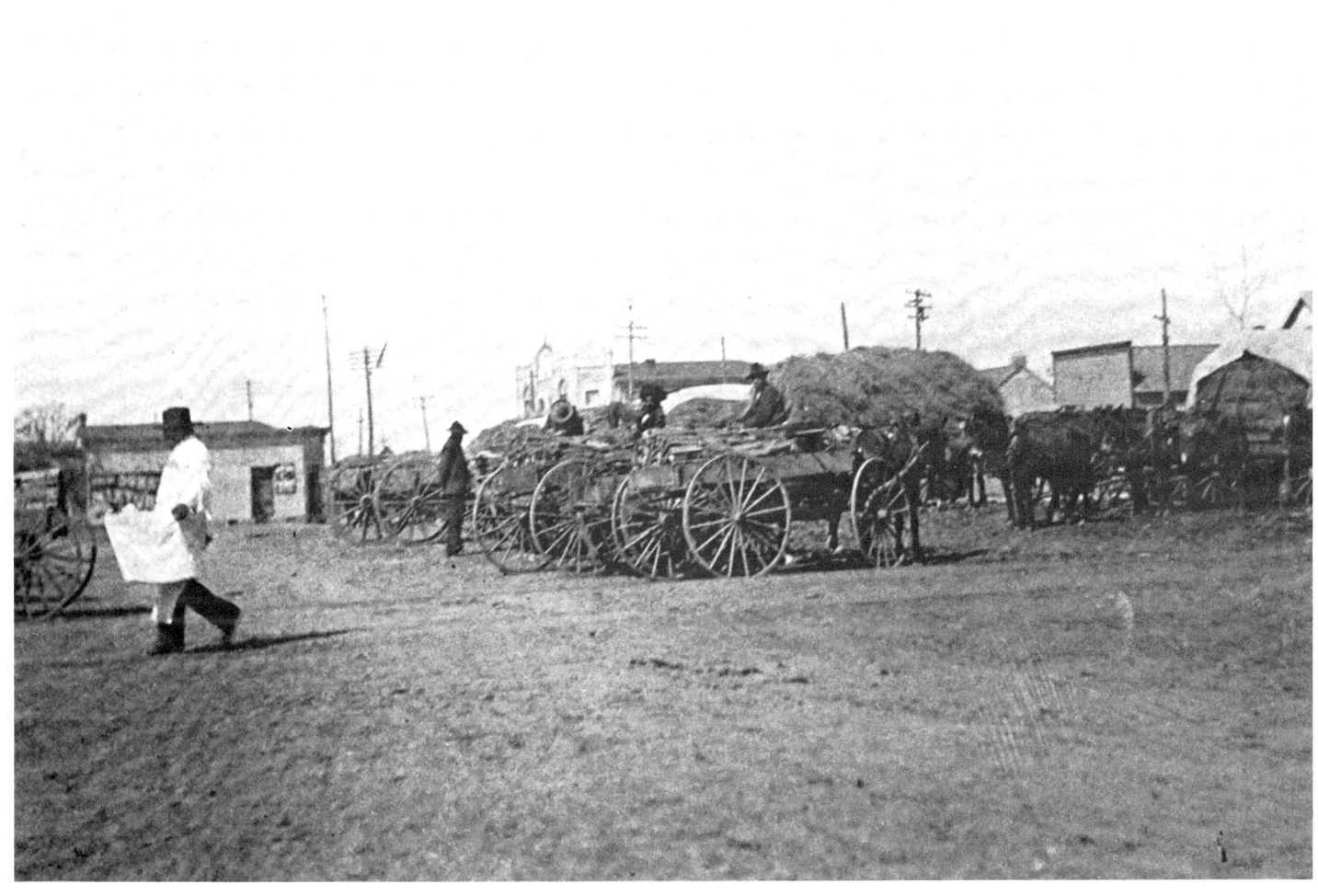

63. Milam Square, San Antonio.

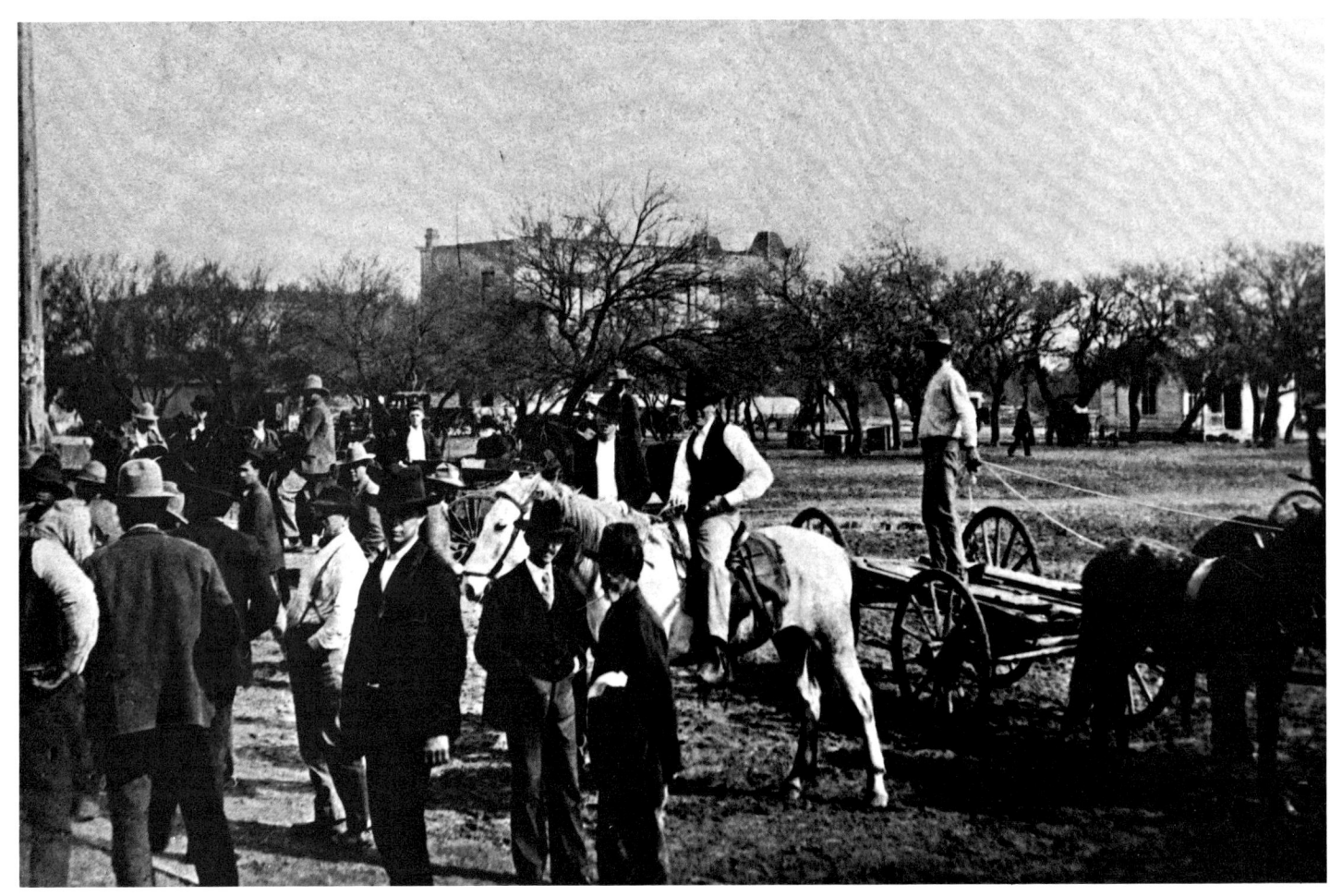

64. "First Monday" in Cotulla.

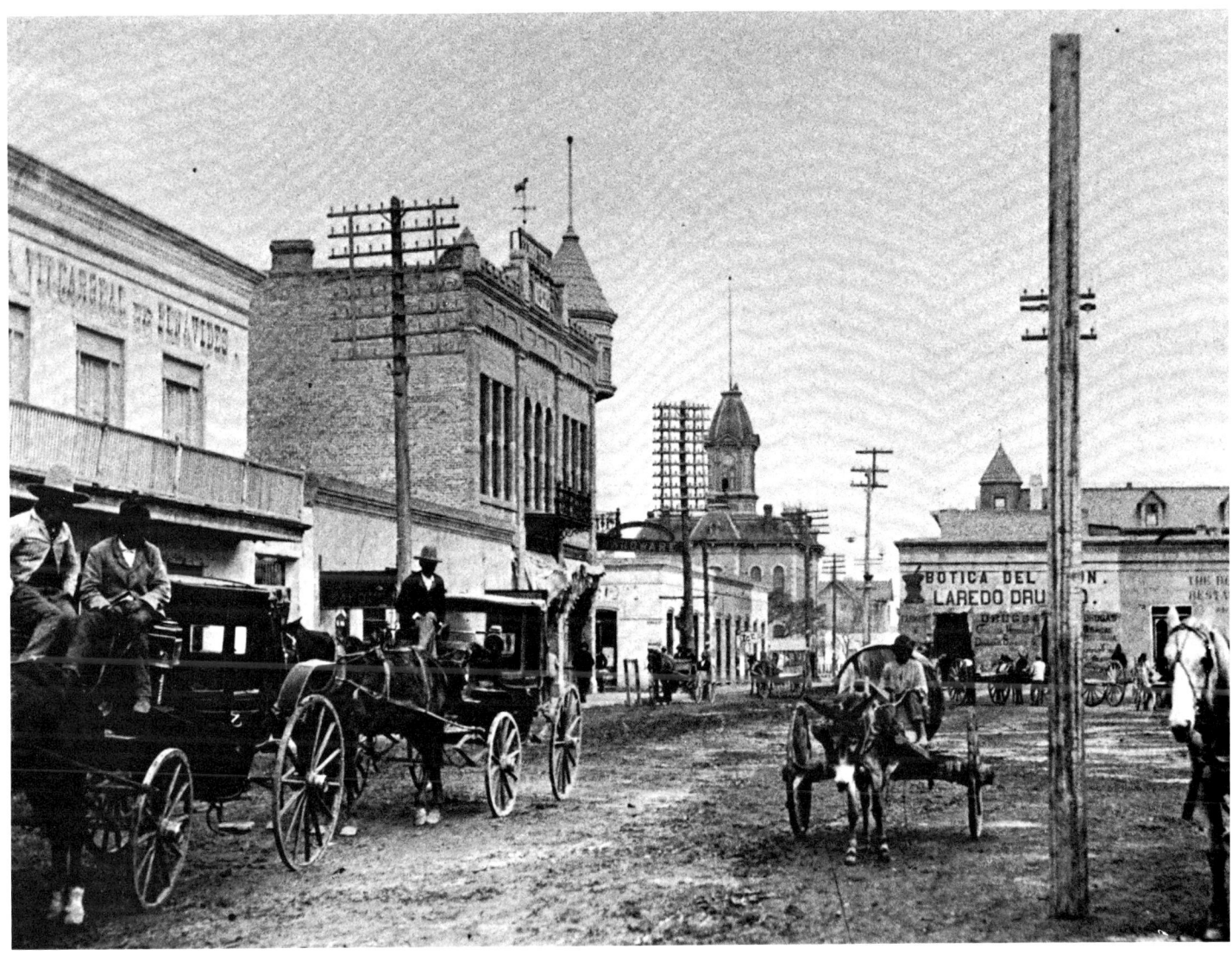

65. A street scene in Laredo.

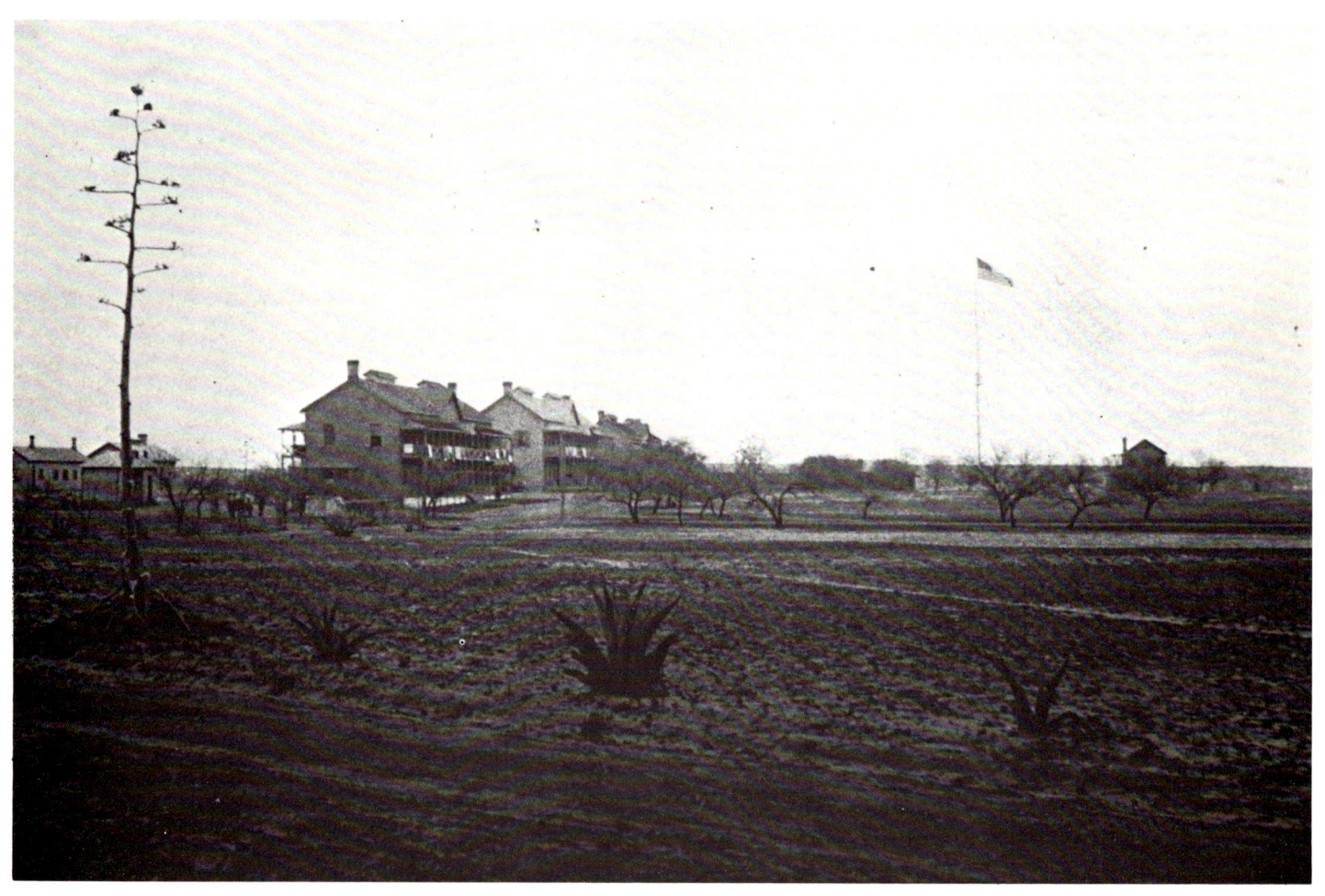

66. Fort McIntosh, Laredo. It was built in 1865 and used by the U. S. Army until 1946.

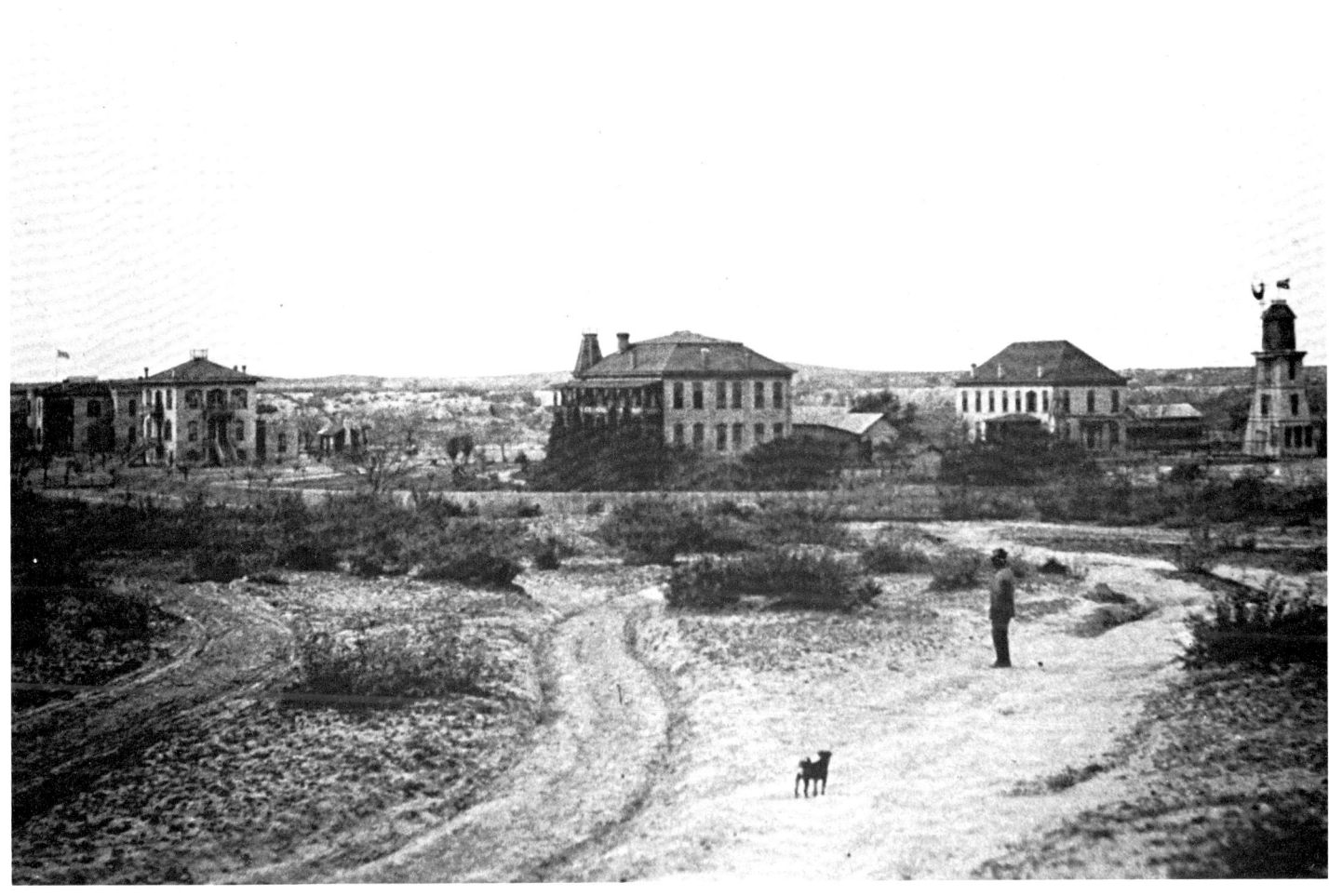
67. Laredo Seminary, later the Holding Institute.

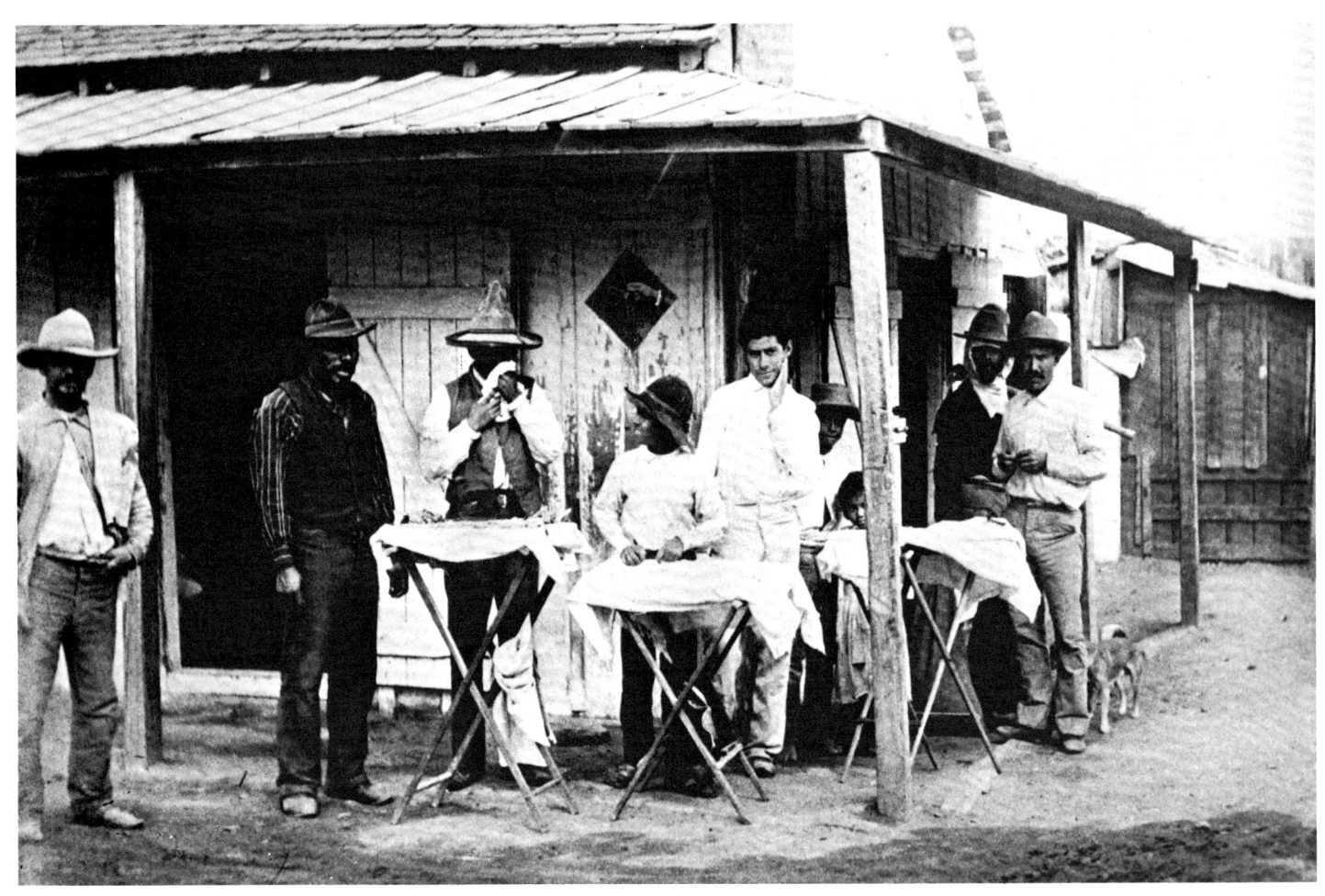

68. Mexican candy vendors, Laredo.

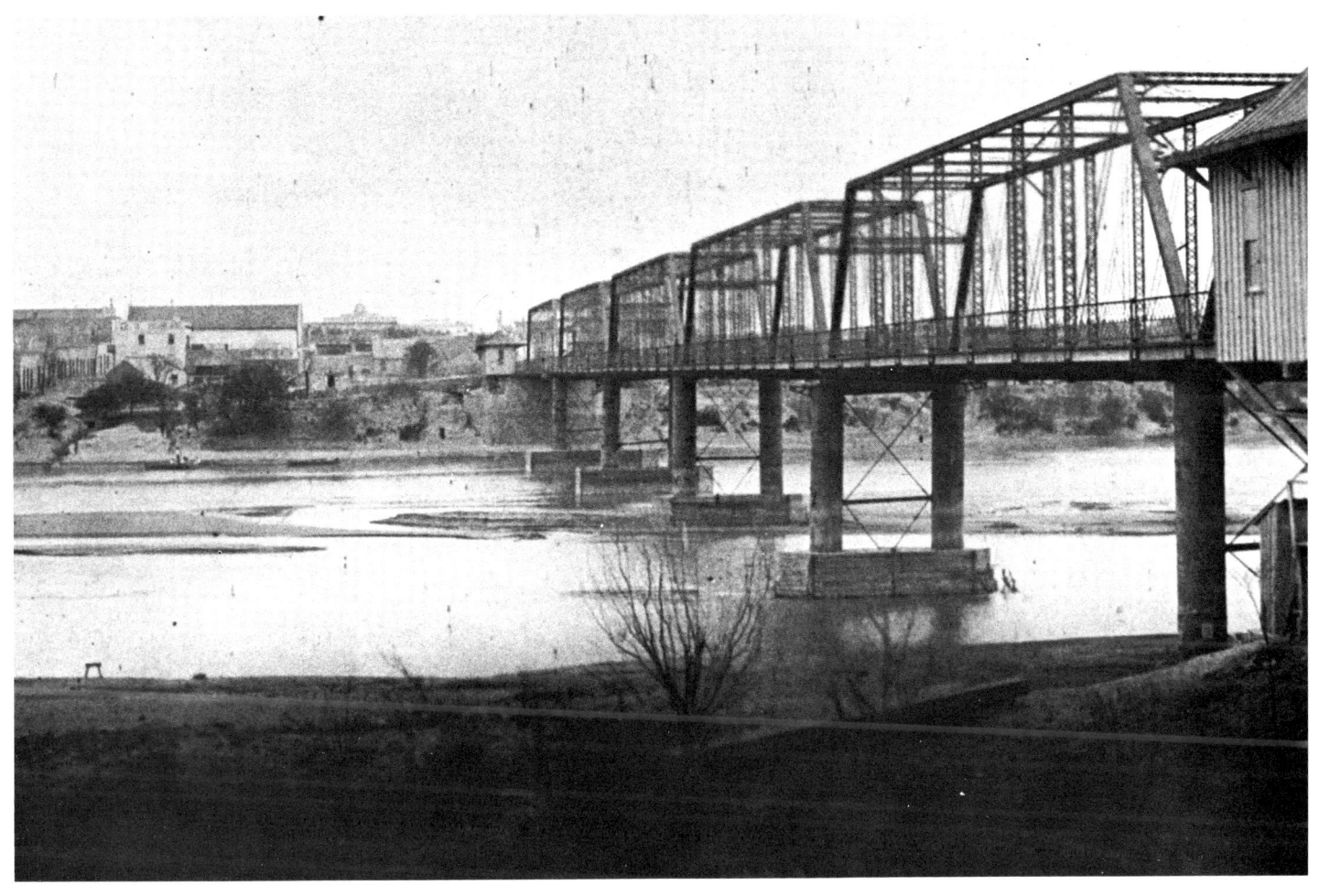

69. International bridge, Laredo to Nuevo Laredo. Built in 1889 to replace a ferry, it was damaged by a tornado in 1905 and burned in 1920.

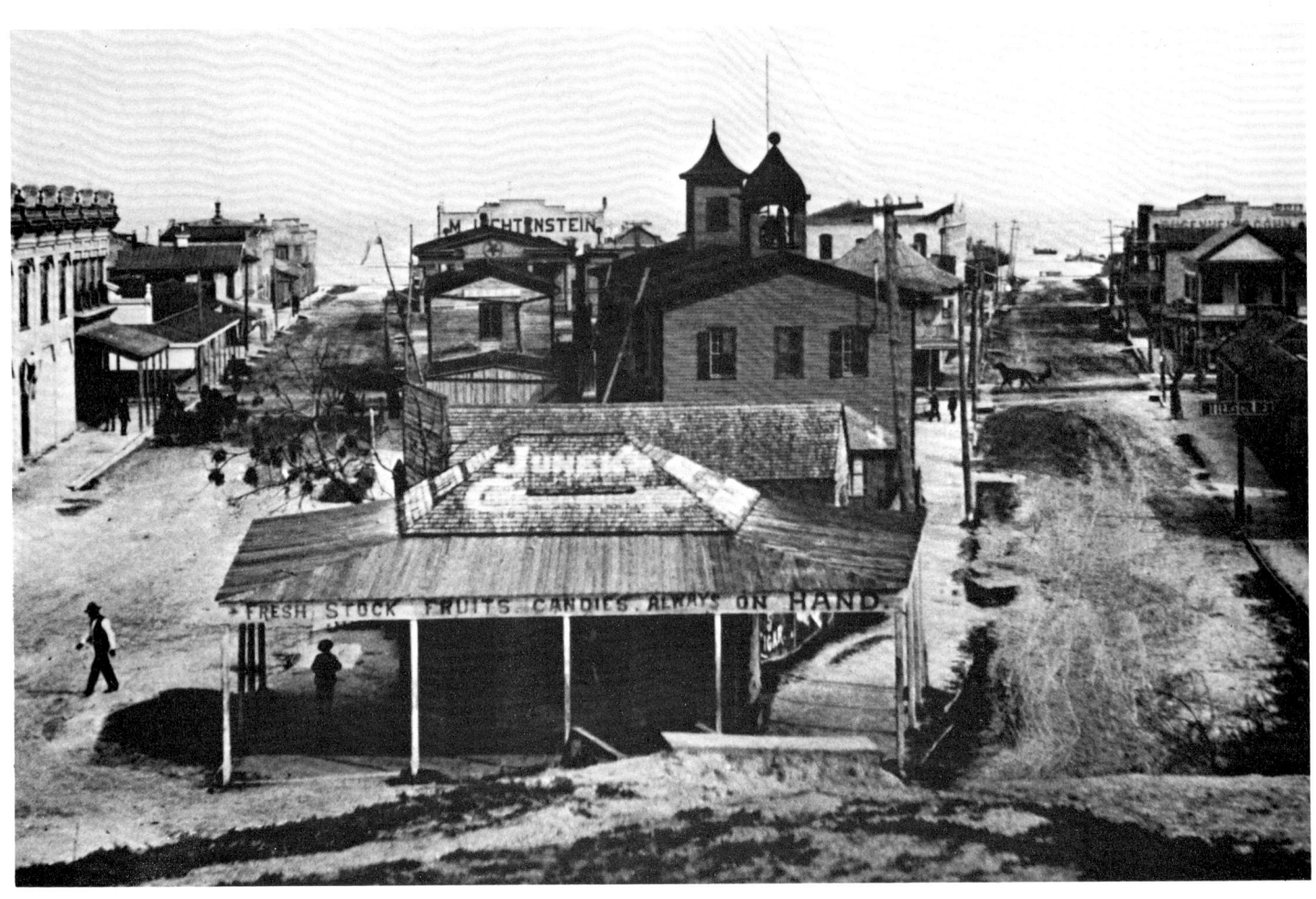

70. Corpus Christi from the bluff. Lichtenstein's is still a major store.

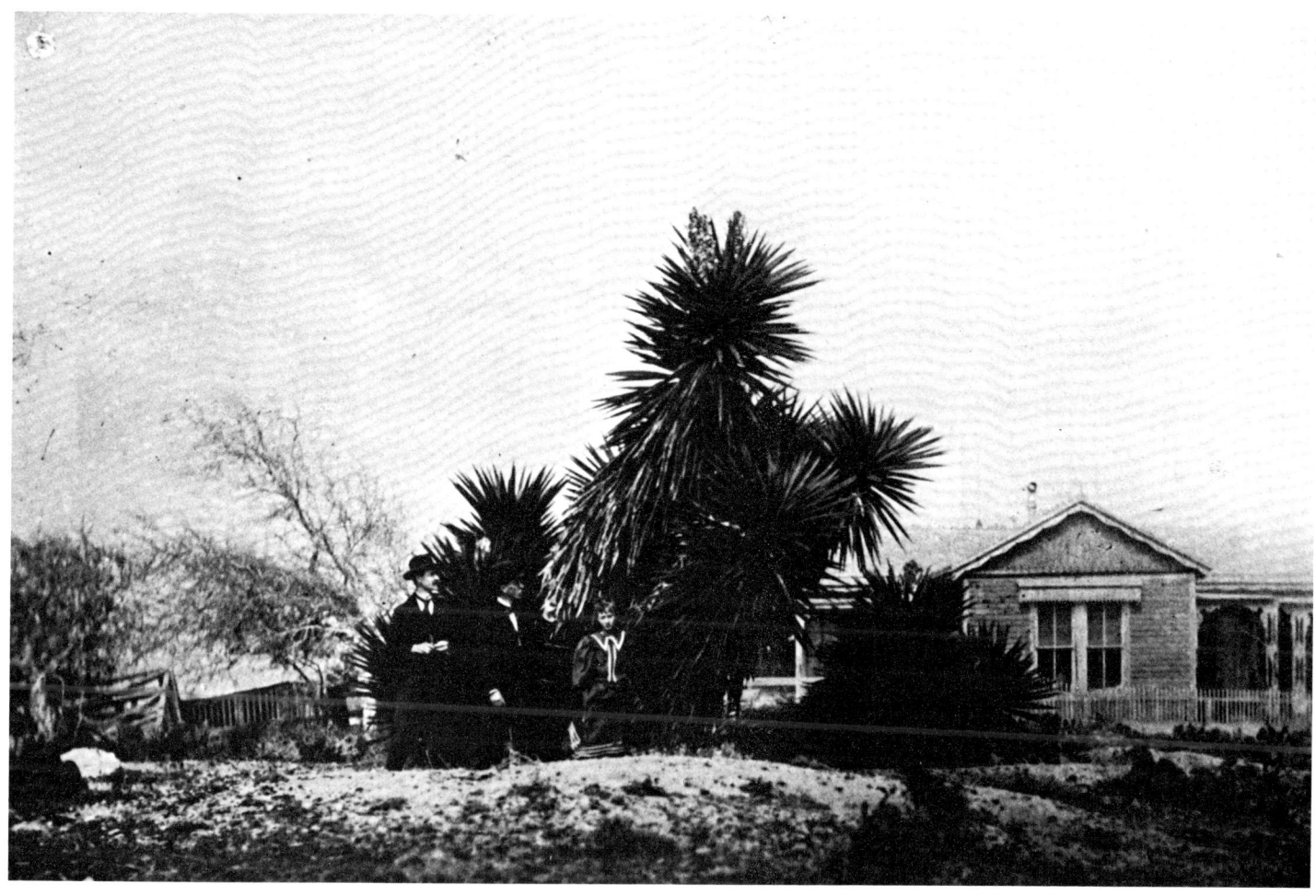

71. A Spanish dagger plant, Rockport.

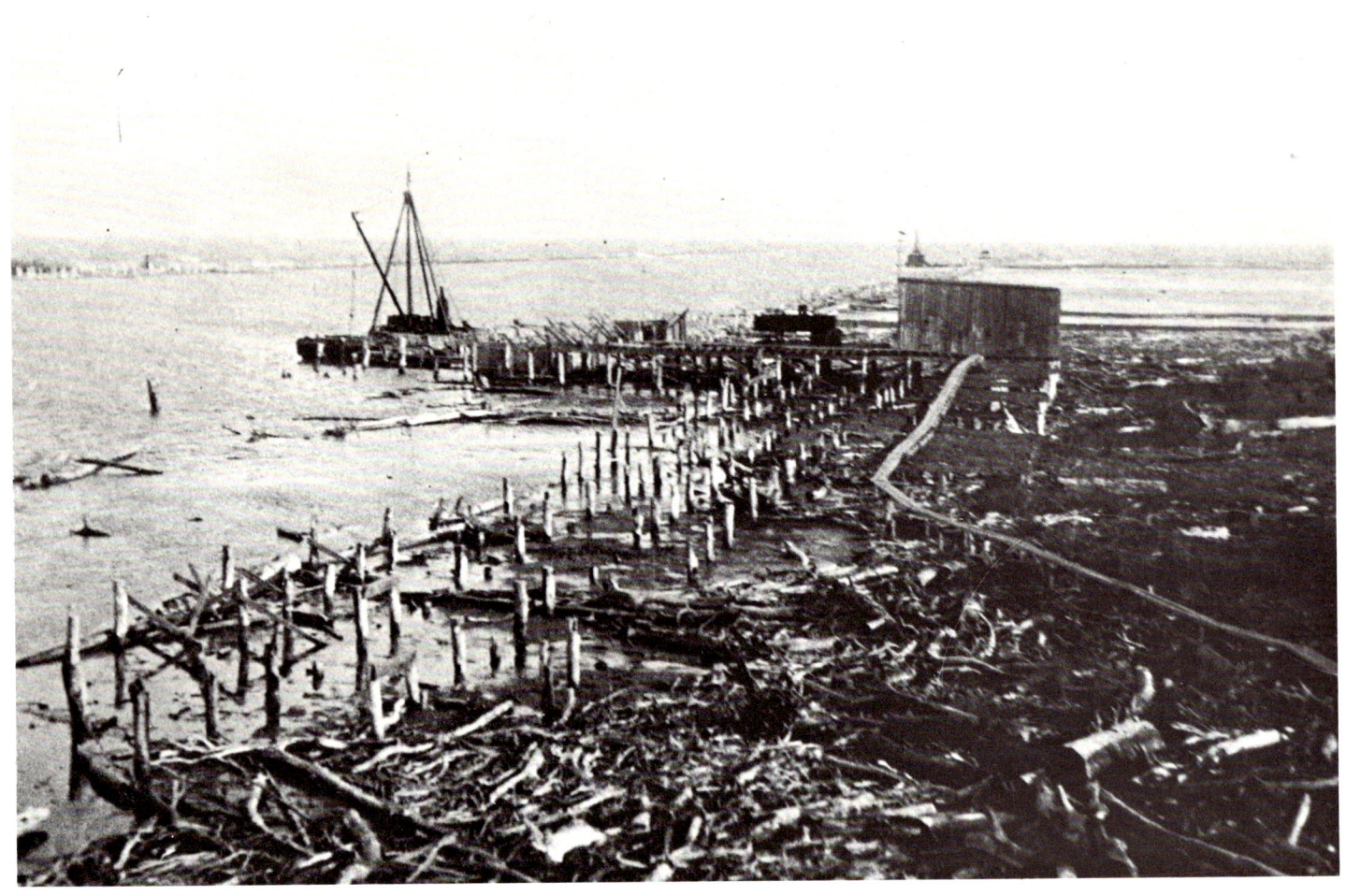

72. The mouth of the Brazos River.

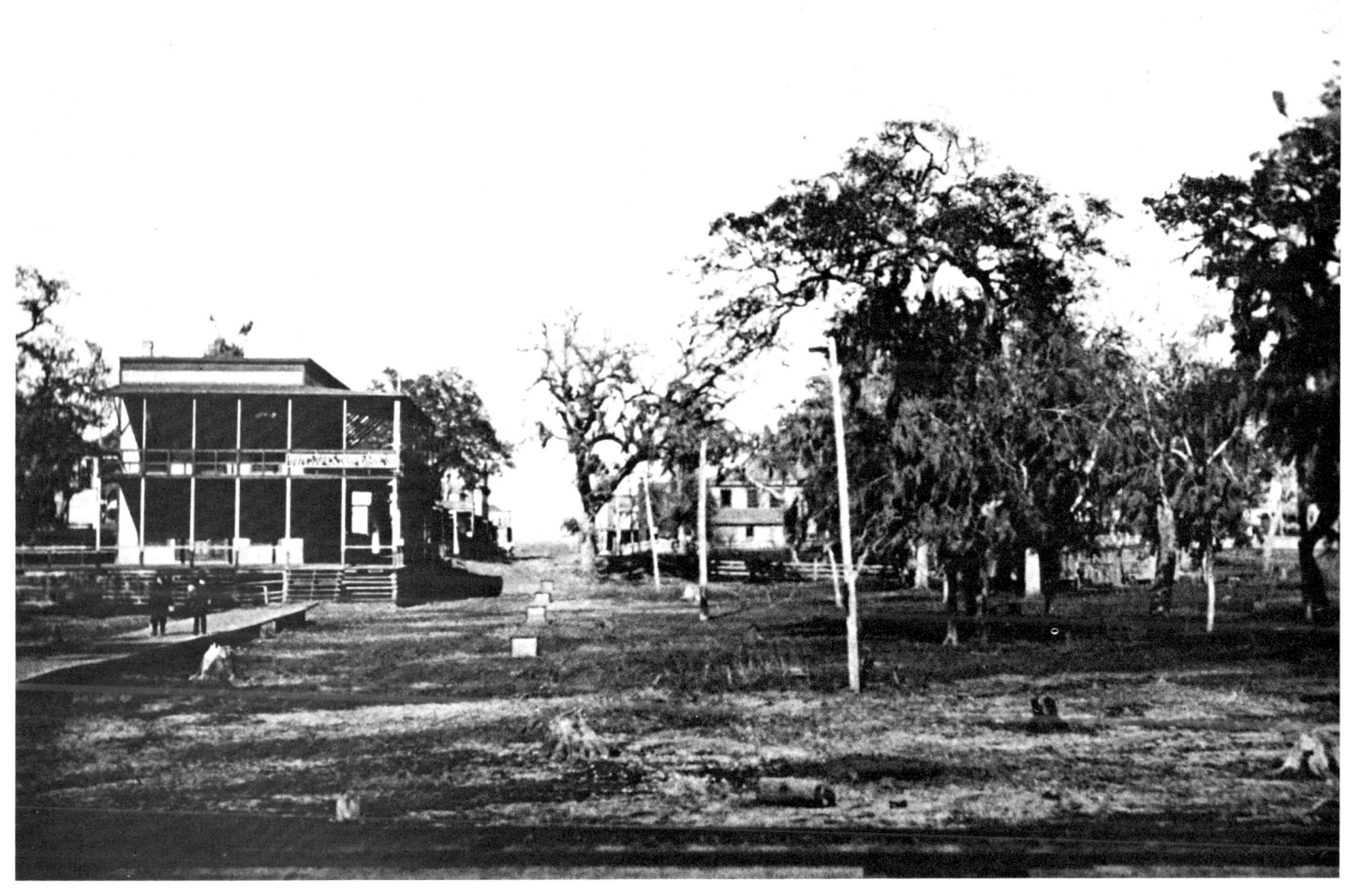

73. Brazos Land & Improvement Co., Velasco.

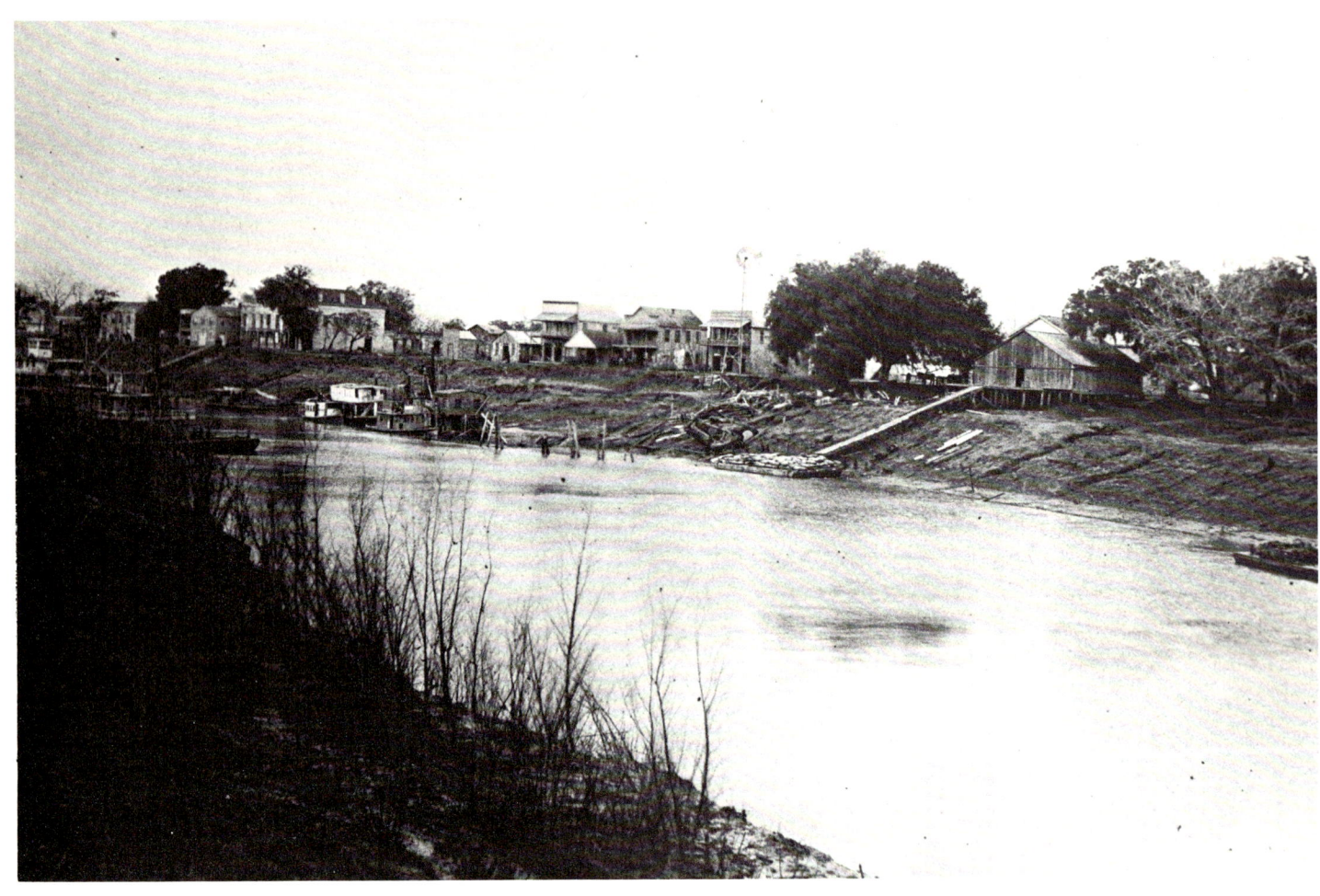

74. Columbia, on the Brazos River.

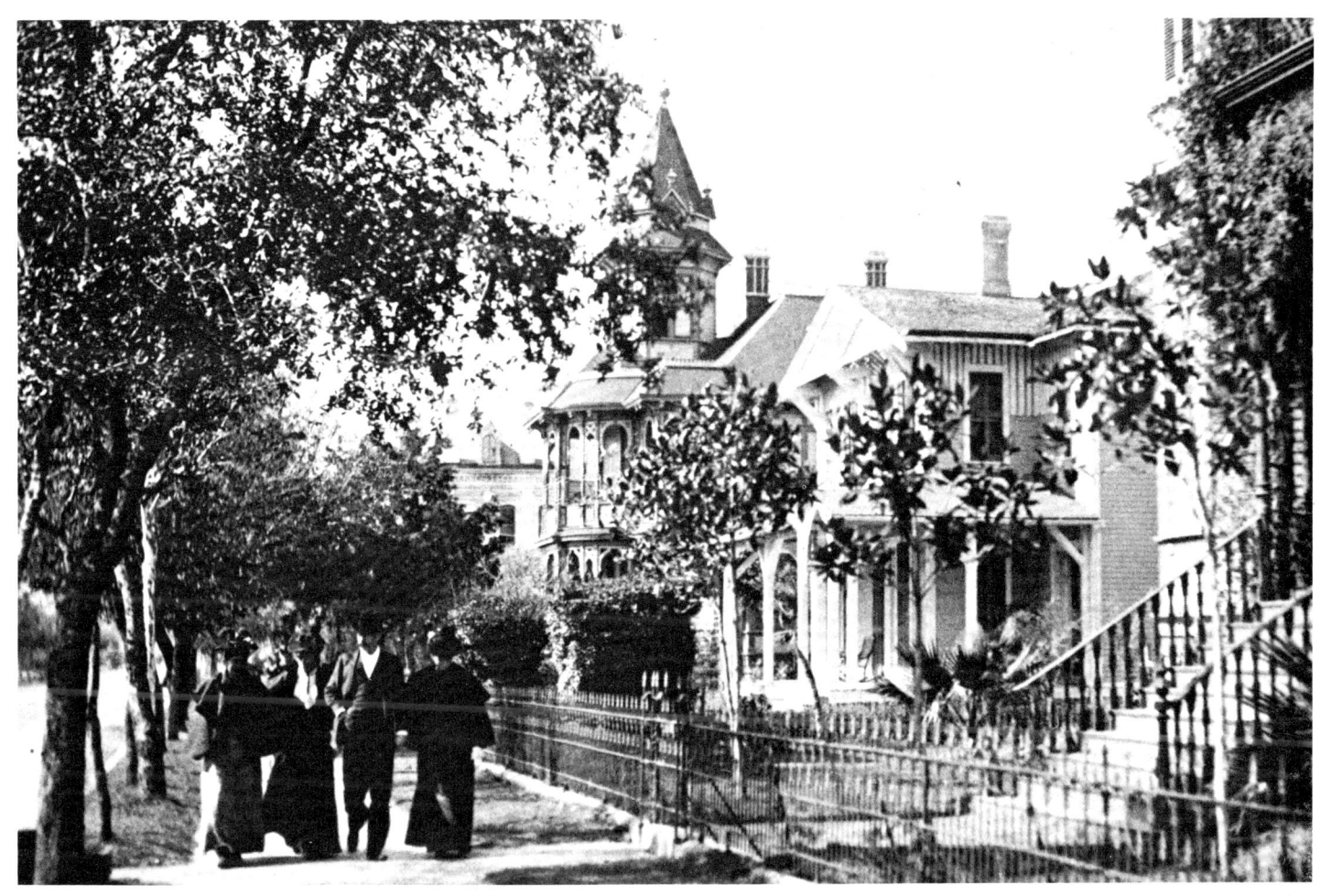

75. A scene on Avenue I in Galveston.

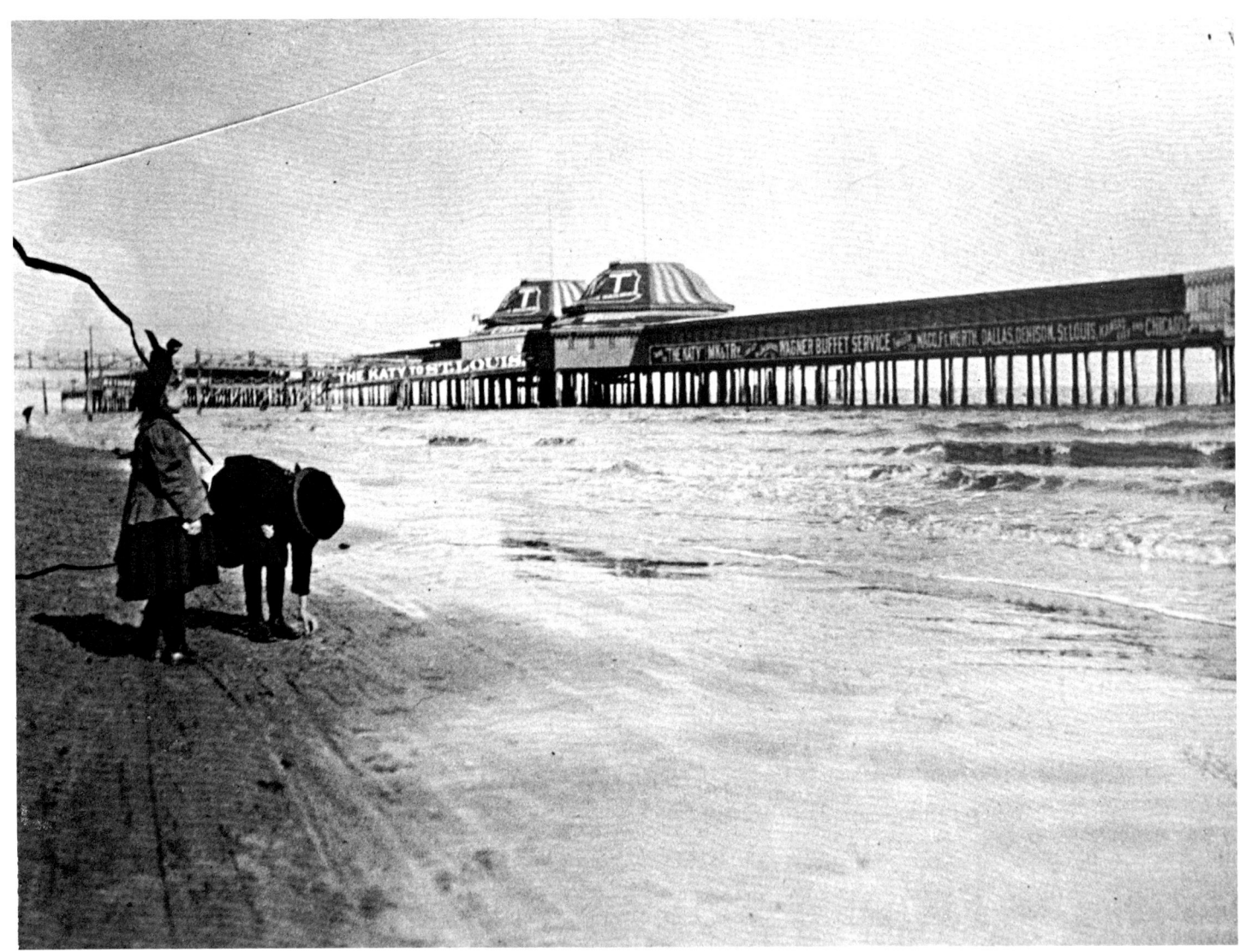

76. On the beach, Galveston.

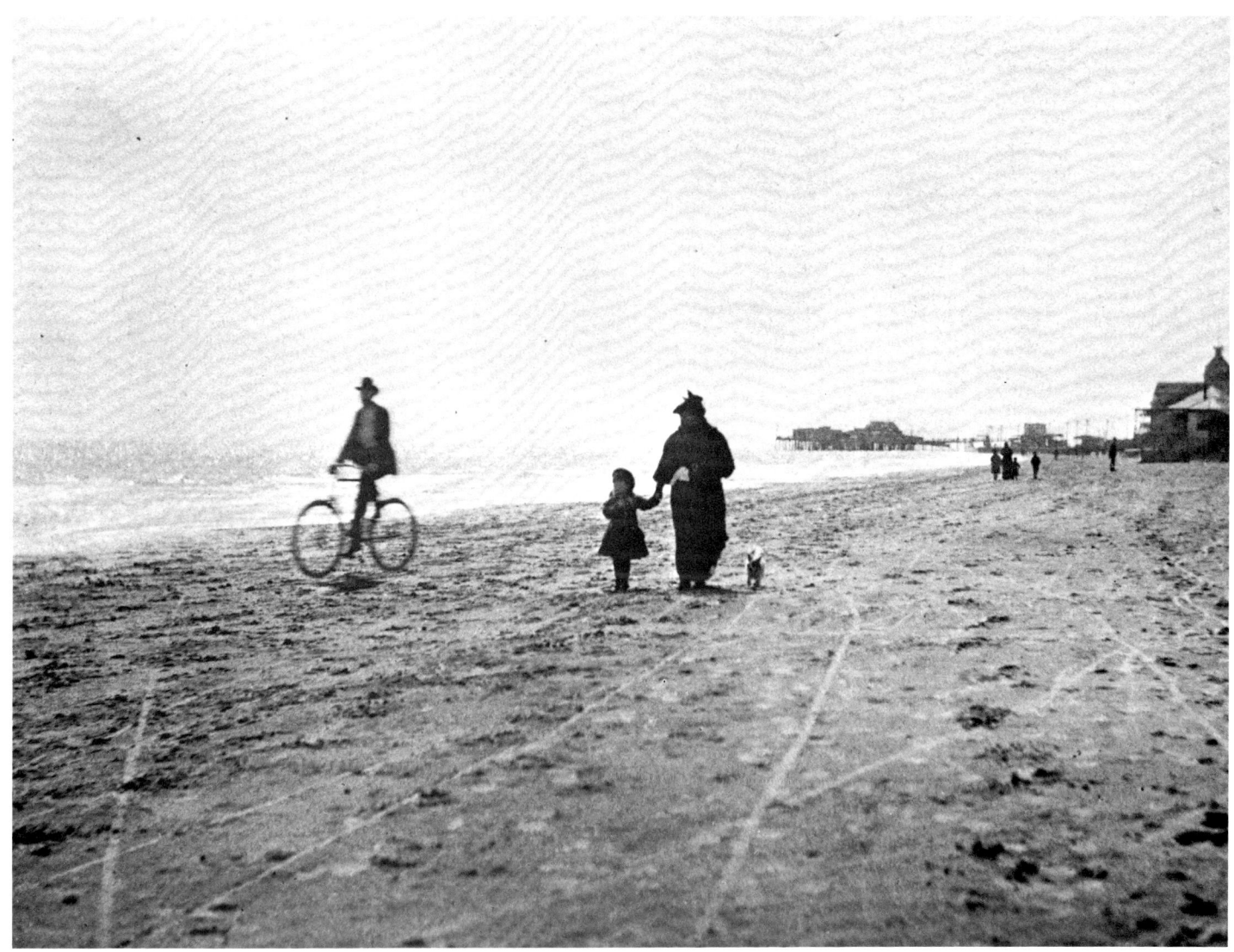

77. On the beach, Galveston.

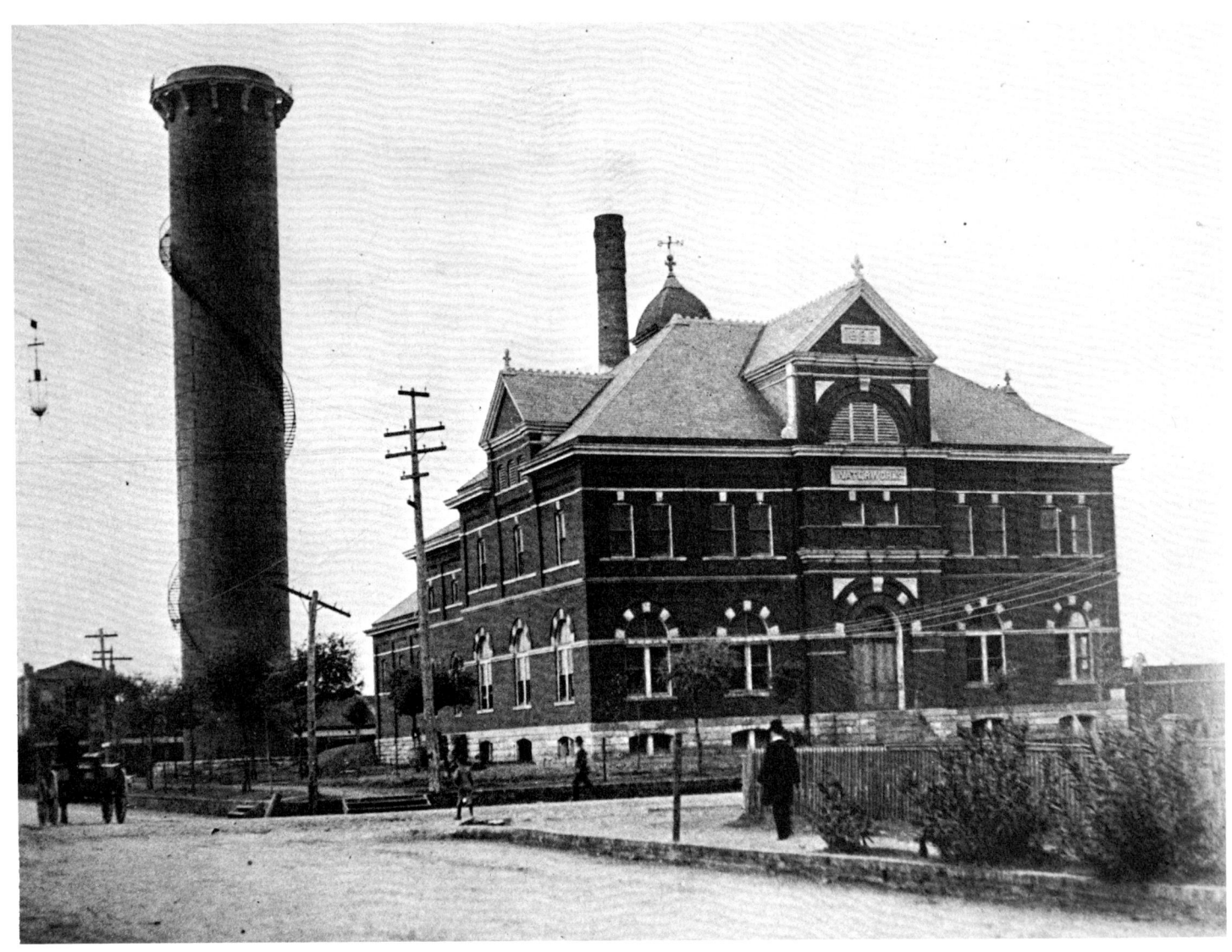

78. Galveston Water Works.

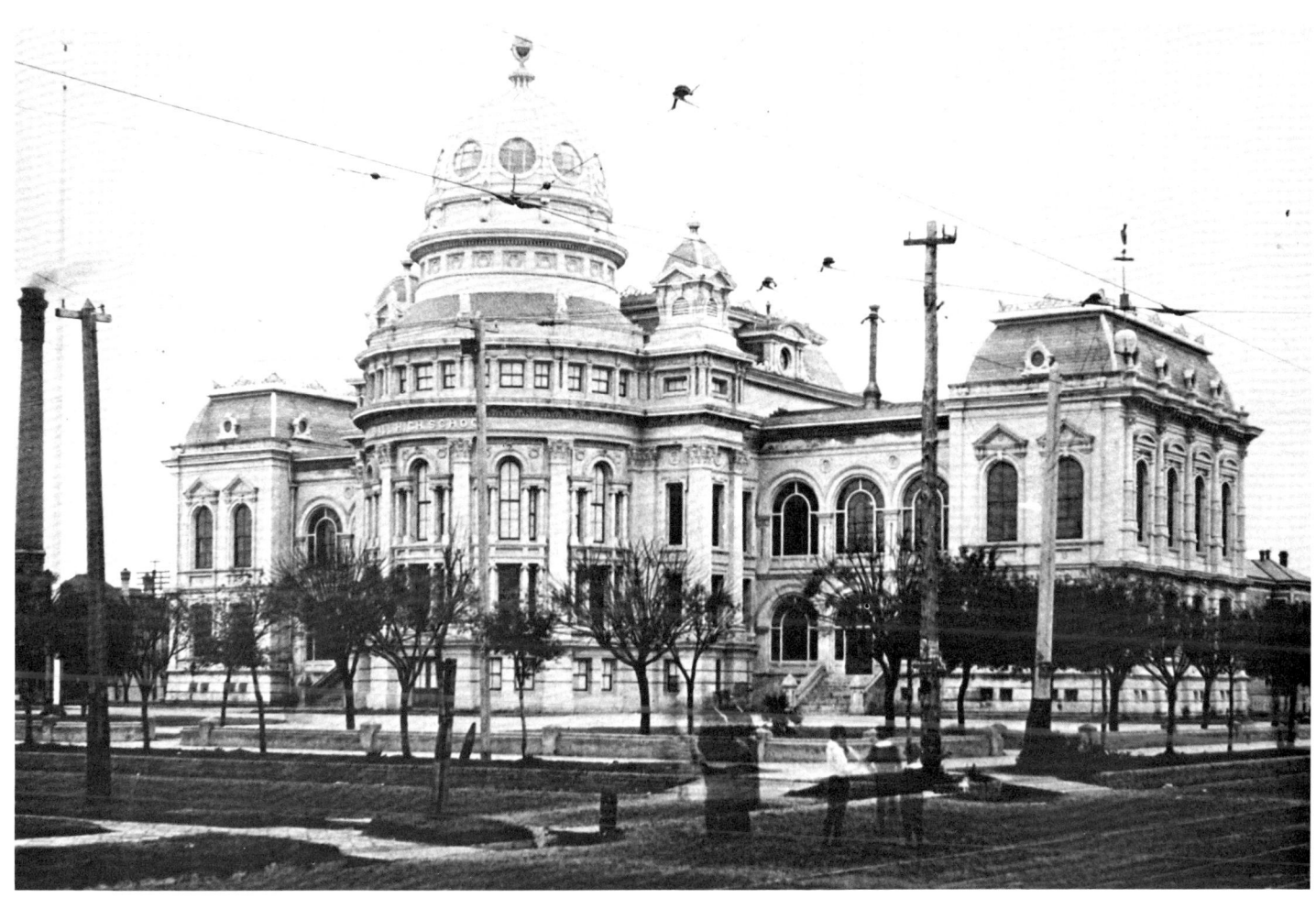

79. Ball High School, Galveston.

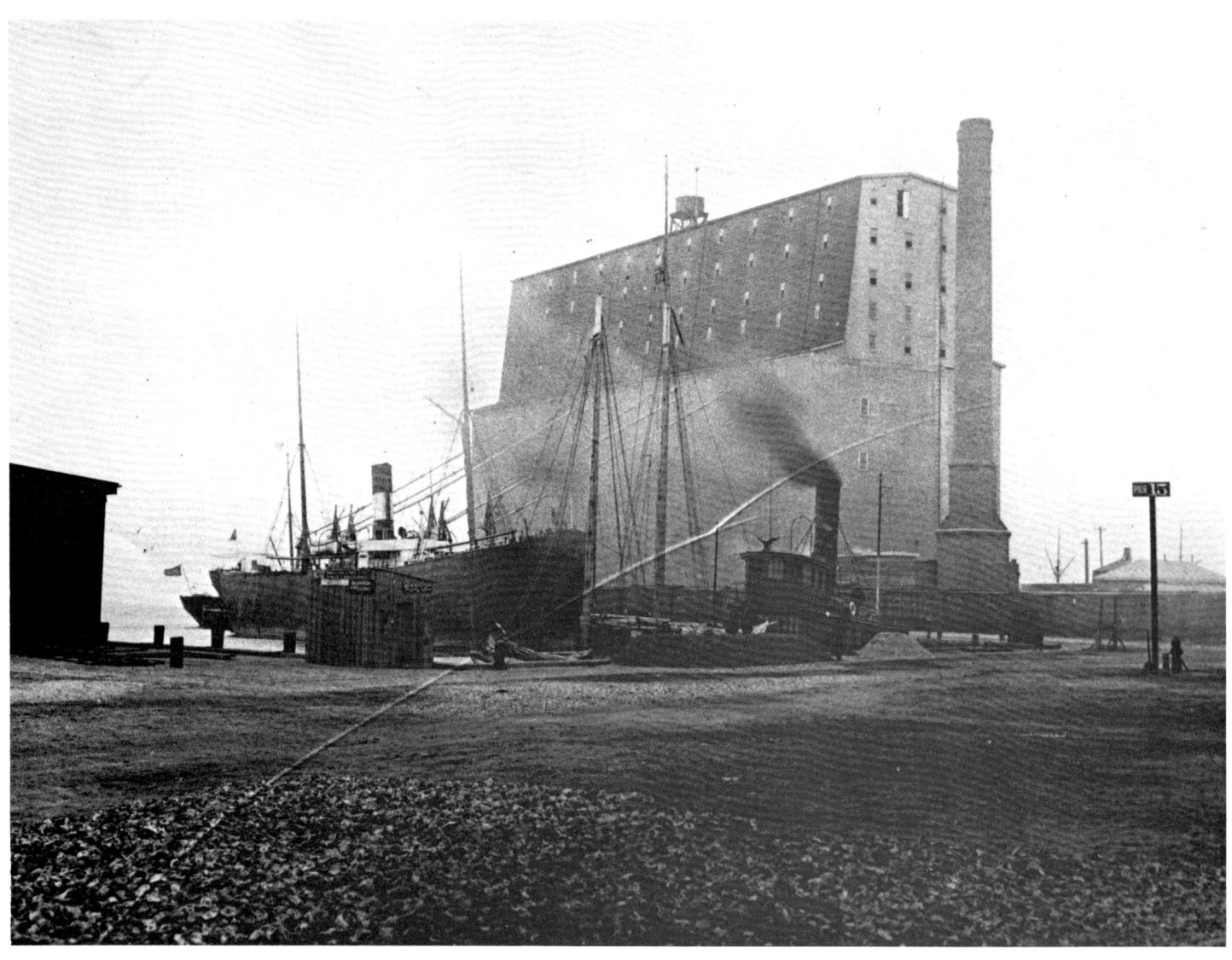

80. Grain elevator, Galveston, the second highest structure in Texas, after the State Capitol.

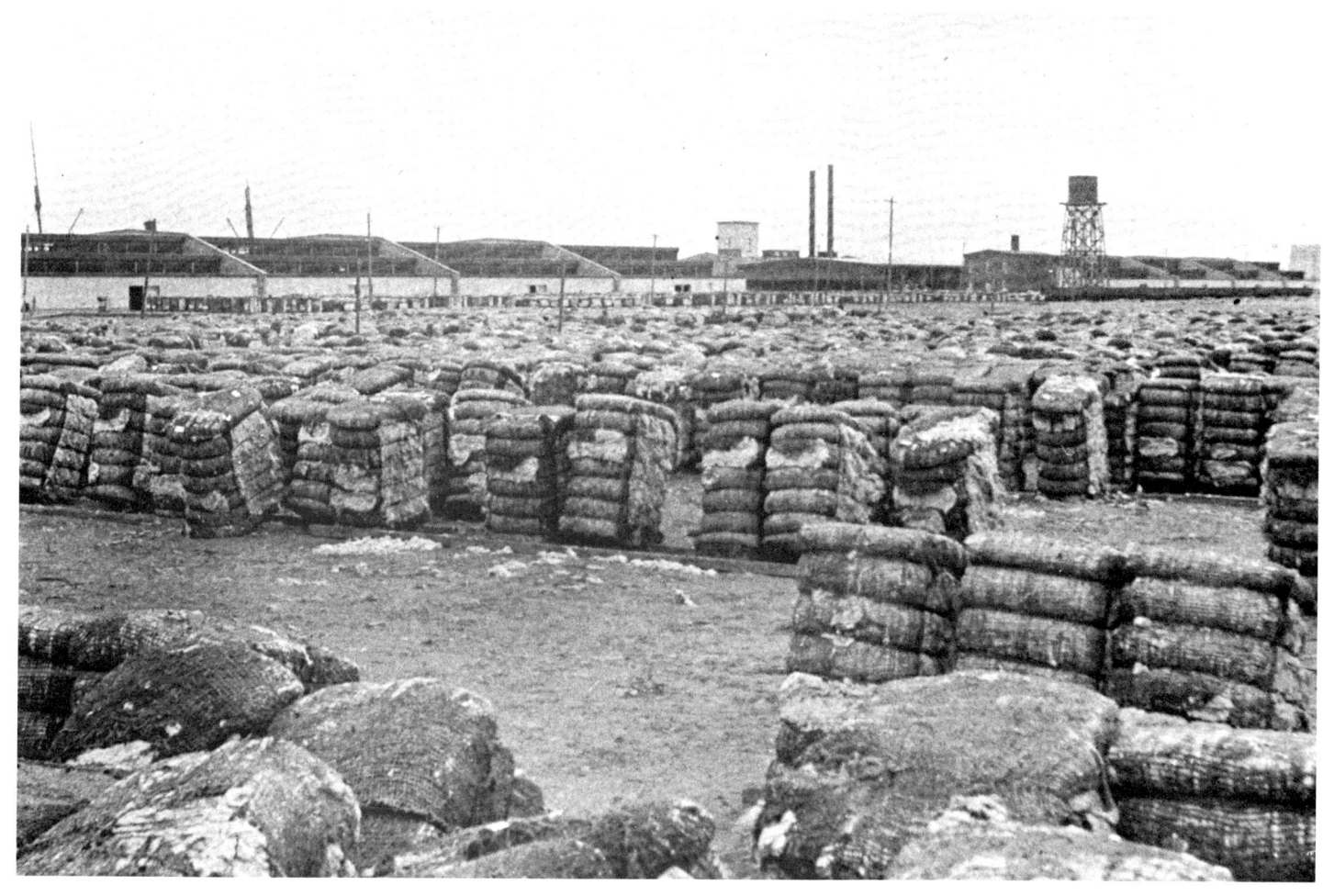

81. Moody Compress, Galveston.

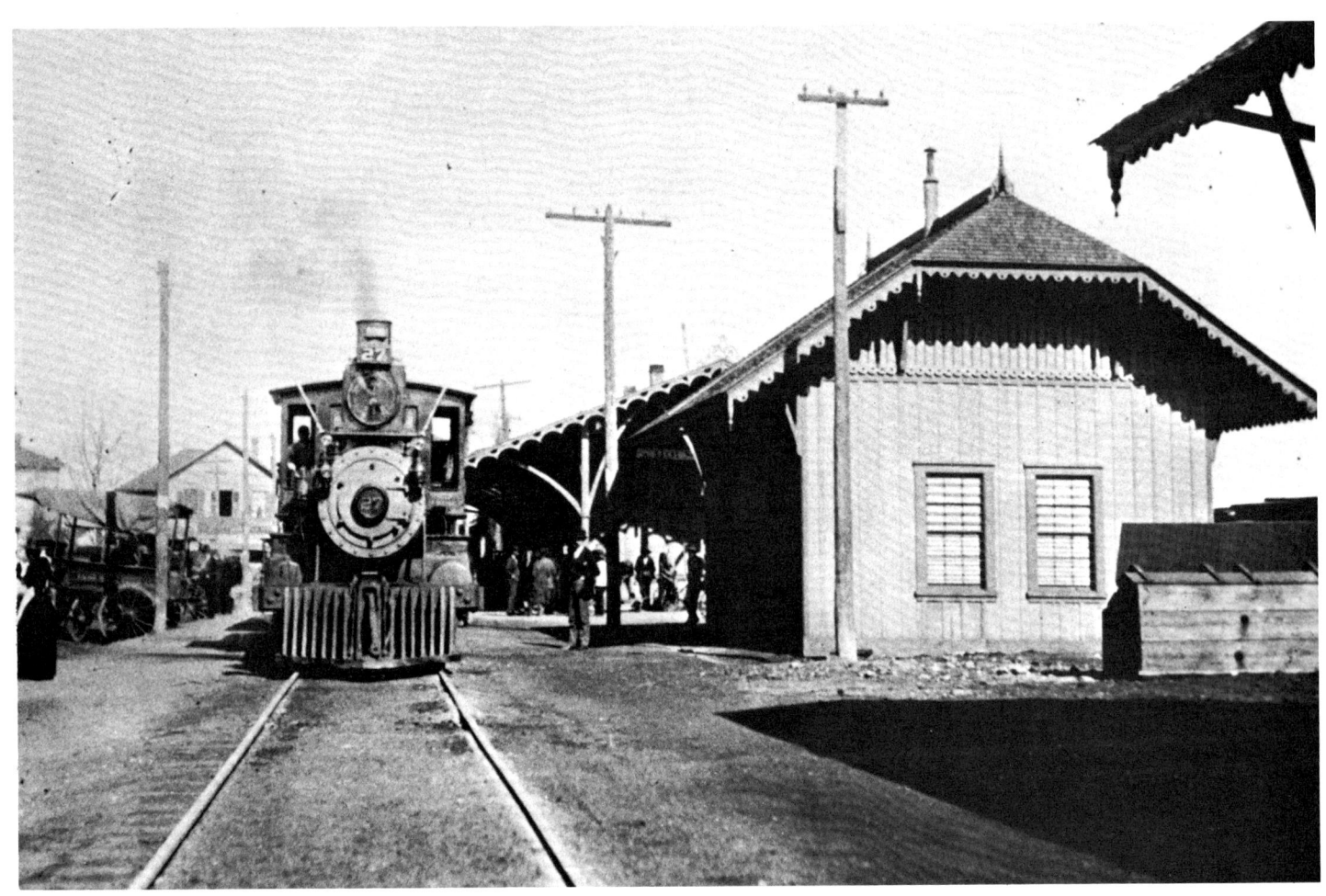

82. I&GN Station, Houston.

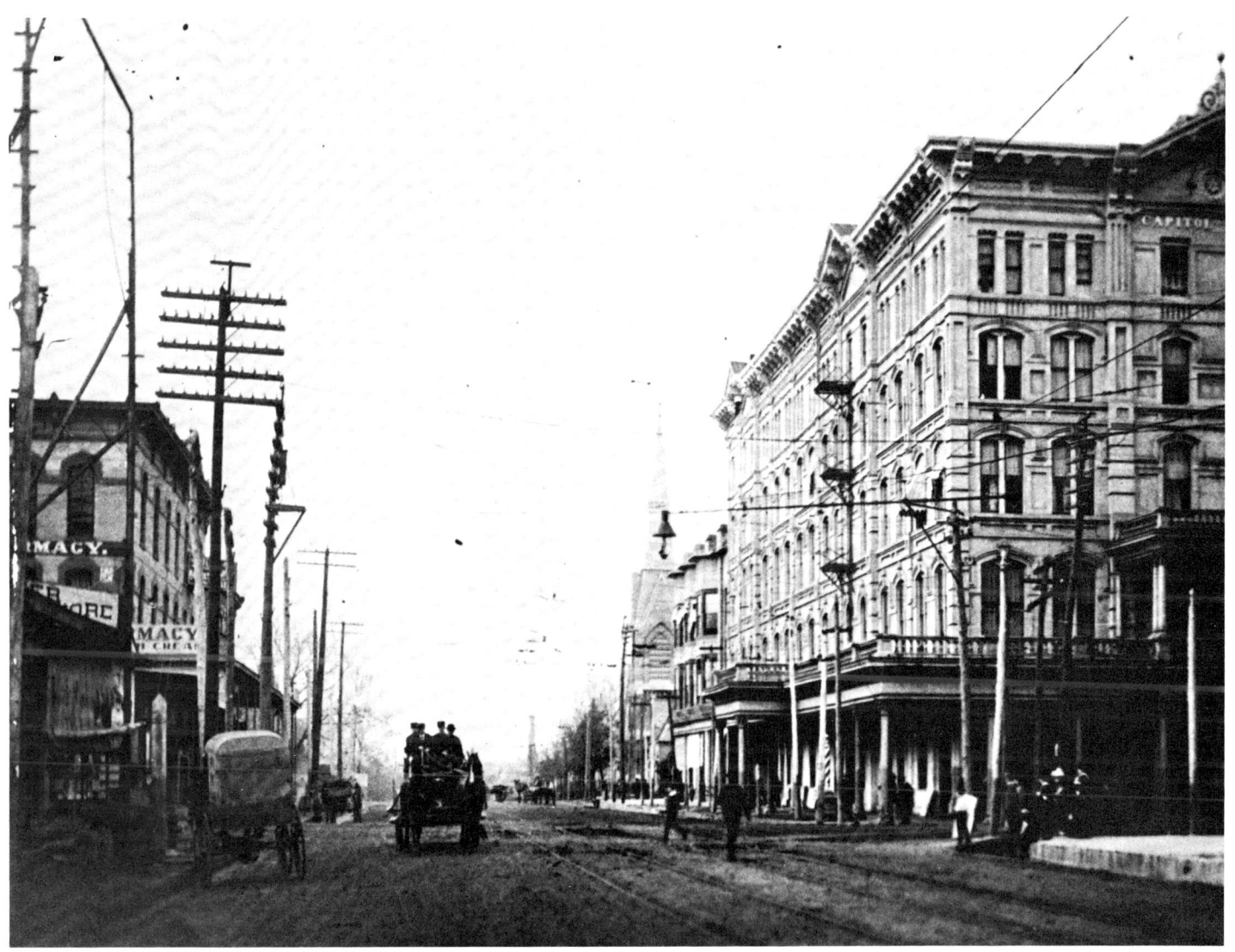

83. Travis Street at Texas in Houston. The Capitol Hotel (right) was on the site of the old capitol of Texas, and later became the Rice Hotel.

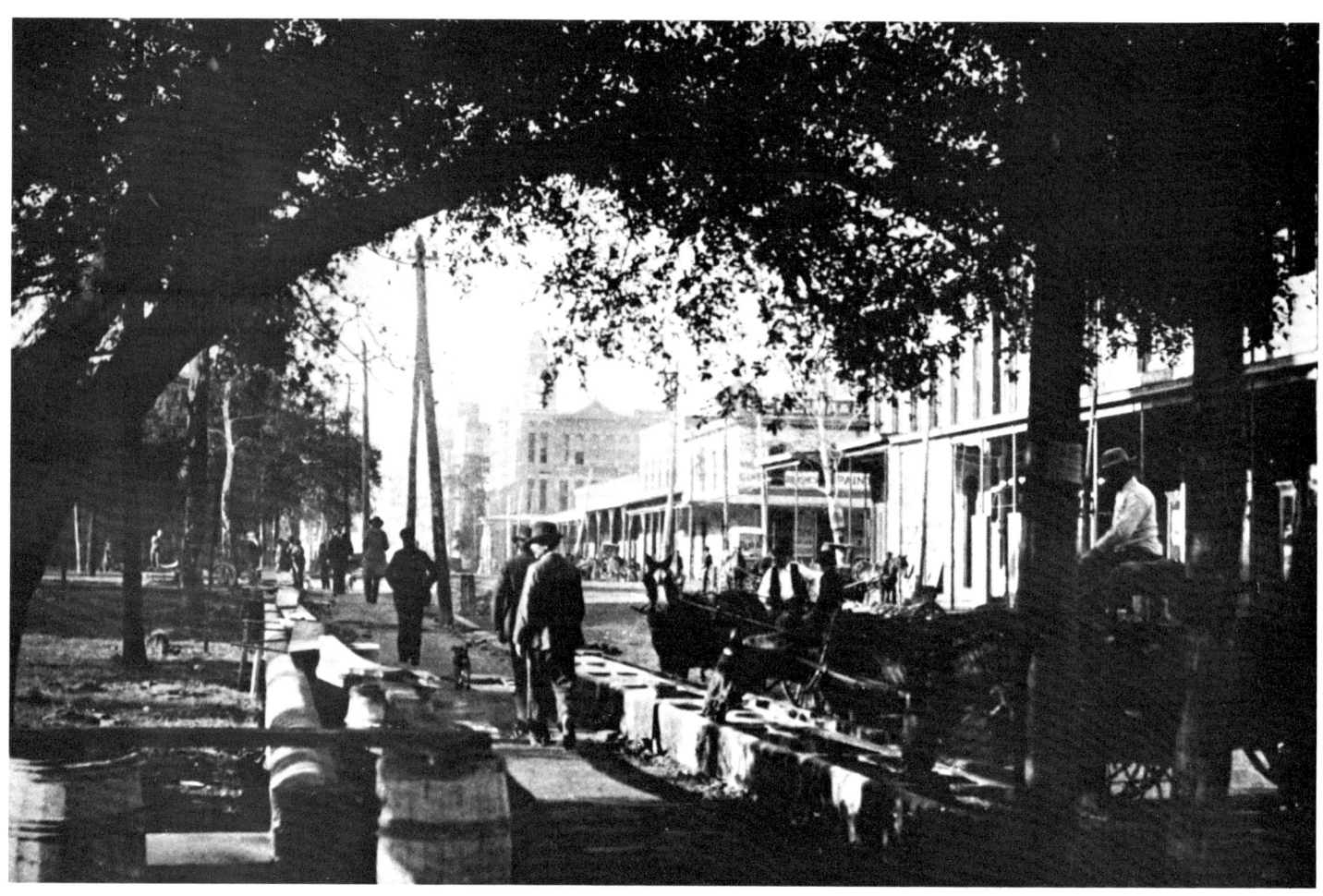

84. Market Square, Houston.

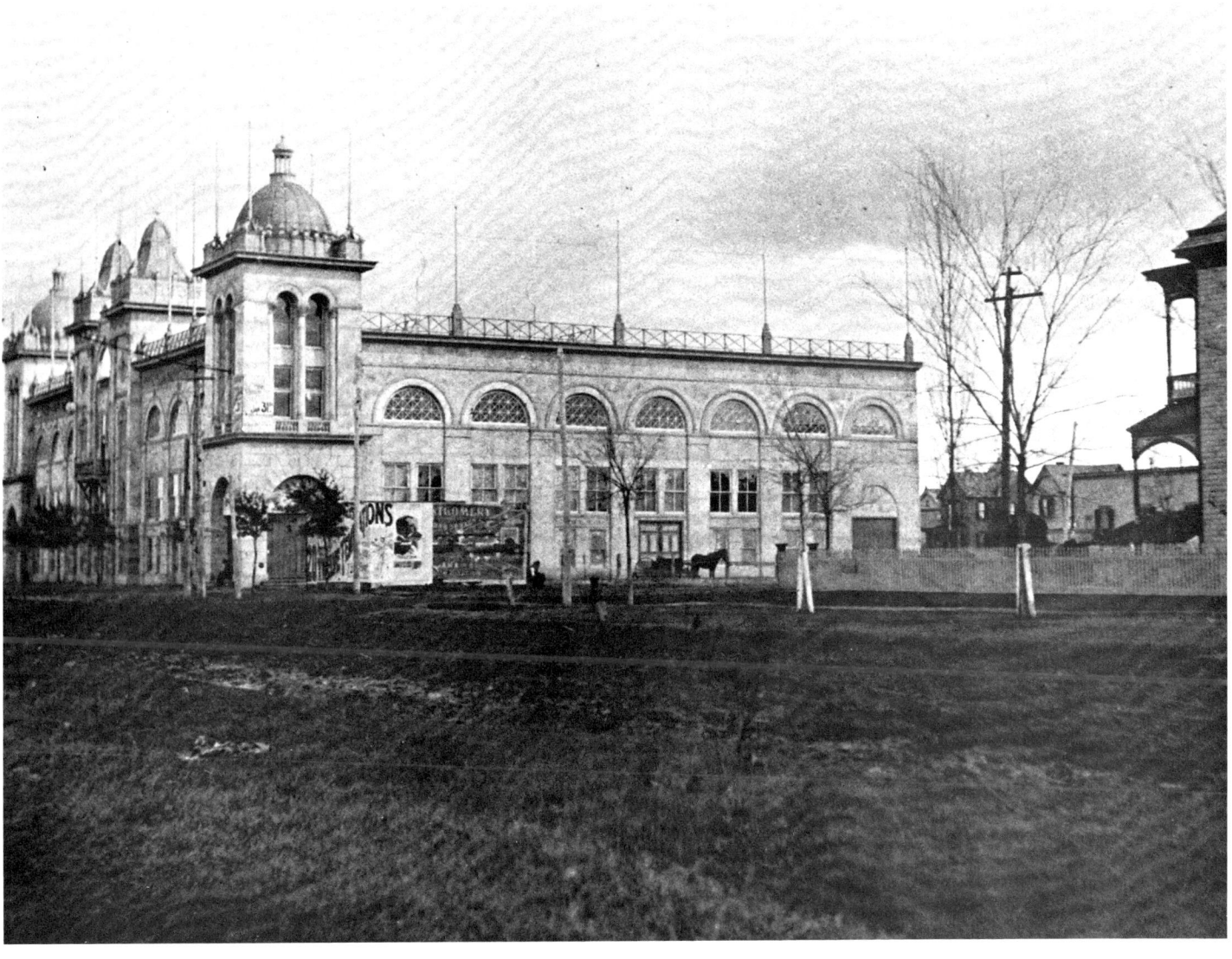

85. The Auditorium, Houston.

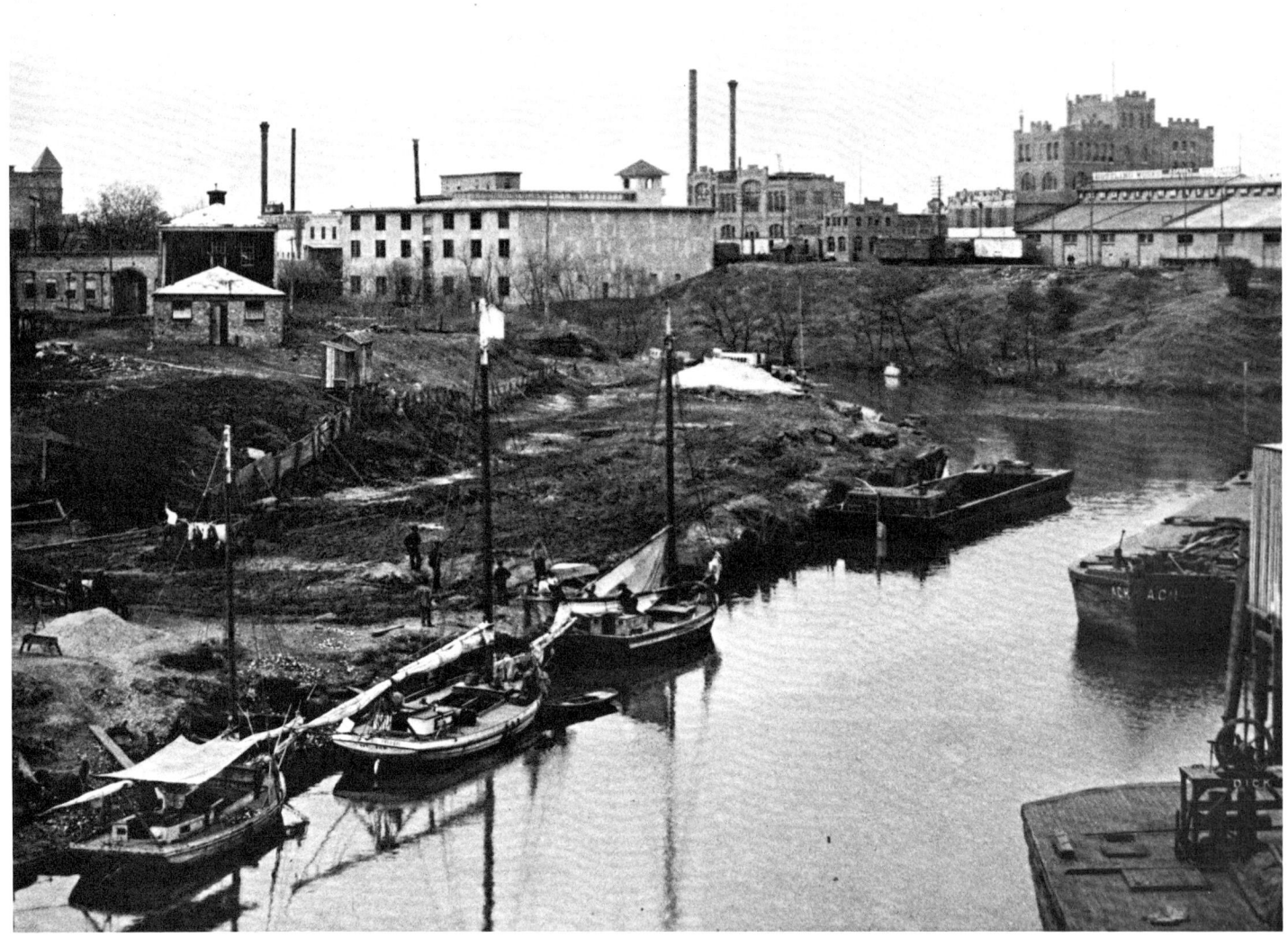

86. A wharf at Houston.

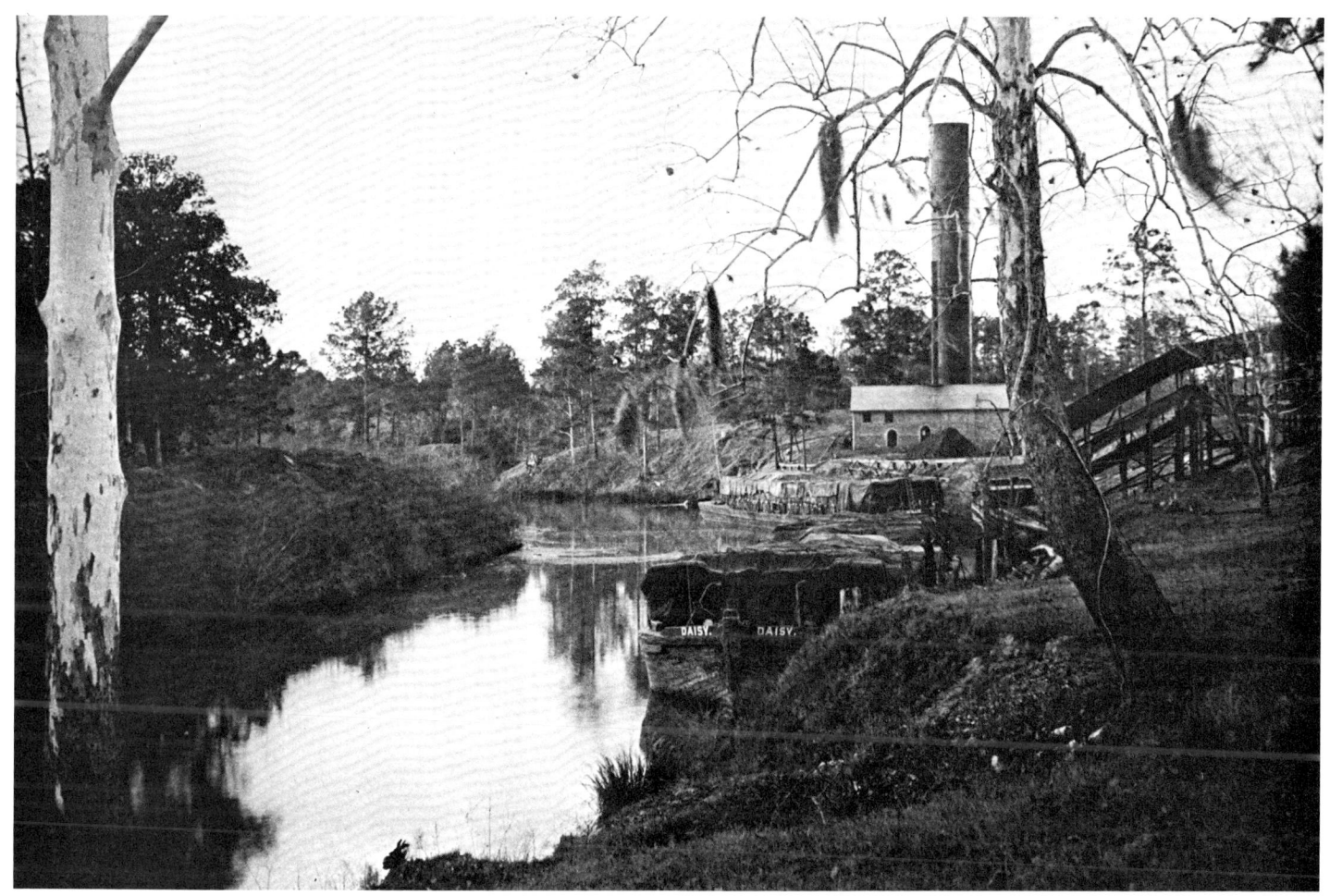

87. Buffalo Bayou, which became the Houston Ship Channel.

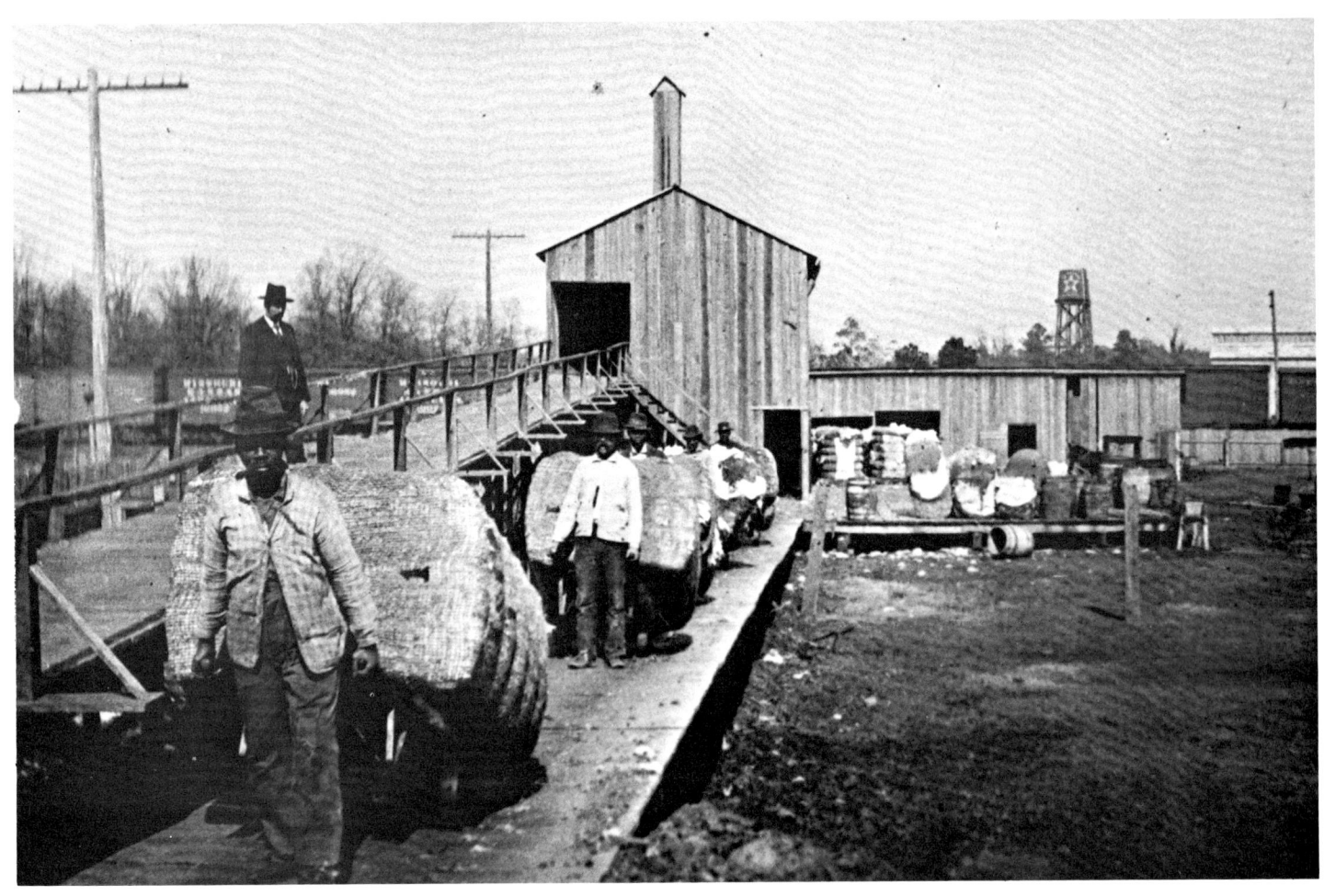

88. Inman Compress, Houston.

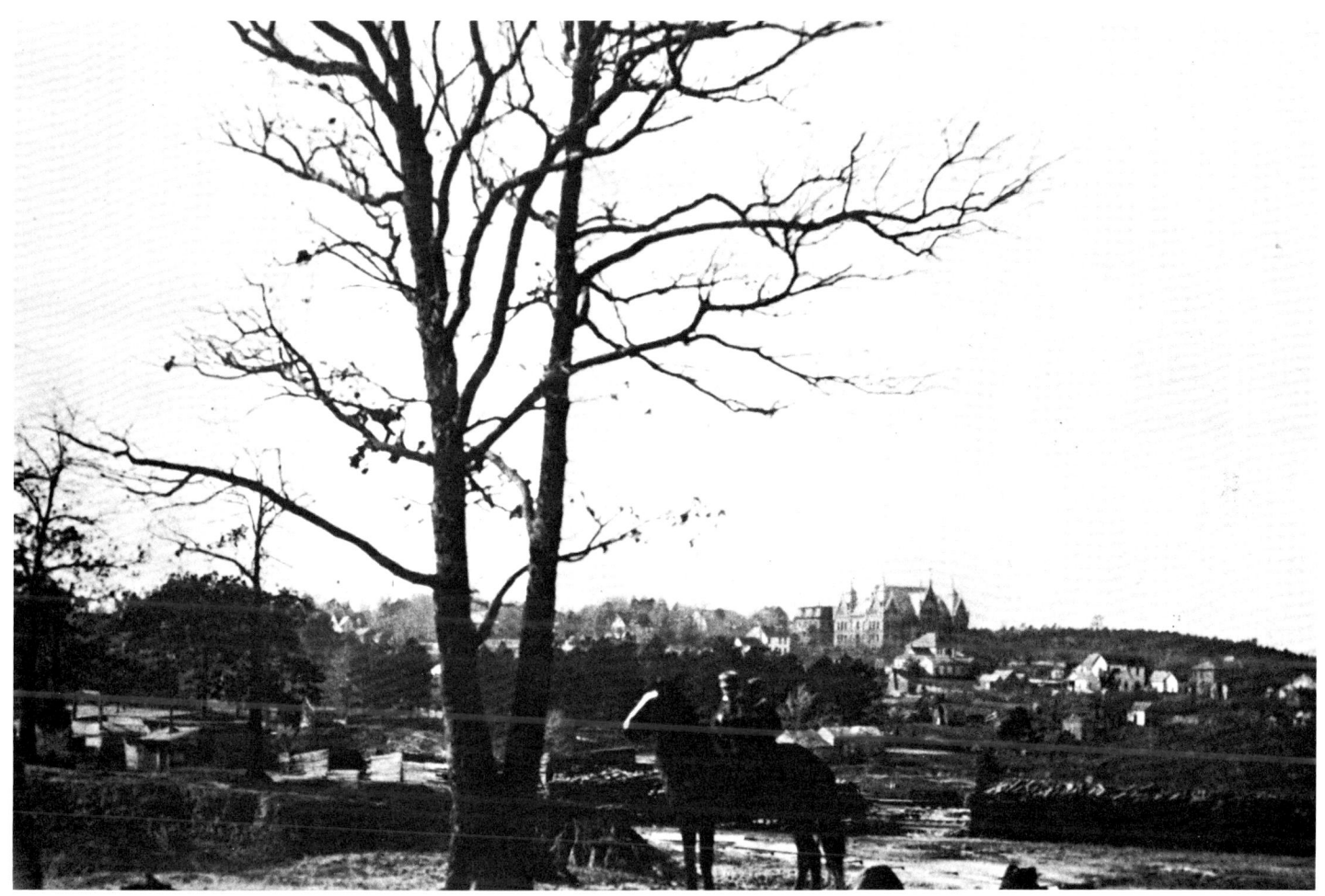

89. Sam Houston State Normal, Huntsville.

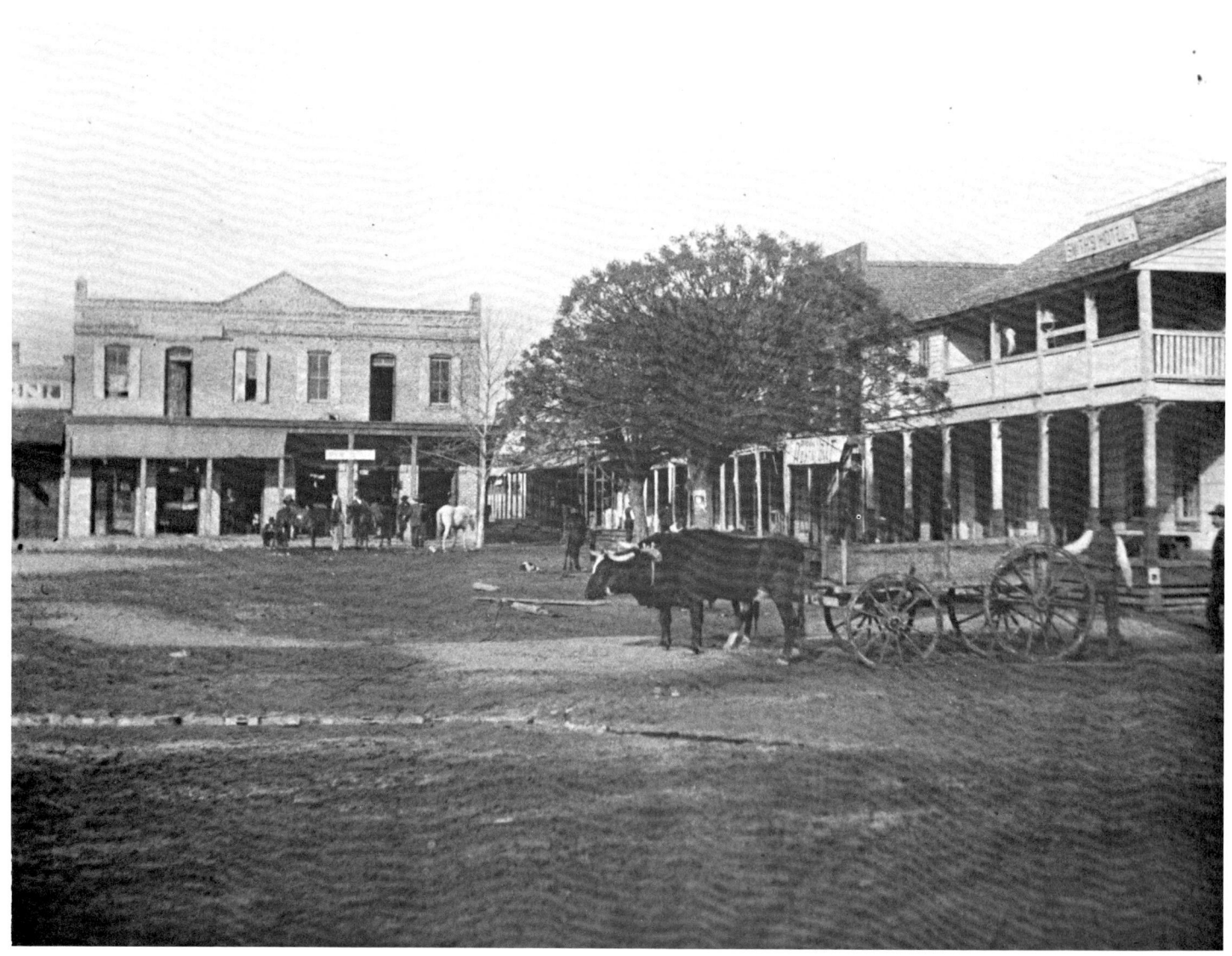

90. Lufkin. Smith's Hotel with the dinner bell is at right.

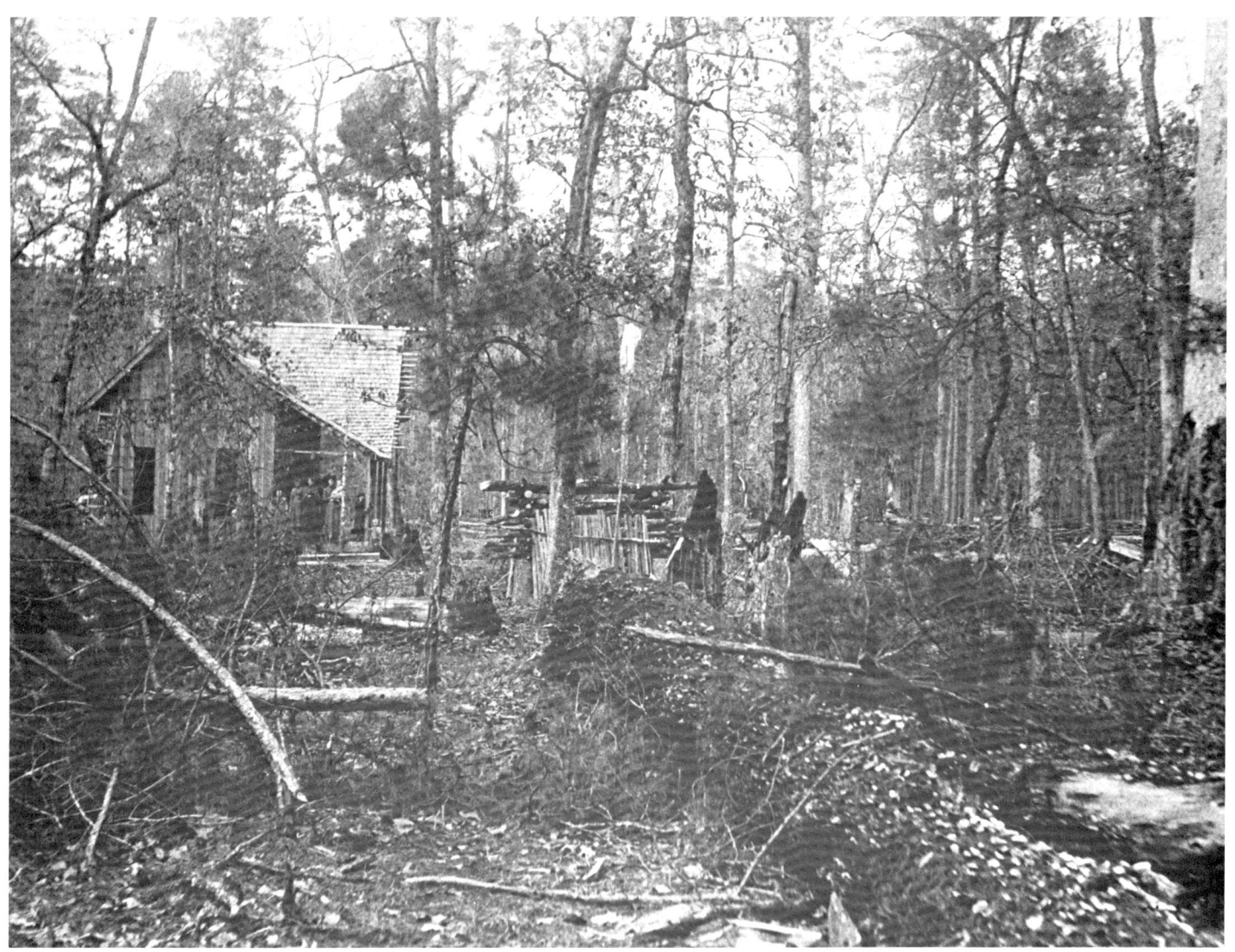

91. A new settler in Angelina County.

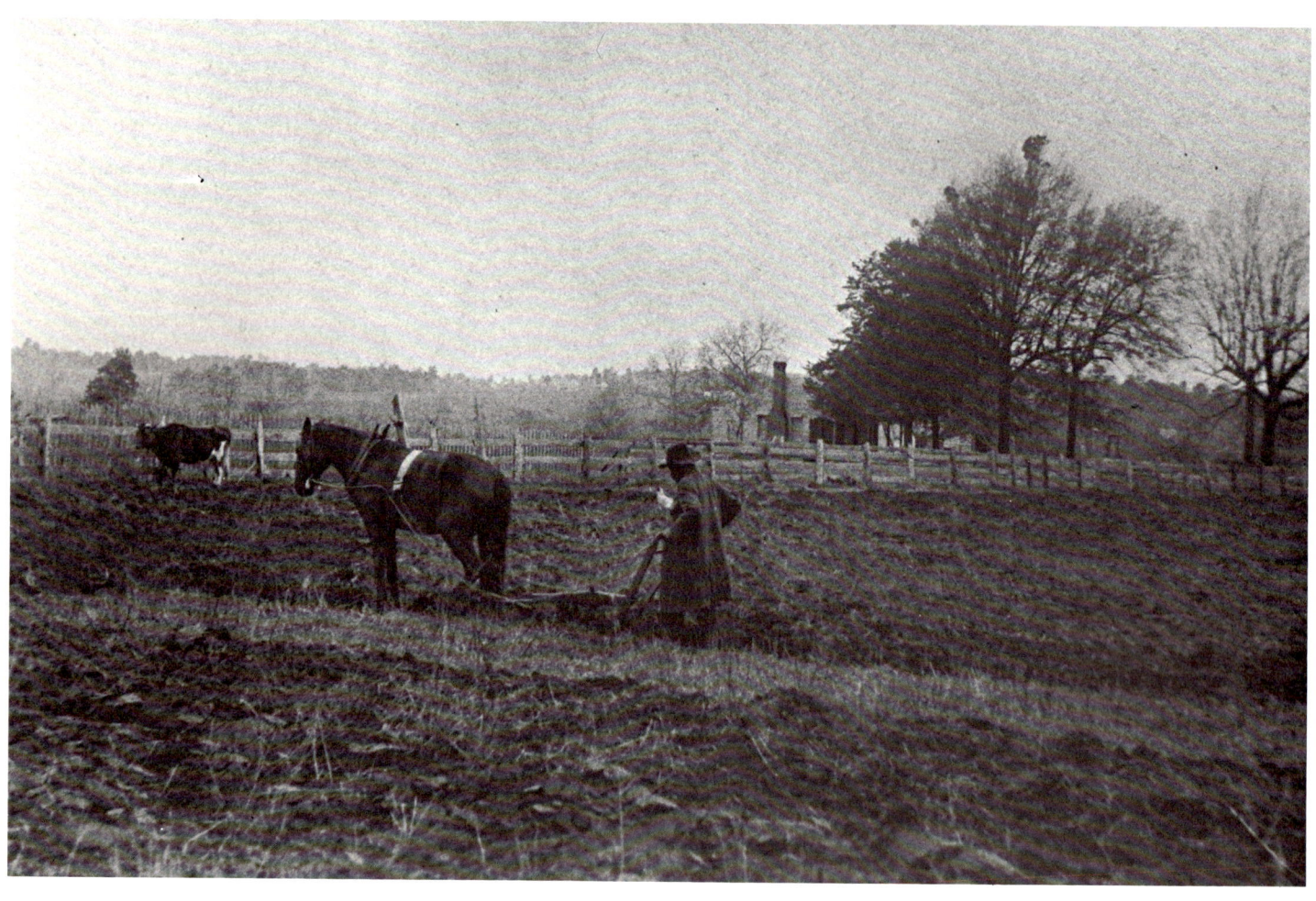

92. A farm in Cherokee County, near Rusk.

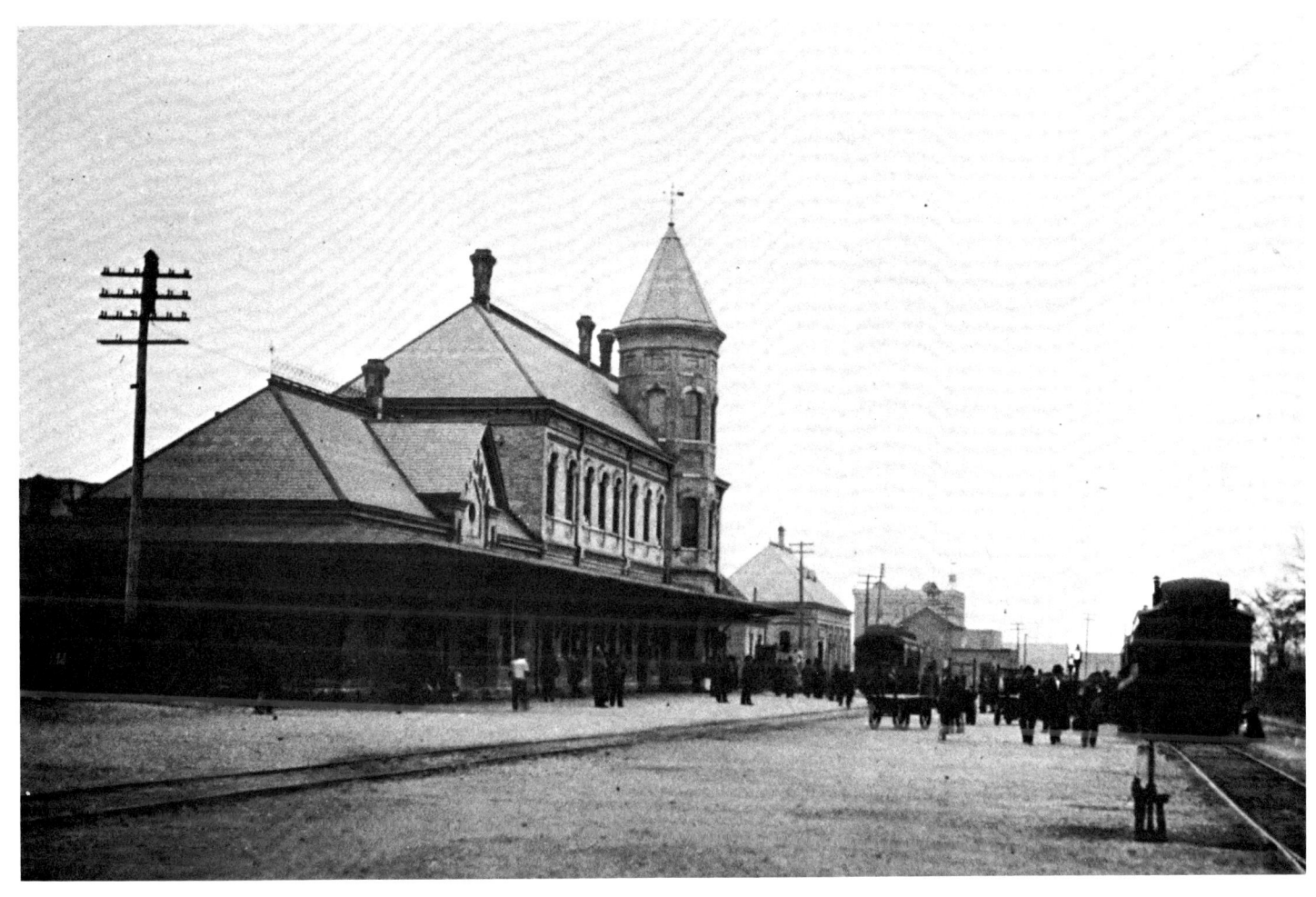

93. I&GN Station at Palestine, built in 1873. The railroad was required to "establish a depot within half a mile of the courthouse."

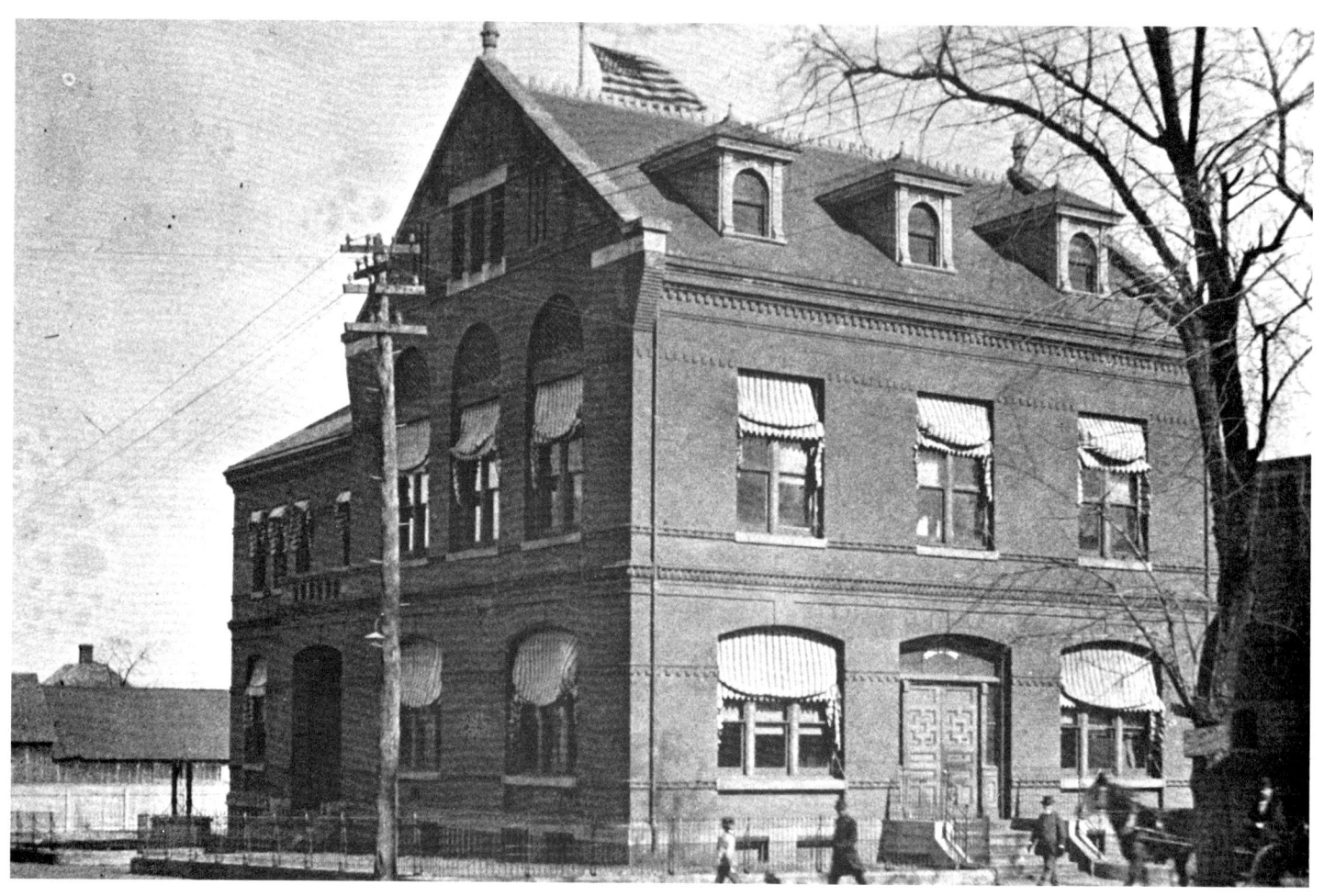

94. Post Office, Tyler.

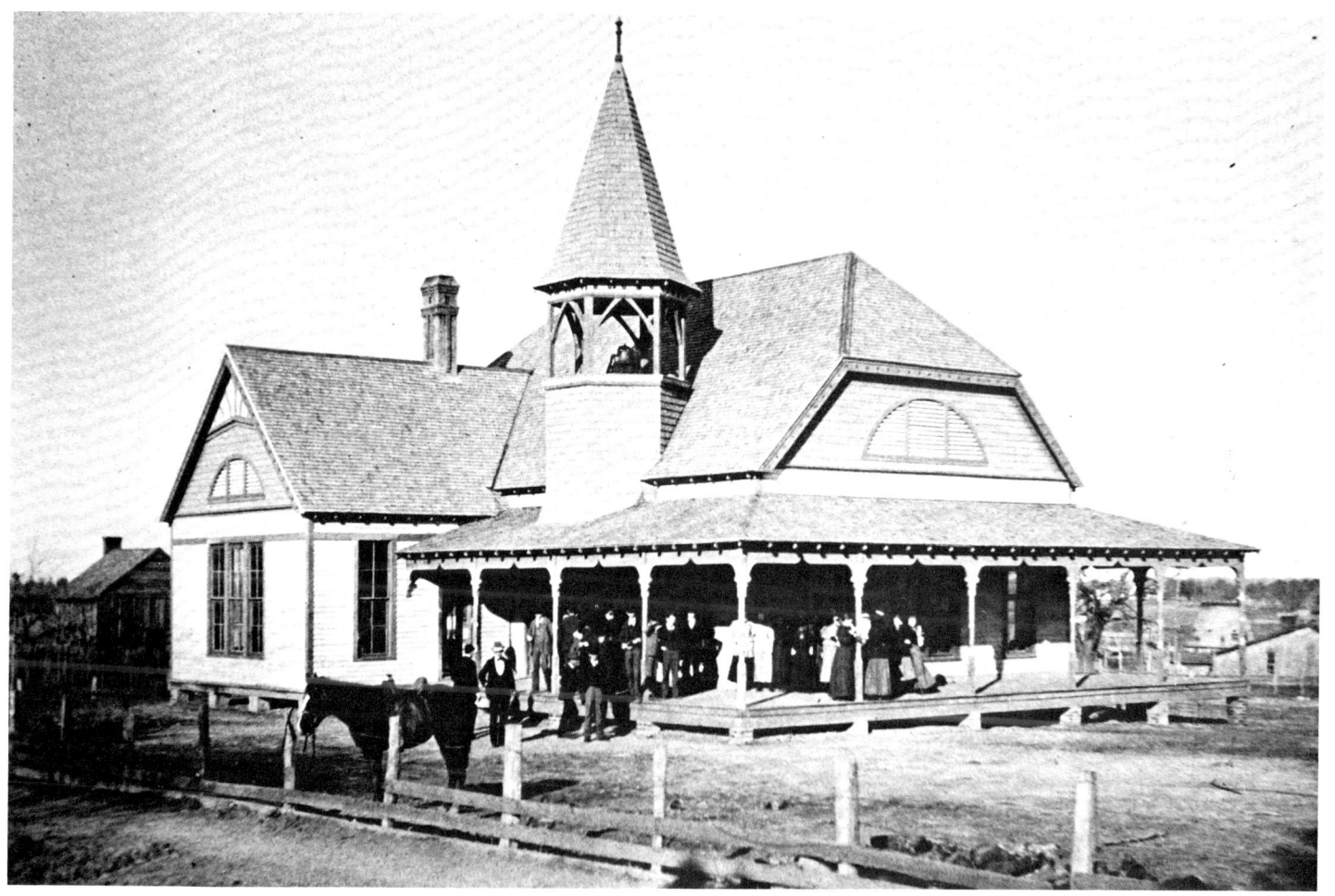

95. Henderson Male and Female College. It closed soon after this picture was made.

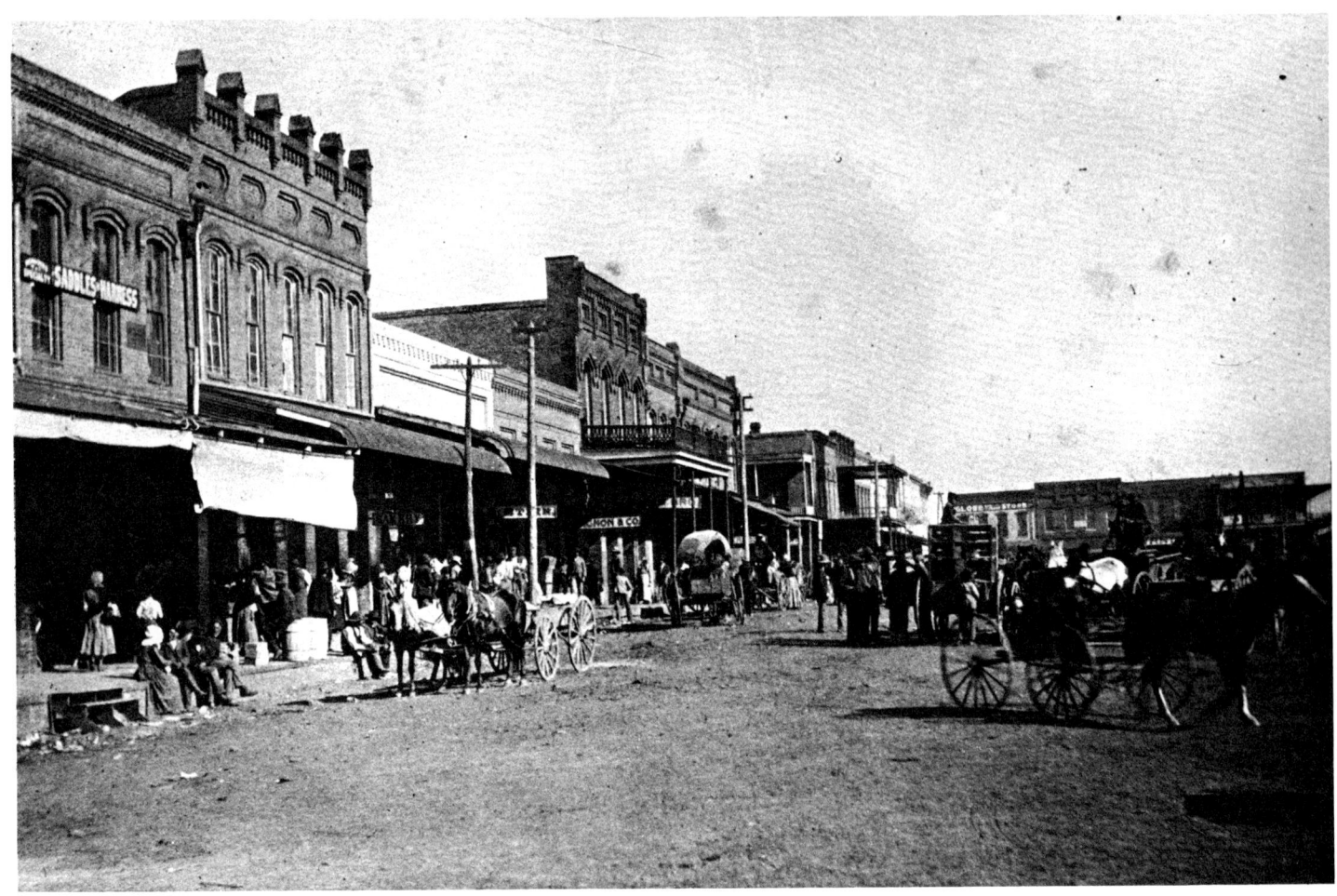

96. A street scene in Marshall.

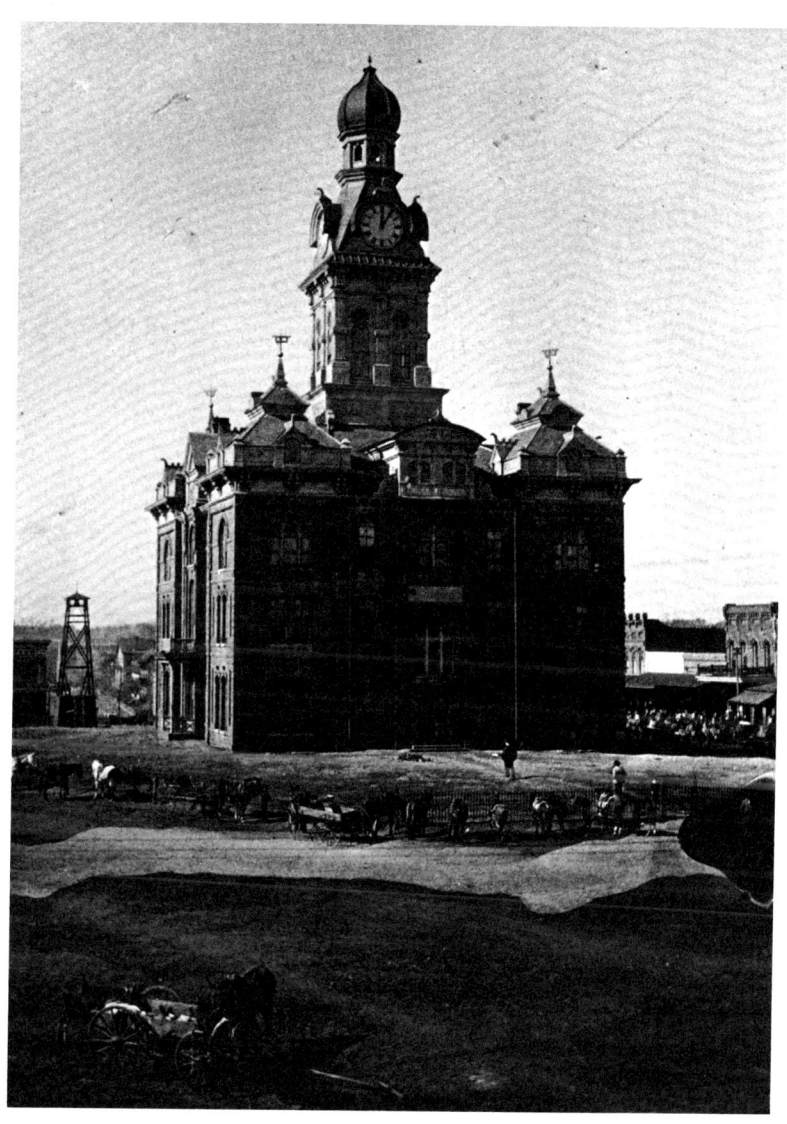

97. Harrison County Courthouse, Marshall.

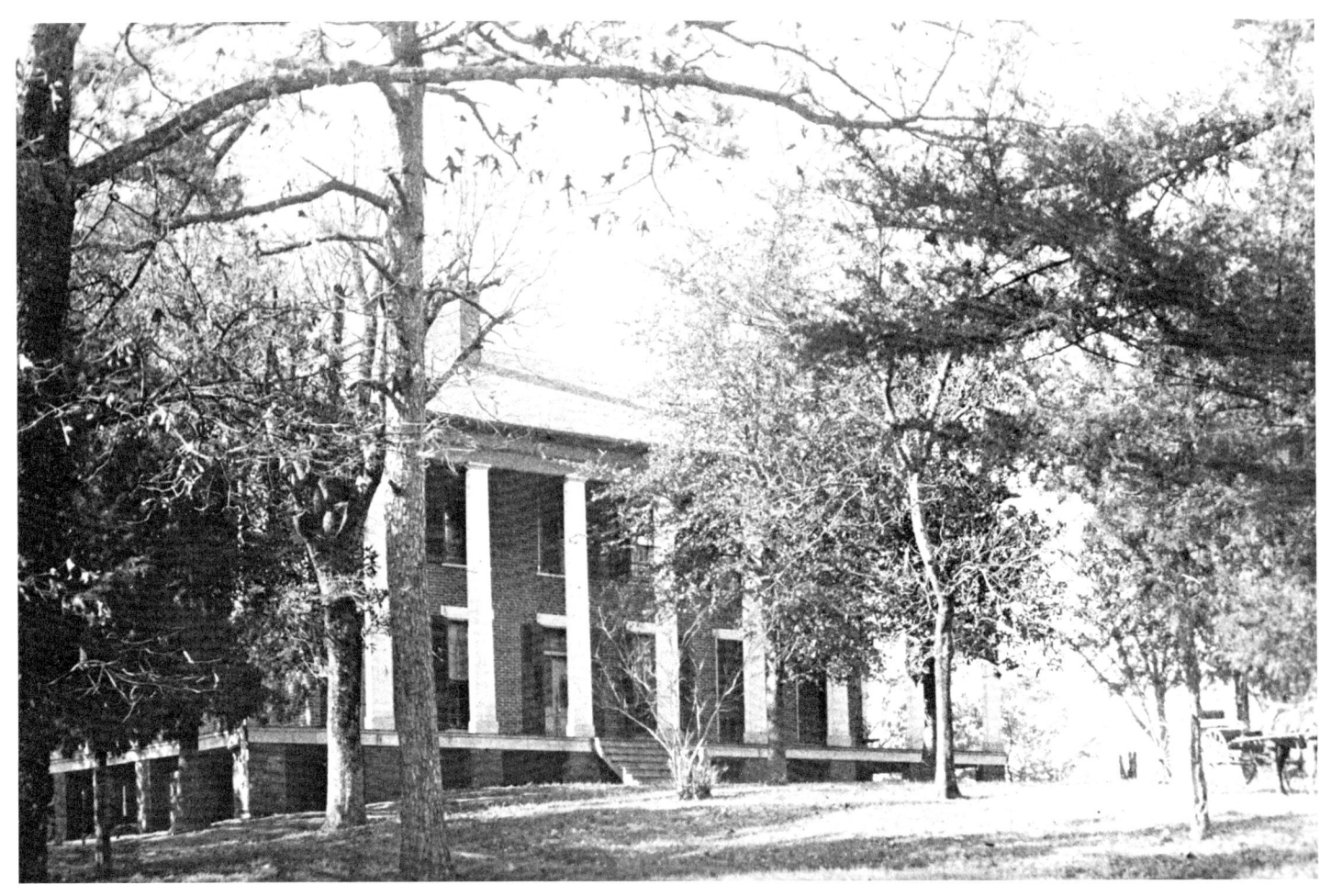

98. "Wyalucing" (Bishop College), Marshall.

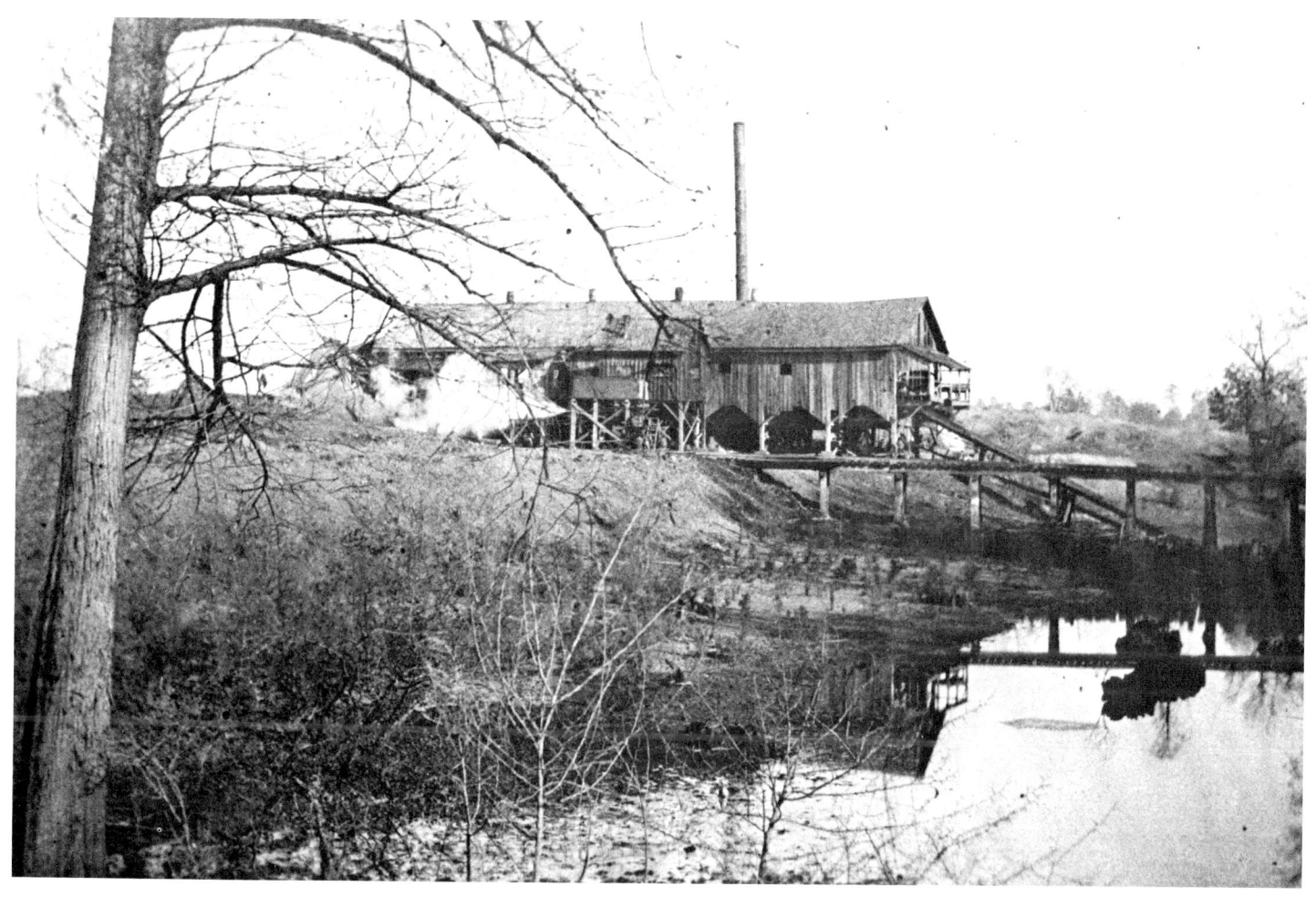

99. Clark & Boyce Lumber Co., Jefferson, Marion County.

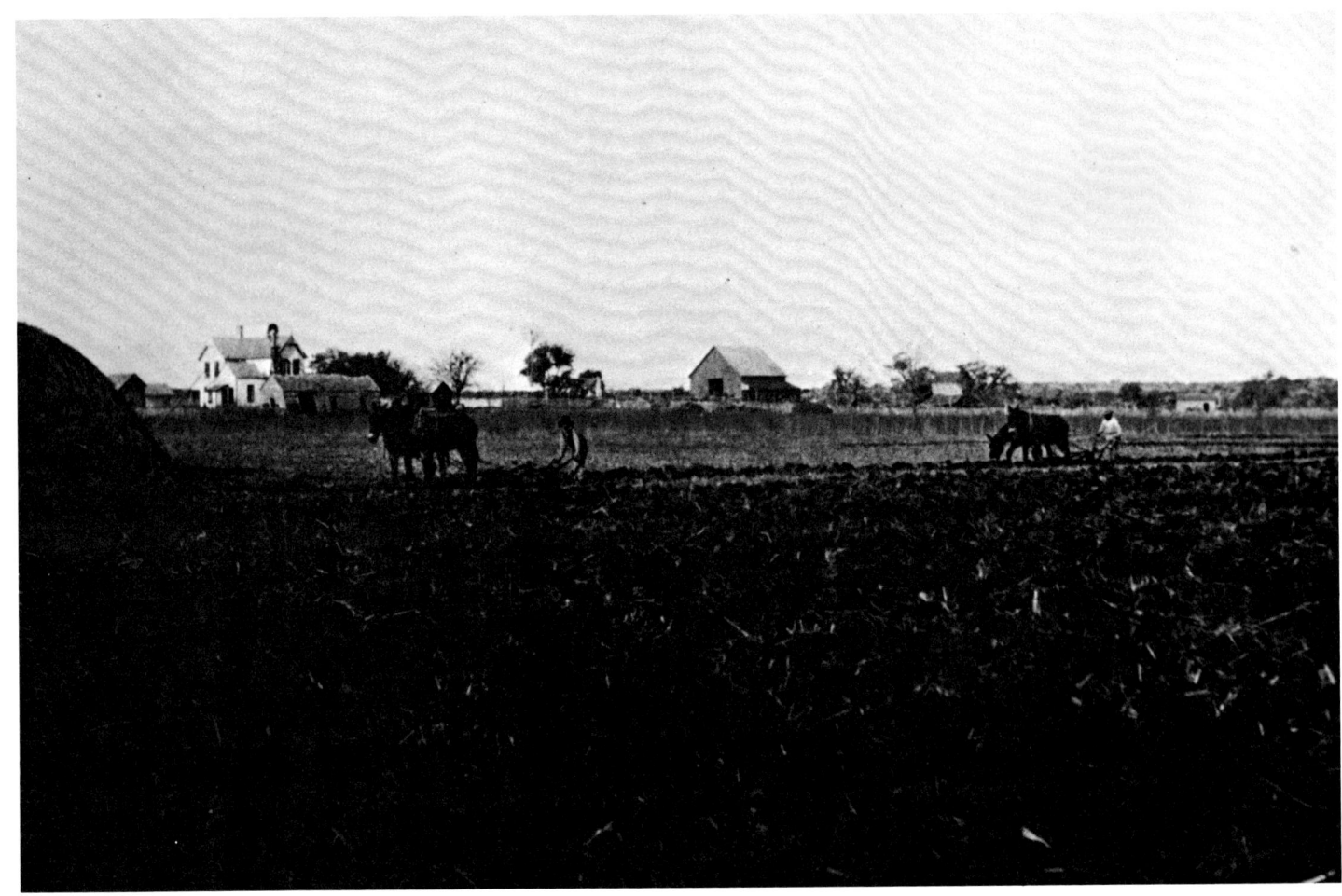

100. A farm in Cass County, near Atlanta.